I0605321

Anthony Benezet

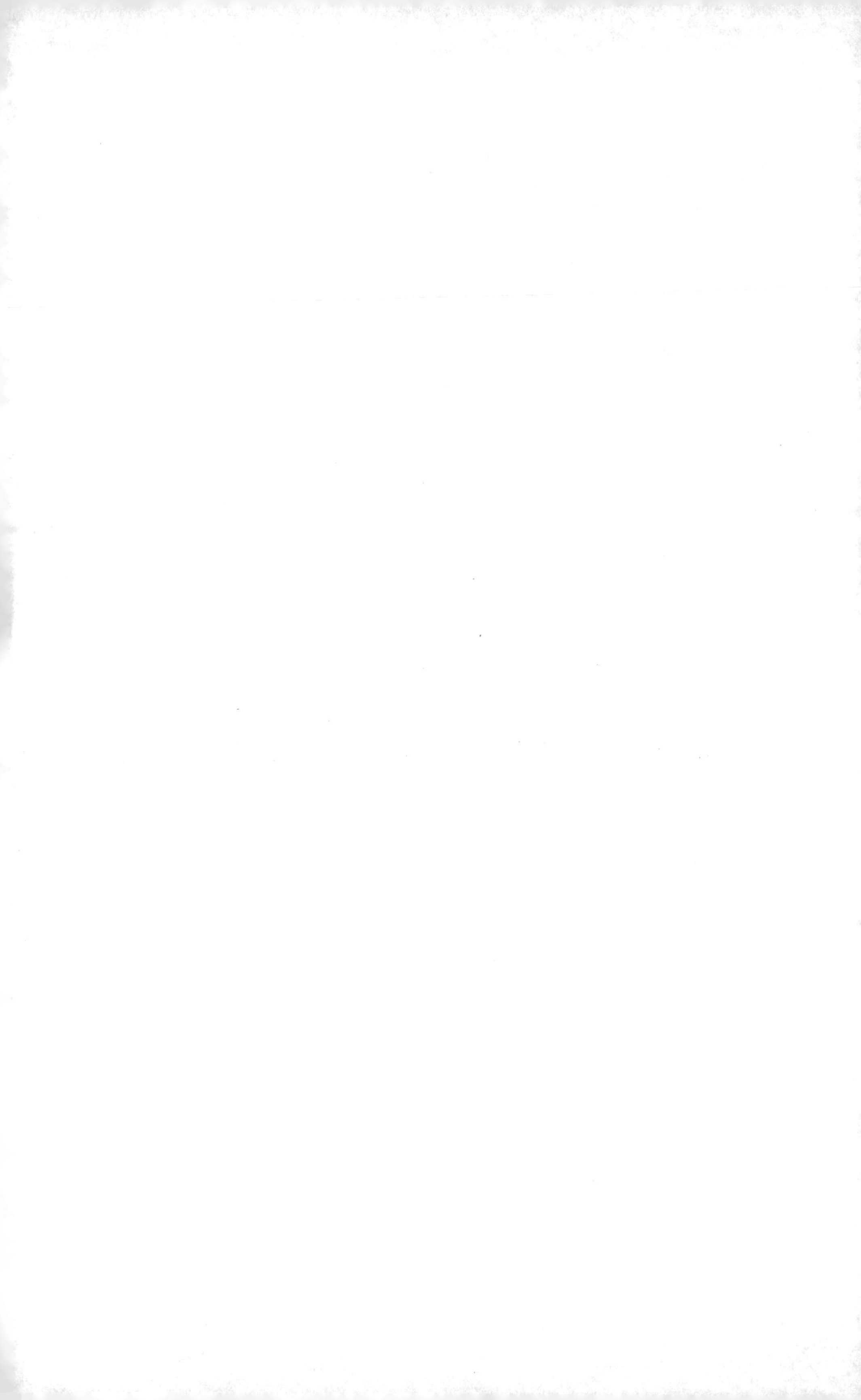

Anthony Benezet

Quaker, Abolitionist, Anti-Racist

David Chanoff

THE UNIVERSITY OF GEORGIA PRESS
ATHENS

A Sarah Mills Hodge Fund Publication
This publication is made possible in part through a grant from the Hodge Foundation in memory of its founder, Sarah Mills Hodge, who devoted her life to the relief and education of African Americans in Savannah, Georgia.

Published by the University of Georgia Press
Athens, Georgia 30602
www.ugapress.org
© 2025 by David Chanoff
All rights reserved
Designed by Melissa Buchanan
Set in Adobe Caslon Pro
Printed and bound by Sheridan Books

The paper in this book meets the guidelines for permanence and durability of the Committee on Production Guidelines for Book Longevity of the Council on Library Resources.

Most University of Georgia Press titles are available from popular e-book vendors.

Printed in the United States of America
25 26 27 28 29 P 5 4 3 2 1

Library of Congress Cataloging-in-Publication Data
Names: Chanoff, David author
Title: Anthony Benezet : Quaker, abolitionist, anti-racist / David Chanoff.
Description: Athens : The University of Georgia Press, [2025] | Includes bibliographical references and index.
Identifiers: LCCN 2025011794 | ISBN 9780820374239 hardback | ISBN 9780820374246 paperback | ISBN 9780820374260 epub | ISBN 9780820374253 pdf
Subjects: LCSH: Benezet, Anthony, 1713–1784 | Abolitionists—United States—Biography | Educators—United States—Biography | Quakers—United States—Biography | Antislavery movements—United States—History—18th century | Antislavery movements—England—History—18th century | LCGFT: Biographies
Classification: LCC E446 .C49 2025 | DDC 973.7/114092 $a B—dc23/eng/20250529
LC record available at https://lccn.loc.gov/2025011794

This book is dedicated to my mother, Golda Chanoff, who embodied compassion, fair-mindedness, and humane values for her children and for all who knew her. She saw people as individuals, not as races or types, and would have considered Anthony Benezet a kindred soul.

CONTENTS

ACKNOWLEDGMENTS

Many years ago, I was researching a potential book on how American Revolutionary ideals impacted other nations when I came across a description of Anthony Benezet's influence on British abolitionism and on the English-dominated Atlantic slave trade. The description I read mentioned *To Be Silent Would Be Criminal*, a book about Benezet by Irv Brendlinger, a professor of church history at George Fox University. Brendlinger detailed the astonishing network of eighteenth-century personalities who were deeply affected by Benezet's antislavery writing, including Benjamin Franklin, John Wesley, Benjamin Rush, the Abbé de Raynal, and others at a somewhat greater distance such as William Wilberforce. Benezet's fingerprints seemed to be all over the abolitionist movements in America as well as England. He was, quite obviously, a person of historic importance, yet I had never heard of him. When I asked some historian colleagues, they knew his name but little more. Not a single nonhistorian I talked to had even heard the name.

How was it that a person of such significance had apparently just slipped out of the country's historical consciousness? That question led me to a lasting interest in this strangely obscure Philadelphia Quaker, and over the years I collected bits and pieces of information about him. Then, in 2009, the University of Pennsylvania Press published a full-length biography, *Let This Voice Be Heard*, by Maurice Jackson. A lucidly written, thoroughly researched examination of Benezet's life, it answered many of the questions I had but left me with a still-obsessive desire to learn more. In the first instance, this current volume owes its existence to both Jackson and Irv Brendlinger, for whom Anthony Benezet exerted the same gravitational pull that I felt, and whose work gave me an enduring motivation to undertake my own study.

The more immediate spur to actually writing was provided by Professors Bernie Lown and Doris Sommer, two friends whose persistence eventually drove me to stop talking about Benezet and start searching for a publisher. In that effort I was fortunate to connect with Nate Holly, editor-in-chief at the University of Georgia Press, a PhD historian himself with an in-depth knowledge of Benezet's era and the early abolitionist movement Benezet, more than anyone, precipitated. Holly rendered succinct but wise guidance that made an essential difference in the direction this project took.

My deepest gratitude goes to Nate, Doris Sommer, and Bernie Lown, who to my great regret passed away before the book was finished. Other friends and colleagues generously volunteered precious time to read and comment on what I was writing.

Foremost among these was Bertrand Van Ruymbeke of the University of Paris. Bertrand is one of the true experts on Benezet, still a small, though now growing, circle of scholars. Nigel Hamilton, a leading biographer whose recent book on Abraham Lincoln and Jefferson Davis gave him a close-up familiarity with slavery issues, also read and commmented on the entire manuscript. I've been grateful to have Nigel's thoughts on writing as well as substance over the years; his suggestions this time around were particularly important. I'm grateful as well to others who offered knowledge, advice, and, in the case of Avi Eden and Emmy Miller, hospitality too. Thoru Pederson, Julie Winch, James Basker, Bob Hall, David Crosby, Bill Madeira, Michele Latimer, and my department chair at Brandeis, John Burt, all weighed in in either large or small ways, as did my brother, Matthew Chanoff, a thinker and writer himself of impressive reach. My thanks go to them and to the members of the Boston Biographers Group, who have been putting up with my month-to-month updates and have given me both intellectual and moral support along the way. One of the group's members, Mary Chitty, has been a diligent and highly resourceful researcher who has unearthed obscure but telling facts, corrected errors, and clarified many of the confusions inevitable in an effort to tell the life story of an individual who lived more than 250 years ago and managed to leave almost no personal information of the kind biographers always expect, or at least hope for.

I'd like to also thank the archivists and librarians who made it possible for me to work the levers of historical investigation from a distance. Among these were Randy Granger, for many years archivist at the William Penn Charter School, where Benezet's tenure as a teacher is still remembered and honored; Mary Crauderueff, curator of Quaker collections at Haverford College; Sofia Akram, archivist at the Wandsworth (England) Libraries; Neil Robson of the Wandsworth Historical Society; and Elizabeth Bridge of the Wandsworth Friends Meeting.

My wife, Lissu (of more than fifty years now), brings the perspective of an insightful general reader to everything I write, as well as providing the comforts of hearth and home that alleviate the anxieties and enhance the pleasures of a writer's always chancy journey into the past.

Anthony Benezet

PROLOGUE

The funeral carriage trundled slowly over the cobbles on Chestnut Street, heading west. The horse moved at a slow, almost dignified pace, as if it sensed the deceased in the coffin it was drawing was someone of importance. Behind the carriage the crowd was already growing, although the cortege had just left the dead man's home, where he had expired thirty-six hours earlier of "a disorder in his stomach and bowells."[1] Toward the end it had been painful, but eventually he had just fallen asleep, and then he was gone, "with seeming great ease," a close friend who was there wrote, "laying on his couch in the outer room about Sunsett."[2] It was May 4, 1784. Anthony Benezet, a revered Quaker elder, had been lucid until his last sleep overtook him.

The carriage moved along Chestnut Street, then turned right onto Fourth toward the Friends Meeting House and burial grounds a half mile ahead. In 1784 Philadelphia was the largest, most vibrant city in the independent nation that had just emerged from nine years of bloody war. But most of the city's forty thousand inhabitants lived in an area that extended only a mile and a half or so north to south along the Delaware River and half a mile west to the Pennsylvania State House, soon to be better known as Independence Hall.

Many of the deceased's close friends and colleagues lived within a few minutes' walk of the house Anthony and his wife, Joyce, had occupied for thirty years. Benjamin Rush, General Washington's surgeon general and a signer of the Declaration of Independence, lived on Walnut Street, less than a block away. Like many Philadelphians, Rush had owned household slaves. But reading Benezet's antislavery pamphlets started him thinking differently, and he and his friend Benjamin Franklin had been drawn into Benezet's orbit and become vocal advocates for the antislavery campaign the quiet Philadelphia Quaker had galvanized across the eighteenth-century Atlantic world. Franklin's own home was just a block down High Street from where the funeral cortege was now passing, the throng of mourners growing larger by the minute as Philadelphians—rich, poor, Black, and white—left their homes to join the procession.

Two blocks east of Franklin's home, High Street met Front, with its docks, warehouses, and maritime enterprises that made and sold sails, rope, tar, gear, and provisions for the coastal packets and deep sea freighters that docked and unloaded their cargoes here—including shipments of captive Africans who had been bought and sold in the city until a decade earlier, when the state legislature effectively ended the practice by imposing a prohibitive ten-pound sales tax per head. Benezet had petitioned and relentlessly lobbied for that act. He and his influential friend Rush had seen it through.

At the corner of Front and High Street (today's Market Steet) stood the London Coffee House. Benezet (he pronounced his name "Benezett") had walked by it almost every day of his adult life. It was here that captains and sailors, merchants, bankers, and politicians gathered to do business, see friends, eat, drink, and learn the latest. Here stagecoaches from other cities and towns let off and picked up passengers, next to an outdoor mart and auction venue that sold horses, carriages, furniture, household implements—and enslaved humans, led straight from the docks onto a wide plank set on two barrels to be inspected—teeth examined, muscles felt, genitals handled, haggled over, then led away by their new owners.

Benezet had been a teacher. The education of children was his calling, he said, and it was true he had a special talent for it. He taught both boys and girls, when educating girls was considered frivolous; he taught Black children, considered by most to be uneducable; he taught children with disabilities when many still believed disabilities were curses from God or demons. But there was something about the sight of those Africans being manhandled and sold that had, eventually, been too much for him, that turned his stomach with disgust—and turned Benezet toward a different, higher calling. He never did stop teaching, but in middle age he declared that when it came to slavery, "to be silent would be criminal."[3]

Human beings, he had thought, can simply not be bought and sold like draft animals or pieces of furniture. That, he said, was as much against natural law as it was against divine law. But it wasn't just that: it was also that he knew these Black Philadelphians. He knew the dockworkers and craftsmen and laborers. For years he had talked with them, heard their stories, about themselves, their parents, their memories, and the fearsome journey that they or their forebears had endured when they were brought out from Africa on the Middle Passage.

He had gotten to know them over many years. He knew their children especially well. Starting in 1750 he had taught them, free and enslaved, at night in the big upper room of his house. Then he had persuaded the Friends Monthly Meeting to build them a school, and he had taught them there. The Black children, he said, were equal to white children in terms of intelligence and creativity; it was, he said, "a vulgar prejudice founded on ignorance to think otherwise, based on fallacious reasoning and absurd sentiments."[4] Now many of those children were walking with their mothers and fathers at the rear of the crowd of mourners, many of the adults weeping openly. It was, an observer said, "the greatest concourse of people that had ever been witnessed on such an occasion in Philadelphia."[5]

When they finally reached the Arch Street burial ground, the throng of mourners spread out on all sides of the open grave, straining to hear a few prayers and remarks by two Society of Friends ministers. Then the coffin was lowered into the unmarked grave. Benezet had wanted no memorials, in stone or otherwise. A Revolutionary War veteran who was there told friends afterward, "I would rather be Anthony Benezet in that coffin than General Washington with all his fame."[6]

So many in that crowd had known him personally—the Quakers, of course, but many others too. Some found him exasperating at times, with his relentless advocacy and soliciting. But though he imposed on them, they understood that what he had stood for and what he had done had changed their lives. They had had that rarest of individuals among them, one whose presence had brought out the better angels of their nature. Those at the grave site, and others who were not, kept him in their hearts and in their minds. Some saw him in their dreams. Rush did. He dreamt about "a little white man, his face grave, placid and full of benignity. In one hand he carried a subscription paper and a petition, in the other a small pamphlet."[7] Rush counted Benezet's memory a blessing. Tens of thousands of others did as well, in England, in France, in the Caribbean, wherever the slavers had plied their trade. "Who," French revolutionary Jacques-Pierre Brissot asked, "had been more useful to mankind than Anthony Benezet?"[8]

Twenty-three years after Benezet's body was lowered into its grave in the Friends' Arch Street burial ground, a momentous event took place three thousand miles away in Great Britain's House of Commons. Following a speech by the indefatigable William Wilberforce, British lawmakers passed a bill outlawing the slave trade by a vote of 283 to 16. Wilberforce had been introducing antislave trade bills every year since 1789, five years after Benezet breathed his last. In his speeches he had incorporated Benezet's ideas, his strategies, even his language. For eighteen exhausting years Wilberforce and his allies had been battling the sugar interests and the shipping industry, and at long last they had prevailed. Two months later the Abolition Bill passed in the House of Lords and became British law. It was, the great historian W. E. H. Lecky wrote, "one of the three or four most virtuous acts in the history of nations."[9]

Thomas Clarkson was one of the group around Wilberforce who celebrated the triumph, some of them in tears. It was Clarkson who, two decades earlier, had enlisted Wilberforce into the war on slavery. He had partnered with Wilberforce ever since, providing dramatic evidence of the slave trade's horrors, and orchestrating the massive petition drives that fueled Wilberforce's campaign. Benezet had turned Clarkson's life around. Reading Benezet's *Some Historical Account of Guinea* had moved him so profoundly that he had had to get down from his horse on his way from Cambridge to London. Sitting on the side of the road with the reins in his hand, he had thought to himself, "It is time some person should see these calamities to their end," and he had given up his aspirations for the clergy to devote his life to the cause of combatting "the crying evil."[10]

John Wesley, the immensely influential founder of Methodism, had himself been brought into the abolitionist fold by Benezet. "I read a very different book, published by an honest Quaker, on that execrable sum of all villainies," he wrote in his journal after receiving Benezet's *Some Historical Account of Guinea*, the same book that had so affected Clarkson.[11] Impelled by Benezet's account, Wesley wrote his own widely disseminated *Thoughts upon Slavery*, borrowing entire sections from Benezet's tracts and initiating a collaboration with England's leading antislavery figures, who themselves had been deeply moved by Benezet.

Wilberforce, Clarkson, Wesley, Britain's great abolitionist activist Granville Sharp, along with many other of the eighteenth-century Atlantic world's most consequential figures, were galvanized by the moral power of this modest Quaker teacher who as an adult never ventured more than a few miles from his home in Philadelphia. Benezet's fingerprints are all over the extinction of the Atlantic slave trade, and the gathering strength of America's own burgeoning abolitionist movement as well. He was a figure of global importance, "a saint," Garry Wills called him, a great bearer to the rest of the world of the American ideals (no matter how compromised) of equality and liberty.[12]

We don't know what Benezet looked like. He said he didn't want his "ugly face" to go down to posterity. People who knew him said he was plain, "far from handsome." But it wasn't his features that caught attention; it was his demeanor, the aura he seems to have projected. "His face beamed with kindly animation," said one acquaintance. "His eyes were kind," said another, "full of humanity." A French visitor, the Marquis de Barbe-Marbois, described him as vivacious, like the French nation generally, referring to Benezet's French origins. An early biographer wrote that Benezet was "quick in his movements."[13] We can assume this refers to his normal way of carrying himself energetically—maybe a bit more sprightly than the stolid English Quakers who still dominated the city. Thomas Paine must have seen him like that, looking out the front window of his rented rooms across Front Street from the London Coffee House where in 1775 he was writing his incendiary pamphlet *Common Sense.*

In the twenty-first century we know Benezet in the sense that we know what he did, the immense reach of his influence on the Atlantic world of his day. But the man himself we do not know. His house is long gone, marked by a plaque only in 2016. His grave is unmarked. He wanted no memorials. He left no diary or journal. His voluminous correspondence contains only sparse personal hints. It's almost as if he wanted to remain unknown, just as he wanted no picture and no memorial. Some specialists on the period have taken note of him. His letters are collected. His writing has been preserved. But he is not present in the collective consciousness, a key figure not just in Western history but in world history. Yet his inner life beckons to be understood. Where, after all, did such a man come from? What lay behind someone who must be considered among the most consequential activists in America's history?

Despite the opaque surface of Benezet's interior biography, it's possible to identify the major inflection points that marked his life, the changes that made him who he was and enabled the immense power of his antislavery crusade. What in his environment did he draw on that gave shape to his fundamental beliefs, that translated themselves so forcefully into action? Bernard Bailyn, the great historian of the American colonies and the Revolution, spoke of "those mysterious impulses that propel the mind beyond familiar ground into unexpected territories—that account for the sudden appearance of creative configurations of thought."[14] My intent in this book is to uncover those "impulses" that propelled Anthony Benezet's mind into unexpected territories, to illuminate them and help reveal what drove him to see things as he did.

Benezet spoke to the evil of human beings violently forcing their will on the vulnerable and helpless—the atrocity against humanity that was slavery. He spoke to the essential equality of Black and white. The principles he fought so hard for 250-plus years ago are no less important now, and hardly less at issue. Benezet lived in an age of conditions and assumptions different from ours. But by tracing the contours of his thinking, we may well find guideposts for ourselves and for our own time.

CHAPTER ONE

The Man We Do Not Know

In the midwinter of 1713 the Benezet family—father Jean-Etienne, mother Judith, two-year-old Anthony (Antoine), and five-year-old Marie-Madeleine—abruptly fled their home in the northern French city of Saint-Quentin, leaving everything behind and heading through the Arrouaise Forest toward the Dutch border, 250 miles to the north.

The Benezets were Huguenots, part of the massive flood of refugees that fled King Louis XIV's suppression of French Protestantism that began with the so-called Sun King's accession in 1661 and lasted up through the early years of the eighteenth century. French Protestants had enjoyed the freedom to worship for almost seventy years, guaranteed by the 1598 Edict of Nantes that had ended the French wars of religion. But from the beginning of his reign Louis had been bent on eliminating the reformed religion in France and turning his realm back into an entirely Catholic nation.

Louis's anti-Protestant laws quickly bore down on the Huguenot population. His decrees excluded Protestants from public offices and various professions, prohibited interfaith marriages, banned Protestant outdoor meetings, restricted and then prohibited Protestant preaching, and forbade Protestant internal migration. Dragoons, the notorious *dragonnades* that wrecked households and goaded families to convert to Catholicism, were quartered in Protestant homes. Then, on October 18, 1685, Louis formally revoked the Edict of Nantes, and Protestantism in France was criminalized.

Louis's revocation (formally the Edict of Fontainebleau) was categorical, uncluttered by any nuance. "We can do nothing better," the revocation read, ". . . to obliterate the memory of the troubles, the confusion, and the evils which the progress of this false religion [Protestantism] has caused in this kingdom" than to revoke the previous edict. All (so-called) Protestant churches were to be "demolished without delay." "We forbid our subjects of the alleged Reformed Church," the Sun King declared, "to meet any more for the exercise of the said religion in any place or private house, under any pretext whatever."[1] Louis's goal, the primary objective of his domestic policy, was the total extirpation of French Protestantism.

A quarter or so of France's Protestant population fled. Those who stayed needed to abjure their faith and convert or suffer the consequences. Some of the extended Benezet family had already paid the price for refusing to conform; one of young Anthony's uncles was hanged, an aunt was immured in a nunnery, and two cousins died in the galleys. Torture, depredations, executions, and massacres ravaged the main Protestant regions of the country. In these circumstances most Protestants did recant and convert; they were called *Nouveaux Catholiques* (new Catholics) or simply *convertis* (converts). Many accepted the change, settled into their new Catholicism, and got on with their lives. But to the authorities all the conversions were suspicious. The *convertis* were monitored for attendance at Mass, at church festivals, marriages, baptisms, funerals. Their names were kept in the conversion rolls. Those who continued to practice their Protestant faith in secret also got on with their lives, but they felt scrutiny and feared the breakdown of their pretense.

Jean-Etienne, Anthony's father, was born into a *Nouveau Catholique* family. He no doubt went to Mass often enough to evade suspicion. Although he and Anthony's mother, Judith, were married by a Huguenot minister, they took the precaution of having their daughter, Marie-Madeleine and baby, Antoine, baptized by a Catholic priest. We don't know the details of Jean-Etienne's adherence to the Calvinist faith he cherished in private. Did he attend secret meetings for worship and join in the hymn singing so characteristic of Huguenot Protestantism? Did he pray the Calvinist forms of prayer or have contact with covert preachers eluding the state's religious police? Whatever form his hidden spiritual life might have taken, for many years he passed as acceptably Catholic. His own father had managed to swim with the tide—a practicing Protestant until it was no longer possible, enough of a Catholic after that not to arouse the inquisitors.

It didn't hurt that the family had money and standing. Anthony's grandfather was a collector of customs, his father a well-to-do linen merchant who had married into the Crommelin family textile dynasty. Given Jean-Etienne's position, it's probable that in Saint-Quentin he enjoyed a certain layer of protection. The textile industry was the city's economic engine, and most of those employed in the industry, from the linen, silk, and felt makers to the marketers, middlemen, and exporters, were Huguenots. By 1685, with the revocation of the Edict of Nantes, many of them had fled, leaving the region's economy in disarray. Given that, it's likely there was some official tolerance operating vis-à-vis Jean-Etienne and his business—until suddenly there wasn't, and the family had to flee on short notice.

In the years before his flight, Jean-Etienne had watched as successive waves of suppression washed over Saint-Quentin. Royal soldiers ran rampant in the region; arrests and killings terrorized the Huguenot population. Huguenot churches ("temples") were torn down, pastors driven out. Little was left of the fabric of French Protestant life that had persisted through the wars of religion, then subterraneously after the revocation. Jean-Etienne had seen all of that. Then his own turn came.

But in a sense, he was lucky. His family had originated in Calvisson, nestled in the foothills of the Vaunage in France's south. Some of his relatives were still there in 1702 when the town emerged as the epicenter of the blood-drenched Huguenot revolt known as the Camisard rebellion.[2] It's possible, perhaps likely, that the Benezet family's martyred relatives had been from the Calvisson region. Unlike Saint-Quentin and other urbanized settings where Huguenots lived alongside majority Catholic populations, the Vaunage region, isolated among the hills in the Nage Valley, was overwhelmingly Huguenot. Also unlike the Huguenot city populations, where Huguenots tended to be craftsmen, professionals, and businesspeople, the Protestants of the Vaunage were largely poor farmers, shepherds, and villagers, who lived out their lives in a remote hinterland separated from the major concentrations of their coreligionists, separated also by the Occitane dialect they spoke and by the widespread illiteracy of the region.

Isolated as they were, the Calvinism they practiced had developed distinctive features, more emotional, inspirational, and ecstatic than the liturgical and doctrinal discipline of the mainstream religion, with a sharper millenarian bent. After the revocation these differences intensified, fed by the ingrown circumstances of life in the region. Huguenots who lived closer to France's borders or to the Atlantic coast found and utilized flight paths out of the country, tens of thousands in steady streams that bled the country of a significant portion of its higher-level artisans and professionals. But from the landlocked hills and valleys of the Vaunage and the neighboring Cevennes massif, there were few escape routes and little in the way of wealth to enable flight. At the same time the concentrated Huguenot population made the area a prime target for the regime's agents of suppression and conversion.

Nowhere was Louis's effort to crush Protestantism pursued more fiercely than in the Benezet family's Vaunage homeland, and nowhere more fiercely there than in their native town of Calvisson. When the infamous archpriest and torturer the abbé du Chayla was given inquisitorial powers over the region in 1687, the persecution began in earnest. Dragoon squads swept into towns and farmsteads. Executions, imprisonments, condemnation to galleys, and incarceration of young women in convents spiraled. Collective punishments escalated the torment.

The people of the region resisted. With their "temples" destroyed, they took to the forests and mountains to hold services and hear the lay preachers who emerged to replace the pastors who had been expelled or hunted down and eliminated. But the rebellion began in earnest when a group of Protestants, enraged by du Chayla's actions, broke into his house, freed the people imprisoned there, set fire to the place, and assassinated the abbé.[3]

After that, it was war to the teeth between hastily organized groups of Protestant farmers, shepherds, mountaineers, and villagers and the king's dragoons and successively larger bodies of royal troops sent to quell a rebellion that was showing the typical effectiveness of guerrillas fighting in their home territory. The rebels, called Camisards from the white shirts they wore to identify themselves, killed priests and burned Catholic churches wherever they could. Their leaders—Abraham Mazel, Roland Cavalier, and Jean Cavalier (no relation to Roland)—proved to be inspired guerrilla chiefs, particularly Jean Cavalier, a twenty-one-year-old shepherd turned baker who demonstrated a native genius for this kind of war, winning victories even though always badly outnumbered and managing successful retreats from defeats. At Vagnas in 1703 he routed royal troops but the next day was overwhelmed in turn, though he managed to escape with enough of his force to renew the campaign. That oscillation, from victory to defeat and from defeat to victory, characterized the carnage, despite the rebels lack of numbers.

The religious conflict meant that the Camisard rebellion saw extreme levels of hatred and brutality. The Camisards massacred captured Catholic troops and civilians in cold blood; government troops reciprocated with even greater ferocity. Over two years of reprisal and atrocity French forces ground down the rebels and carried out a reign of terror in the Cevennes that horrified Protestants in England, Holland, Scotland, and elsewhere, pillaging and burning town after town, hanging rebels and sympathizers, and burning many at the stake. "Determined to end the ongoing resistance," writes historian Catherine Randall, "the king and his counselors decided to devastate the Cevennes through a scorched earth policy. The Marechal de Montrevel published an official decree that, if necessary, every Camisard town and village was to be destroyed."[4] After he put that policy in motion in the fall of 1703, hundreds of villages and hamlets were razed or burned and their surviving populations relocated to Catholic areas.

News of the destruction of France's Protestant heartland generated waves of anger among France's Protestant neighbors. Writing campaigns decrying the savagery were launched, and the Anglo-Dutch coalition sent several expeditions with the idea of providing military support for the Camisards. The rebellion itself may have taken place in a remote and relatively isolated region, but it was known, commented on, and acted on beyond France's borders.[5]

There's no doubt at all that Jean-Etienne Benezet, who had relatives in the Vaunage and was connected internationally through family networks, was acutely aware of what was happening in the South. He was only twenty years old when the Camisard rebellion ignited, but he came from an old Huguenot family and he himself, although growing up a *Nouveau Catholique*, nurtured in secret a deeply felt Protestant spirituality. Given the extreme violence against Protestants in the South and the ongoing suppression of Protestantism in Saint-Quentin, one can assume that as the years passed and his linen business flourished, Jean-Etienne experienced a painful degree of inner conflict. His success at making money was contingent on his pretense of Catholicism, uncomfortable, to say the least, given the depth of his hidden faith. Professor Gregory Monahan described the situation of many, like Jean-Etienne, who had been forced to abjure their faith. They "[had accepted] through gritted teeth a church they had been taught all their lives was Satan's child. The misery of accepting the Mass was so traumatic that some never got over it."[6] That was likely Jean-Etienne's mindset. One refugee wrote, "*J'ai damné mon âme, pour sauver mes biens*" (I damned my soul to preserve my goods.)[7] That his coreligionists, including his extended family, were being terrorized and murdered in Cevennes and elsewhere no doubt turned Jean-Etienne's inner turmoil acute.

When he finally did flee in 1715, Jean-Etienne was profoundly relieved at being in a place where he was free to practice his "holy religion." His experience left him with a lasting antipathy toward clerical hierarchies, an emotion he shared with many fellow Huguenot refugees, "born," says historian Margaret Jacob, "out of profound anger at being persecuted and forced out of their homeland."[8] Jean-Etienne's history of suppressed, searching spirituality shaped the family environment in which young Anthony Benezet grew up. The boy understood at least the gist of his father's inner conflicts, and while we don't know the dynamics of the Benezet family's domestic life, we can reasonably conjecture that Anthony's father was more open than closed about spiritual matters, which would have been normal for religious families then. Jean-Etienne was, we know, "deeply preoccupied by his spirituality and salvation."[9] We can imagine too, what a vast relief it was to finally get himself and his family away from France and its cruel persecutions.

When Jean-Etienne, Judith, and the children fled their home in Saint-Quentin, they abandoned the comforts of their previous well-off life, taking with them only the possessions they could carry. It was a rough, dangerous journey. Judith was heavily pregnant, close to term. The roads had checkpoints. After the revocation of the Edict of Nantes, the flood of departing businessmen, artisans, and key workers prompted King Louis to shut down the border crossings, locking in Protestants who could then be forcibly converted to Catholicism.

When Jean-Etienne and his family fled, they knew they stood a chance of being stopped and arrested, which could easily end in disaster, with Jean-Etienne in jail, in the galleys, possibly even executed (the Saint-Quentin authorities did hang him in effigy, a symbolic execution); Judith imprisoned; and the children cast to who knew what wind. Detained children, as they knew too well, were often separated from their families and converted by the authorities. But "God put it into our hearts," Jean-Etienne later wrote in the family record, "to leave France and retire to a Protestant country where we may freely profess our religion."[10]

The journey to Rotterdam took the Benezets twelve days in the midwinter cold of the Little Ice Age, when temperatures plummeted in France, England, and elsewhere in Europe. There's no direct record of what happened along the way, but a family story survived that Jean-Etienne had brought along someone he could trust, a young man to help them get through. At a roadblock or guard post, this companion approached the guard with a pistol in one hand and a purse of gold coins in the other. "These are good people," he supposedly told the guard. "They *are* going to pass." The guard took the gold and let them through.[11]

The Benezets left Saint-Quentin on February 3, 1715; they arrived in Rotterdam on February 15. Two weeks later Judith gave birth to a baby girl, whom they presented for baptism at Rotterdam's Walloon church. "God be praised," Jean-Etienne wrote, "that this child was baptized in a Protestant church."[12]

In the France the Benezets fled, Protestantism was being stamped out. The Netherlands, in contrast, had become a clearinghouse for Protestantism in its standard forms, as well as for a hodgepodge of radical sects in search of freedom to gather and worship—"a receiving station for all the sects of Christendom," as one scholar put it.[13] A hundred thousand French Protestants had resettled in Holland's cities, especially Rotterdam and Amsterdam;

there they found themselves among Anabaptists, Pietists, Arminians, Socinians, Quakers, Mennonites, Familists, and other lesser-known sects, with all the turmoil, confusion, and doctrinal conflict inherent in "a social, cultural, linguistic, and especially religious diversity of a sort never seen before in Europe."[14]

How Jean-Etienne reacted to this whirlwind of religions we don't know. What we do know is that he stayed for only six months before taking his family across the channel to England. He may have decided on this second emigration in the belief that England would be a better place to restart his linen business. But Jean-Etienne Benezet was also concerned about his spiritual life. Many fleeing Huguenots followed the road to Holland and then to England, where they established their own churches. One was in the village of Wandsworth, just south of London, home to what was already a small, settled Huguenot community. After the trauma of the family's escape and the wild religious turbulence of Rotterdam, Wandsworth may have seemed a relatively tranquil setting for both Jean-Etienne's business and his spiritual needs that had been so miserably suppressed in Saint-Quentin.

Huguenots called the lands of their exile "the Refuge." These places—Germany, Holland, Switzerland, England, America—offered freedom of worship, though sometimes those with established religions imposed requirements and restrictions on dissenters. But by and large the exiles succeeded in creating vital religious communities for themselves. Most thrived economically as well. Many exiles were skilled artisans in textiles—silk, felt, and cloth; others were entrepreneurial and established businesses, local and sometimes as part of French-speaking global trade networks. But successful or not, all the exiles carried with them vivid experiences of persecution, inexpungible memories of what they had suffered back in their homeland.

CHAPTER TWO

The Benezets in England

Anthony was barely two when the family undertook their hard trek through the Arrouaise Forest to Holland. The humanitarian concerns of his mature years lay in his distant and unimagined future. But the formation of his spirituality was an ongoing enterprise from his earliest youth—one is tempted to say from the dawn of his awareness, as it would have been in that age when religion was the matrix for how most people understood the meaning of their lives. His exposure to the world of religion—which eventually led him at age eighteen to his Quaker faith, and then to all else—came first through his family, then through the steeped religiosity that surrounded him as he came of age in the Huguenot refuge.

In Rotterdam, where the Benezet family lived for six months after crossing the border from France, enthusiastic religion was at a high pitch. The variety of sects gathered there included some of the Reformation era's most insistent voices regarding the worshipper's ability to make a direct, personal connection with the divine. The English Puritans, devoted to the quest for personal salvation through an immediate infusion of God's grace, had settled first in Holland for a dozen years before moving in 1620 to the New World. They chose Holland because even then, almost a hundred years before the Benezets arrived, the United Provinces was a haven for sectarians. As time passed, Amsterdam, Leiden, Rotterdam, and other safe harbors saw larger and larger concentrations of sects—Pietists, Quakers, Baptists, Socinians, and others—along with the outpouring of religious emotion they brought with them. "You could scarcely go through the streets of [any of] the Townes and Cittys of the Reformed Netherlands," wrote one minister, "but upon the Lord's day in the intervals of Sermons you should heare in the Streets Scriptures read, Sermons repeated, Psalms sung, Parents and Masters at prayers with their children & families."[1]

In the midst of this overflow of piety and enthusiasm, Jean-Etienne made what was called a *reconnaissance*, a formal recognition and recantation of his "error" in having conformed to Catholicism and attended Mass.

He did this before a consistory of Huguenot elders at Rotterdam's Walloon church, which had become a center for Huguenot worship. The Walloons were French-speaking Spanish Protestant refugees who welcomed the later arriving Huguenots. Their Rotterdam church was deeply involved not only with Huguenot refugees but with the prophetic movement that drove the Camisards in their insurgency.

In the violent cauldron of the Camisard rebellion, the region's Calvinist religion had evolved its own distinctive features. The heightened enthusiasm that characterized the South's Protestant spirituality transmuted: ecstatic worship with its trances, raptures, supranatural visions, and auditory hallucinations had been a regional quirk, but by 1702 these extremes had become Cevennes Protestantism's identifying characteristics.

As the rebellion progressed, ecstatic worship reached a fevered pitch. Camisard tenaciousness and ferocity on the battlefield were spurred by the so-called "prophetic" sermonizing of a large number of lay preachers, many of them young, who preached while seemingly possessed by the spirit of God or Jesus. A Camisard soldier, Jacques Bonbonnoux, described the experience in his *Memoir d'un Camisard.* "We prayed to God day and night," he wrote. "We sang psalms, we read the Bible. A young boy of seventeen years . . . spoke to us every day with prophecies and sermons. . . . Our worship ravished me with wonder. . . . Before we went into battle a young preacher . . . would exhort us with great zeal to fight even unto the death."[2] The enthusiastic excitement Bonbonnoux describes had arisen in the southern Huguenot stronghold as far back as the 1680s during the growing religious suppression leading up to the revocation. It marked the divergence of the Cevennes region's religion from that of mainstream Calvinism.

For the Calvinist Huguenots in Holland, the Rotterdam Walloon church's alignment with the prophetism of the Camisards was unusual. But the Walloon church pastor for thirty-two years was Pierre Jurieu, a leading Huguenot theologian and a fierce advocate for the suppressed *Nouveaux Catholiques* back in France as well as for the Camisards in their quixotic rebellion. Jurieu ran a spy network out of his church that penetrated France's ports and commercial institutions and fed information to the British. His *Pastoral Letters*, which circulated surreptitiously through France and openly all through Protestant Europe, excoriated the papacy as the great Antichrist and declared imminent salvation for French Protestantism through the fast-approaching Second Coming. "We must endeavor to open the eyes of the princes and the peoples of the earth," Jurieu wrote, "for, behold! The time is coming quickly when they are to eat the flesh of the beast and to burn it with fire; strip naked the whore of Babylon [the Papacy], tear off her ornaments, and make a full end of her, within a little while, great things must come to pass."[3]

Jurieu exhorted Huguenots to hold fast to their faith in the face of the Catholic campaign to eradicate French Protestantism. They would soon, he said, be vindicated by the triumph of the Holy Spirit overthrowing "the [Roman] beast." Those who died for the faith were martyrs whose memory would strengthen their brothers and sisters. Jurieu and others produced extensive martyrologies, extolling those who died for their steadfastness, to the extent that the idea of martyrdom embedded itself in the Huguenot consciousness.[4]

The Camisard rebellion was the last paroxysm of Europe's religious wars. Waged in an obscure corner of the continent, it burned hot for only a short time. But its "legacy," writes historian Lionel Laborie, "remained in everyone's mind throughout the eighteenth century," in part due to the reach of Jurieu's *Pastoral Letters*.[5] That legacy of martyrdom was no doubt a painful note in Jean-Etienne's mind as he recanted his Catholicism in the church that bore the distinctive imprint of Jurieu's long tenure. The fiery pastor had died two years before the Benezets escaped France, but his influence was pervasive; his apocalyptic pronouncements and martyrologies had become an important feature in the Huguenot identity narrative.

That was true throughout the Huguenot diaspora, including in England, where the Benezet family moved in August 1715—first to Greenwich, then London, then finally to the town of Wandsworth just south of the capital. Wandsworth is now a southern district of London city, but when the Benezets arrived there more than three hundred years ago it was a small town known for its market gardens, which supplied London's Covent Garden, and its corn mills, much of whose output went to the kitchens of the royal household. The Wandle River, from which Wandsworth took its name, meandered through the town, its banks dotted with mills and factories, including an iron foundry and a pots-and-pans factory founded by Dutch émigrés at Point Pleasant, where the Wandle flowed into the Thames. The town was also known for its cloth manufacturing, which no doubt attracted the Huguenot refugees who began arriving in the late seventeenth century and who, by the Benezets' time, constituted a thriving, if small, community, with its own French-language church and nearby burial ground. Huguenot refugees, with their skill at working textiles, began hat making and dyeing businesses and other cloth-related enterprises, which made Wandsworth a likely location for Jean-Etienne to reestablish the linen enterprise he had abandoned when the family fled Saint-Quentin.

The Huguenot arrivals, in Wandsworth and elsewhere, brought with them skills the British economy welcomed, and in terms of employment many quickly integrated. At the same time, their struggle against the Catholic Church and the Catholic power of France made them natural allies. But like all refugees attempting settlement in foreign places, they had their problems. The English might have been sympathetic to the Huguenots' plight, but they also had a history of xenophobia and antagonism toward the French generally, and now a flood of French people had descended on them.

With so many immigrants settling in the country, the initial compassionate welcome was, by the turn of the century, wearing thin. In some places around London the refugee population was so dense that French was heard on the streets more often than English, to the irritation of many English-speaking natives. Questions were raised about the policy of permitting foreigners to settle and why the Crown provided aid to foreigners rather than poor Englishmen. French foods were disparaged, French ways of dress, French idiosyncrasies noted and frowned on. British weavers objected, sometimes violently, to the arrival of large numbers of French clothworkers.[6] The artist and satirist William Hogarth in his drawing *Noon* depicted a group of dour Huguenots dressed in dark clothing as they left church services, contrasting them with the happier, enthusiastic English enjoying their midday activities.[7] Religious differences, too, began to loom in significance. Huguenots and the English were both Protestant, but they were different kinds of Protestant, and that became more telling as time went by.

While we know little about the daily lives of Anthony and his family as they strove to settle into their new home, we do have a good deal of information about the French community they became part of. The immigrants' lives were conditioned by the Calvinism they practiced and the way they accommodated themselves, or didn't, to the English religious world they found themselves in. That world was dominated by the Church of England but encompassed a variety of dissenting confessions, including Quakers, whom the Benezets got to know as neighbors. The Huguenot newcomers also brought with them their own trailing memories and sometimes experiences with the ecstatic prophetism of their Cevennes compatriots.

When large numbers of French refugees began arriving in the latter seventeenth century, there was a common feeling that England was the protector of Europe's suppressed Protestants. But by the early eighteenth century, public sentiment increasingly linked British identity with membership in the Anglican Church.[8] Some of the Huguenots' French churches conformed to the national church, using a French translation of the *Book of Common Prayer* as the service liturgy, but others dissented, adhering to Calvinist forms of worship. As British sentiment cooled toward foreigners and their un-British ideas and customs, religious differences received heightened concern.

In such a conflicted and in some ways fraught environment, the Huguenot community treated the sensitivities of their hosts with extreme care. Many, perhaps most, of the Huguenot refugees had not yet been naturalized, which subjected them to special taxes and various restrictions.[9] For many reasons they needed to be accepted and to assimilate, not to stand out for their differences. But in 1706 an exacerbation injected itself into the fragile religious situation in the form of three "prophets" fleeing the bloody terminal phase of the Camisard rebellion.

Elie Marion, a former captain in the Camisard army, was on his way to Switzerland when he was suddenly overcome by a voice telling him to go to England instead. Two other prophets, Durant Fage and Jean Cavalier (no relation to the Camisard war chief), were already there, preaching the apocalypse and the destruction of the Antichrist (the pope), prophesying from the midst of ecstatic trances, and drawing first small, then larger audiences.

It's likely that the prophets' original hope was to raise an army from the English Huguenot community and from British supporters of the Camisard cause. "The trumpet is ready to sound," Cavalier prophesied, channeling the Holy Spirit. "Fire, Lightenings and Thunderbolts are prepared for thine enemies. . . . Prepare thyself to depart within a short time out of this Country, and go to thy Brethren, to fight there more than ever."[10] But while some of the refugee Huguenots were receptive to Cavalier's call, as were a number of Englishmen, few had any appetite to actually go to France and engage in armed struggle.

At the same time, the manner of the prophets' preaching—the trances, the convulsions, the glossolalia—attracted not only the curious but also some who saw the spirit of God at work in something like the way God had manifested himself in Biblical times. Most were familiar with the description of the newly anointed king of Israel, Saul, who fell in among a group of wandering prophets: "Thereupon the spirit of God gripped him and he spoke in ecstasy among them" (1 Sam. 10:10b). And if God was again bestowing the gifts of prophecy, was it not possibly a precursor or announcement that the promised millennium was indeed at hand, as the prophets were proclaiming?

There was, initially, a wave of emotional support for the three survivors of the Cevennes war. Public collections were ordered throughout the country for their relief, which met with a generous response. The prophets had fought courageously against the brutal might of the Catholic Church and its French minions. There was great sympathy for that. Antipathy toward the Roman church was at a peak in England, which had been at war with France for twenty years, fueled by fear of Louis XIV's hegemonistic aspirations and by the threat of a French-led expansion of Catholicism. In this context the Camisards were admired for their valiant resistance to Louis's drive to eliminate French Protestantism.[11]

But while the Huguenot refugee community may have sympathized with the prophets, they were also wary of the effect they might have. Their concern was prescient. If the three prophets had kept a low profile, there likely would have been nothing but sympathy. But they had not arrived in England to keep a low profile, and in any event their inspiration by the Holy Spirit was not to be denied.

The result was not only that they drew a small contingent of followers from the refugee Huguenot community; worse, their apocalyptic declarations appealed to a segment of British believers with their own millenarian hopes and expectations, some of whom thought the persecution of the Camisards itself prefigured the end-time. To them the "French Prophets" appeared as potential heralds of the Second Coming, and they joined a growing following.[12]

The millenarian impulse was never far beneath the surface of English religious life. Muggletonians, Fifth Monarchy Men, Ranters, Seekers, and other enthusiastic sects were only the most visible manifestations of the deep desire for the advent of the promised new dispensation so central to Christian eschatology. In that regard the three French prophets (*les Inspirés*) were an unwelcome visitation to a British government doing its best to cope with the unsettled and potentially destabilizing post-Cromwellian state of the country's religious affairs. "Appealing as frequently to Anglicans as to dissenters, the French Prophets would confront English society with a turbulent and menacing millenarianism," writes Hillel Schwartz, the preeminent expert on the Prophets. "The potential power of the French Prophets lay in their unusual ability to attract millenarians of all persuasions and of every ethos. Fear of this power . . . was a major factor in the English reception of the *Inspirés*."[13]

The Prophets' distinctive appeal lay in their claim to speak not with their own voices but as channels for the Godhead communicating through them. The episodes of possession—their "inspirations"—were announced by violent body movements, seizures, respiratory distress, and swelling in bellies and throats. One of their former adherents described "violent and strange Agitations or Shakings of the Body, loud and terrifying Hiccups, and Throbs, with many odd and surprising Postures."[14]

The Prophets' bizarre physical manifestations—the convulsions, the trance states, and the rest—along with the spiritual channeling are hard for us, more than three hundred years later, to think of as anything other than hysteria or possibly group psychogenesis (if they were not simply fabrications). But although many in England were either amused or scandalized by them, the Prophets did not represent something distinctly alien. The belief that individuals had at least the potential for personal, unmediated infusion of the Holy Spirit was threaded through all of the Reformed communions, carefully hemmed about in Anglicanism but free of constraints in some of the radical sects.[15]

Prophetism took this essential Protestant tenet to an extreme, which to some of those attracted to their meetings gave incontrovertible, visible proof of the Holy Spirit's presence among the faithful, a tangible manifestation.[16] Before long, that attraction bore fruit in the conversion of small but growing numbers in London and then other English cities. Bristol, Birmingham, Manchester, Salisbury, Ipswich, and Yarmouth all had their prophetic enclaves. Scotland was even more fertile ground, in Edinburgh and Montrose especially.[17]

The leading Huguenot churches, determined to distance the refugee community from the Camisard Prophets and their increasingly volatile messages of coming destruction, issued a combined statement repudiating the *Inspirés*: "The agitation of these pretended Prophets are only the Effect of voluntary Habit, of which they are entirely Masters, though in their Fits they seem to be agitated by a Superior Cause." The churches expressed indignation at "[their] perpetual hesitations, puerile repetitions, absolute gibberish, gross contradictions, palpable lies, conjectures disguised as predictions, predictions already refuted by events, morality that . . . has nothing new about it other than the grimaces."[18]

According to the Huguenot clergy, the Prophets were fakers and frauds, especially dangerous because their activities had the potential to upset the refugees' delicate relations with the established church and the government. "[They] might bring down dishonor on our Religion and censure upon our Refuge," as the Huguenot Threadneedle Street church consistory put it in a 1707 condemnation. After some Huguenots physically assaulted the Prophets, the Threadneedle elders warned their congregants not to let their anger "degenerate into an unrestrained fury that might border on sedition and might disturb the public peace." The Huguenots should remember, the consistory declared, "the clemency which our sovereign has shown us, but gives us no right to expect any further proof of it."[19]

Subsequently the churches refused communion for the three, and shortly afterward Marion and two of the scribes were brought to trial in front of the Queen's Bench Court, accused of blasphemy. Convicted there, Marion was sentenced to stand on the scaffold at Charing Cross with a placard in his hat declaring, "Elias Marion, convicted for falsely and profanely proclaiming himself to be a true prophet, and printing and uttering many things as dictated and revealed to him by the Spirit of God to terrifie the Queen's people."[20] The scribes, likewise convicted, stood on the scaffold next to him with their own placards in their hats.

They stood there for two days as a crowd jeered and pelted them with garbage and excrement. It wasn't the last incident that would seem to belie the Prophets' authenticity. Several days later, one of their English followers, a Dr. Emes, fell ill and died. Some of the newly converted Prophets had declared that he would recover. When he didn't, it was announced that the Holy Spirit had decreed that in five months Dr. Emes would rise from the dead. Five months to the day of his death, a crowd estimated at twenty thousand gathered at the Bunhill Fields cemetery to watch Dr. Emes ascend from the grave. But to their great disappointment, the doctor remained firmly in his coffin, which made the Prophets a laughingstock among a good proportion of those following their English career—though not, by any means, all.[21]

Despite these setbacks, the Prophets continued as an active, proselytizing sect for another decade, after which they maintained a presence into the 1730s, well into young Anthony Benezet's teen years. But even after that, they were far from forgotten. The ethos of their peculiar enthusiasm seeped into the beginnings of Moravianism and Methodism. They profoundly influenced the earliest Shakers. In important ways French Prophetism foreshadowed the Great Awakening, the revivalist phenomenon that gripped Pennsylvania and the other American colonies after the Benezet family emigrated to Philadelphia. "As a religious force in England," Schwartz writes, "as a specter haunting subsequent evangelical efforts, the French Prophets had been etched in many memories."[22] They were etched as well in Jean-Etienne's memory, and they were in young Anthony's mental world, too, as he grew toward maturity in the Huguenot diaspora.

Little has been written about the effect of Benezet's refugee experience on the motives that ultimately guided him. But we know from the experiences of refugees in the twentieth and twenty-first centuries that the trauma of being torn violently from home and displaced elsewhere almost always has lifetime consequences. It imprints itself on personal identity and embeds itself in the narrative of lives. So often it contributes to the moral formation and values of those who undergo the experience; it imparts itself even to the children of victims.[23]

In his later years Anthony Benezet rarely talked about himself, but on several occasions, he permitted others to draw him out. "I ought to be allowed to talk with eagerness about such an important subject," he told the Marquis Barbe-Marbois, the French diplomat who visited with him in Philadelphia during the Revolutionary War. "It was by the intolerant that one of my uncles was hanged, that an aunt was sent to a convent, that two of my cousins are dead in the galleys, and that my father, a fugitive, was ruined by the confiscation of all his goods."[24] "Friend," he told another French visitor, Francois-Jean de Chastellux, "this persecution is a strange thing. I can hardly believe what has happened to myself. My father was a Frenchman, and I am a native of thy country. It is not sixty years since he was obliged to seek asylum in England, taking with him his children, the only treasure he could save in his misfortunes. Justice, or what is so-called in thy country, ordered him to be hung in effigy, for explaining the gospel differently from thy priests."[25]

In his mature correspondence, as well as in his more formal writing, Benezet was almost always strategic. With few exceptions he wrote about the immediate humanitarian causes that engrossed him, what they were, why they were, and what needed to be done about them. He had causes other than ending slavery. He took a hand in relieving settlers in western Pennsylvania marauded and abducted by the Shawnee and Delaware during the French and Indian War; he did everything he could to work for peace with the same tribes. When hundreds of French refugees from the British ethnic cleansing of Nova Scotia were kept isolated in boats off Philadelphia's Delaware River port, Benezet arranged for their food and care.

These concerns drew his compassionate nature. He no doubt felt a special connection with the refugee French Acadians; he shared their ethnicity and spoke their language. Suppression, violence, forcible removal from their homes—his own family had experienced the same ordeals. That feeling for people oppressed and violated exploded into the antislavery activism of the second part of his life. But we can tell from his discussions with Barbe-Marbois and Chastellux that the pain of his own background occupied a permanent place in the landscape of his inner life.

Anthony Benezet was heir to the disaster that drove Huguenots out of France. That defining event shaped the spiritual world he grew up in; it led his family from their home in France to Holland, to England, and then to America. It stayed with Anthony over the years—"I can scarcely believe what has happened to myself," he told Chastellux when he was sixty-seven, a lifetime away from the family's sudden flight from Saint-Quentin. As he entered what then was considered old age the original event was still with him, an indelible part of who he was.

The refugee experience is almost never simply an individual trauma. It conditions the identity of a community as well; it incorporates itself into the collective memory and creates meanings and a distinctive orientation that often persist over many generations. Anthony Benezet grew up in a community still suffering raw wounds, in an environment where martyrdom, suffering, and the pain of remaking lives were built into the culture of displacement. The elements of that culture reflected the struggle of a religious community to sustain itself, whether that meant practicing Calvinism in its standard form or embracing idiosyncratic deviations that empowered armed resistance to the French (and Catholic) oppressor. "The traditions of the past," a nineteenth-century commentator wrote, "were never forgotten by the fugitives in their 'strange land;' . . . the song of praise sung by their ancestors for fear of danger in some mountain fortress of southern France, re-echoed in these crowded London churches. The book that was read out loud . . . spoke of the mental courage and suffering of their forefathers, who . . . had braved persecution."[26] All of this was present in the social, political, and religious sea the Benezets swam in alongside their Huguenot brethren. It was a narrative that played a continuing role in Anthony's interior world as he came of age in the Huguenot Refuge.

CHAPTER THREE

Quakers

The Benezet family were refugees, but the mental and emotional trauma of their flight and disrupted lives undoubtedly faded over time as new experiences took over and they adjusted to their new surroundings. For the two older Benezet children, Marie-Madeleine and Anthony, the adjustments wouldn't have been particularly challenging. For their parents, it would have been more difficult. But with time Jean-Etienne and Judith would have grown more comfortable with the language, more at home with English ways of doing things and with the sometimes surprising customs of their new neighbors. Wandsworth was home to immigrant Hollanders as well as to displaced Huguenots. There was also a small but well-established Quaker community with a meetinghouse, a burial ground, a school, and a schoolmaster.

Anthony wasn't yet three when the family arrived in Wandsworth. In his early years there the Benezets would have gotten to know some of their neighbors, and it seems they enrolled Anthony in the Quaker school overseen by schoolmaster John Kuweidt. While we have little or no information about Anthony's early religious development, we do know that sixteen years later, when the Benezet family arrived in Pennsylvania, both he and his father immediately joined the Philadelphia Quaker Meeting. That tells us they must have known the Society of Friends back in England and that they were already familiar with Quaker beliefs and Quaker ways.

The fundamental element of Anthony Benezet's identity, without which his later antislavery compulsion can hardly be imagined, was his Quaker spirituality. But despite his early exposure to Quaker neighbors in Wandsworth, Anthony's path to Quaker principles and the Quaker way of life was not foreordained. The Benezet family had escaped from Louis XIV's bloody suppression of Protestants in France. Quakers too had been a suppressed minority, suffering cruelly in earlier times from the harsh persecution of a hostile English government and the hatred of mobs inflamed by what must have seemed to them the Quakers' intolerable arrogance and semi-insane fanaticism. But despite the similarities in their histories, Huguenots generally had little to do with Quakers. "All sources," writes University of Paris professor of American civilization Bertrand Van Ruymbeke, "converge to show that Huguenots held Quakers in contempt."[1] They were denounced, for example, as a fanatical sect by the leading Huguenot preacher in exile, Pierre Jurieu. On the essential question of salvation, the Calvinist Huguenots' strict dogma of predestination contrasted sharply with the Quaker belief in the universal indwelling of divine love. Huguenots who resettled in America almost always chose South Carolina or New York as their preferred destination, not William Penn's "Holy Experiment." "Huguenot letters about the Quakers and Pennsylvania in the 1680s and early 1700s were all negative," Van Ruymbeke writes.[2] "This colony's Quakery (in French *la Quaquerie*) is not a pleasant thing," one refugee pastor wrote to his brother.[3] Benezet's father, Jean-Etienne, wrote about being "mocked, despised, and disapproved" for his decision to join the Quakers.[4]

By the time the Benezets arrived in Wandsworth, the Society of Friends was a regulated, largely institutionalized organization, but the Quakers previously had been as wild in their own way as the Prophets were in theirs. Anthony certainly learned about that history; he no doubt absorbed knowledge of the Quakers' fractious, turbulent past as his contacts with the Society matured. That knowledge might well have contributed to his own mature spirituality by repelling him from the intercommunal heat of his times and toward the inner peace and unspoken security that marked the Quaker faith he committed to in Pennsylvania. He had been born into a world of deadly religious violence, and from childhood he lived in the midst of acrimonious conflicts between sects and communions. Given all that, it's tempting to imagine the young Anthony in a Quaker school experiencing the meditative quiet of a meeting for worship, which would have been a regular part of his school week.

Unfortunately, there is no extant account of Anthony's early religious development. All we know with certainty is that he and his father joined the Philadelphia Friends Meeting shortly after their arrival in Pennsylvania in 1731, which leaves open the question of why at the age of eighteen he made such a commitment.

One answer may be his alienation from religious controversy, which held no attraction for him whatsoever. He was, Marbois wrote later, "by character and by religion, the enemy of all controversy."[5] Quakers started off as fierce controversialists, vehemently attacking the established religion with its vainglorious "steeple houses" and its "hireling priests." So disruptive were the early Quakers that Oliver Cromwell at one point regarded them as "the most dangerous" of revolutionary and rebellious sects.[6] But by the time Benezet was growing up in England, the Friends had long since turned inward and away from the militance that had enabled them to grow so quickly in their early period. They had "[left] behind their enthusiastic and ecstatic escapades," writes Larry Ingle, biographer of Quakerism's founder, George Fox, "and withdrew from confrontation. . . . To a large degree, they separated themselves from the outside world."[7] Fox himself urged Friends "not to medle with ye powers of ye earth, to kepe out of all such things . . . to kepe out of all vaine Janglinge."[8] Benezet joined a communion that had freed itself from religious controversy, a rarity in the religious firmament of the early eighteenth century.

He may also have been attracted by the Quaker concept of salvation, which came directly from George Fox's personal experience. According to Catholic scholar Ronald Knox, Fox strode like "a giant figure" through the "muddy pools of forlorn controversy" to infuse a new life into the religion of England.[9] Fox's apprehension of what it meant to be saved convinced tens of thousands of English people and many thousands more outside of England. That idea was so convincing and so comfortable for Anthony Benezet that he never questioned it, even though his father, who converted with him, later left the Quakers for the Moravians and then left the Moravians as well. Also telling is that neither Anthony's mother nor any of his seven siblings joined the Quakers with him. Benezet was the only one in his family who found in Quaker salvational thought an approach entirely congenial to his own mind and spirit.

Fox's experience of salvation, an event that took place when he was twenty-three, was *the* defining moment in his life, and it became the foundational belief of the religion he founded. It came upon him only after a tortured early search for spiritual fulfillment. But when it did come, it came suddenly and without warning.

Fox had grown up in a Presbyterian household, but he was appalled by what he considered the hypocrisy and corruption of clerics and church leaders. Filled with spiritual longing he left home when he was nineteen hoping to find some means of relieving the devastating inner emptiness he felt. After several years wandering, talking with orthodox clerics, dissenting preachers, reading the Bible, isolating himself in contemplation, he had reached a point of desperation. "I had forsaken the priests," he wrote in his journal, "so I left the separate [dissenting] preachers also, and those esteemed the most experienced people; for I saw there was none among them all that could speak to my condition. And when all my hopes in them and in all men were gone, so that I had nothing outwardly to help me, nor could tell what to do, then, oh, then, I heard a voice which said, 'There is one, even Christ Jesus, that can speak to thy condition,' and when I heard it, my heart did leap for joy."[10]

That simple revelation transformed him into a new man. "Now I was come up in spirit," he wrote, ". . . into the paradise of God. All things were new, and all the creation gave another smell unto me than before, beyond what words can utter. I knew nothing but pureness, innocence, and righteousness, being renewed into the image of God by Christ Jesus; so that I was come up to the state of Adam, which he was in before he fell."[11]

What differentiates George Fox from many other seekers after salvation is that once that voice spoke to him he found himself in a state of assured serenity. Whether salvation was by faith alone, or faith and works, or mysteriously predestined, or somewhere in the offing if God granted him sufficient grace—suddenly those questions about the condition of his soul ceased to concern him. He dwelt in the light. And it came to him that if he dwelt in the light, others did too, if only they knew it. In 1647 he set out on a lifetime journey to convince them that they did.

At the age of twenty-three, Fox was suddenly overcome by the understanding that not only was he himself renewed in the image of God, all pureness, innocence, and righteousness, but the same sanctification was the birthright of everyone. He saw that "every man was enlightened by the divine Light of Christ." He saw the Light "shine through all." "I was sent," he says, "to turn people from darkness to the Light that they might receive Christ Jesus; for to as many as should receive Him in His light, I saw He would give power to become the sons of God."[12]

It was the simplest of messages. Fox was offering the light of Christ, which required no suffering, no appeal to scripture, no delving into sin and repentance or searching for signs of salvation. It required only acceptance of that which Fox's listeners had within them already. In a sense he had, as one commentator put it, "his audience with him beforehand." Those who were moved by his preaching were not "converted"; they were "convinced"—that is, "persuaded" to see in themselves something they simply hadn't previously seen.[13] It's no wonder he was so successful, preaching first in the Midlands, then in the North Country—Lancashire, Yorkshire, Westmoreland—and gathering adherents, a group of whom also started traveling and preaching. He began in marketplaces, in the fields, in meetings of other sects, anywhere he could find people who might listen, shouting out his message in churches on Sunday, disrupting services, then being dragged off to jail, where he continued preaching.

Fox began his ministry in 1647. By the mid-1650s, he and his fellow missionaries had attracted perhaps fifty thousand believers. Today we don't think of Quakers as evangelists. But they were then. They went everywhere. They tried to convert the pope; they traveled to Istanbul to confront the sultan. In 1656 three Quaker missionaries were hanged in Puritan Boston; a year later, another went to the gallows there—a woman named Mary Dyer, who had been ejected from the colony with a warning but who persisted in coming back to preach.

Fox's Quaker message may have been simple, but it often had an overwhelming emotional effect. A petition against Quakers in Lancashire maintained, "Men, women, and little children are strangely wrought upon their bodies, and brought to fall, foam at the mouth, roar and swell in their bellies." Puritan leader Richard Baxter wrote, "At first, they did use to fall into violent Tremblings and sometimes Vomitings in their meetings."[14] When William Penn went to his first Quaker meeting after being convinced by the itinerant preacher Thomas Loe, he "was exceedingly reached so that he wept much." He heard a voice telling him to "stand on thy feet." Hearing it, he got up and stood.[15]

The power of Fox's preaching was often overwhelming. His inspiration triggered similar inspiration in a great many who heard him. The picture we have is of large numbers of English men and women thirsting for a path to salvation but frustrated by what they regarded as the failures and inadequacies of institutionalized religion, Anglican and Roman Catholic, and dissatisfied with the answers provided by the various dissenting sects. Fox's message addressed a deep, unfulfilled longing, bringing a relief so profound that some of those affected were carried to extremes of feeling about him. "Dear G:ff" [George Fox], one adherent wrote in a letter offering to lay down his life for Fox: "Dear G:ff, Whose beauty and comeliness in words cannot be exprest."[16] "O thou bread of life," his convert and later his wife, Margaret Fell, wrote, "without which bread our souls will starve. . . . O thou fountain of eternal life, our souls thirst after thee, for in thee alone is our life and peace."[17]

For many Fox had a messianic aura about him. He seems to have felt that about himself as well. "The Lord commanded me to go abroad into the world," he wrote in his *Journal*,

> which was like a briery, thorny wilderness. When I came in the Lord's mighty power with the Word of life into the world, the world swelled,

> and made a noise like the great raging waves of the sea. Priests and professors, magistrates and people, were all like a sea when I came to proclaim the day of the Lord amongst them, and to preach repentance to them.
>
> I was sent to turn people from darkness to the Light, that they might receive Christ Jesus; . . . to direct people to the Spirit . . . by which they might be led into all truth, and up to Christ and God."[18]

Fell, says William Braithwaite, believed that Fox was "possessed by the spirit of Christ."[19] But being "possessed," in this sense, carried with it spiritual dangers, which Fox's closest companions may not have seen. The potential danger of enthusiasm is that for certain personalities a sense of being possessed by the Godhead can lead to a feeling that the believer's own identity has been subsumed by the divine, that ego, personality, motivations have all fallen away and been replaced by something holy, that the self has been transformed. Think of the French Prophets, their bodies and voices taken over, if only temporarily, by the Holy Spirit. At least for the period of their "inspiration," the demarcation between man and God was dissolved. The great mystics historically believed they were progressing toward union with the divine, though only rarely did they claim what William James called "becoming one with the Absolute."[20]

George Fox never confused himself with Jesus, but he did believe he had been perfected and was sinless in the same way that Adam was in the Garden of Eden ("I was come up to the state of Adam, which he was in before he fell"). That was a kind of apotheosis. But the idea that the indwelling Christ might take over the personality altogether was always a potential buried in Fox's Inner Light theology. And that potential revealed itself in the person of Fox's close colleague James Nayler.

Nayler was one of Fox's early converts. Brilliant, eloquent, persuasive, he became a prominent member of the so-called Valiant Sixty, the large group of ardent Quaker evangelists who were key to the growth of the movement. Nayler's effectiveness was especially evident not just in the north of England, where he was from, but in the difficult proselytizing terrain of London. To some of his converts and companions, his charisma seemed more than natural, and some began to see him as a fuller, more powerful embodiment of the Holy Spirit than Fox. Almost inevitably tension developed between the two men, exacerbated by the fact that in a movement with no hierarchy, leadership was inherently prone to conflict. Also, where spiritual authenticity is based on an indwelling of the spirit, which all possess, who is to say that one individual's connection with the Light is more genuine than another's?

The emerging conflict between Fox and Nayler was intensified by their personalities. Fox might have had no official standing, but he was the originator of the movement and was, at least until Nayler, universally acknowledged as its leader. And Fox was not the man to brook a challenge. He had little of the forgiving, accommodating spirit in him. He expected deference and bristled when it didn't seem to be forthcoming.

Nayler, meanwhile, suffered from a precarious emotional constitution, badly weakened by his habit of extended fasts and the stress of long periods of imprisonment. When he was released from his latest confinement in Exeter jail, his mental state seemed undermined. Under ordinary circumstances he was unsure of the extent to which the inward light was, in fact, a kind of divinization, let alone when he was in emotional distress. He had even, apparently, cultivated in his long hair and beard a resemblance to the images of Jesus widely known in his day. When he emerged from his latest imprisonment his most passionate followers greeted him, individuals who had signified in one way or another their adoration. "The everlasting Son of Righteousness," one had called him. "The only begotten Son of God." "Thy name," wrote another, "shall no more be James Nayler, but Jesus."[21]

In 1656, on his release from his latest confinement, a small group of these followers decided to present a "sign" of Nayler's Jesus-like stature. Signs—performative portrayals meant to startle onlookers with their prophetic implications—were a feature in the repertoires of some of the more radical sects, including the Quakers. A figure dressed in sackcloth scattering ashes on his (or her) head might appear in a marketplace or church service, representing the sorrow and mourning sinners would experience at the fast-approaching day of judgment. More shocking was the occasional appearance of naked people running through the streets or even preaching to onlookers. This was "going naked as a sign," meant to signify that the Lord would strip away sinners' vanities and false posturings and expose their evil ways to the world. The intended meaning might have been clear enough to Quakers, but possibly not to onlookers scandalized by the obscenity. But the sign Nayler and his adherents performed was obvious to anyone who happened to see it.

A few days after Nayler's release, a peculiar procession made its way toward Bristol. It was described in a letter written by a witness and from testimony at the trial that followed. A young man, bare-headed, led Nayler's horse along the muddy cart-way, while another walked in front. Two men followed on horseback, each with a woman behind him. Two other women walked alongside, up to their knees in mud—it was raining heavily. "But they trudged along, singing 'Holy, holy, holy Lord God of Israel,' with a buzzing melodious noise, not easy to understand, and the women spread garments before Nayler."[22] Nayler sat on his horse, rain pouring down on him, a bedraggled figure emulating Christ's triumphal entry into Jerusalem. The procession made its way to the center of Bristol, where the participants were apprehended and brought in front of the magistrate.

It isn't clear to what extent Nayler participated in the planning of this event or if he was so emotionally and physically exhausted by his just-completed monthlong fast in jail that he simply went along with his followers' intentions. In any event, a week later he was on trial before a committee of the House of Commons, charged with blasphemy, the punishment for which was anything the committee decided on, up to and including death. The committee asked if anyone had called him Jesus or adored him as Jesus. Although he was undoubtedly aware of what they were after, Nayler's scruples about the inward light led him to the confusion apparent in his answers.

> Had anyone called him by the name of Jesus?
>
> "As I am visible here before you I believe they have not, but that the Word of the Lord is in me, that I dare not deny. . . . If they have given it to any other than to the Son of God that is in me, I do deny what they have said."[23]
>
> "Art thou the everlasting Son of God?"
>
> "Where God is manifest in the flesh, there is the everlasting Son, and I do witness God in the flesh; I am the Son of God, and the Son of God is but one."[24]

His answers were enigmatic, ambiguous, probably as much to Nayler himself as to his inquisitors.

The parliamentary committee came near condemning him to death but finally concluded that a lesser but still severe punishment was in order. Nayler was pilloried and branded on the forehead with a *B* for *Blasphemer*. His tongue was bored through with a hot iron, he was whipped through the streets, then remanded to the Bridewell prison, where he was to serve his sentence of two years of solitary confinement at hard labor, followed by further incarceration at the will of Parliament.

Nayler's catastrophe was, of course, far more than personal. Quakers were subject to widespread attacks for "spawning such as Nayler and his ilk." "The Quaker Jesus," one pamphleteer called him. "Archbishop Nayler," the "false Christ," wrote another.[25] The Quaker community felt the consequences internally as well. In the aftermath Nayler expressed his sorrow and repentance for having caused such a serious disruption to the community's harmony. But Fox didn't grasp the outstretched hand, despite the implorations of some of his colleagues, who were afraid that without some kind of reconciliation, Nayler's adherents would continue to cause trouble. Fox, though, remained adamant, ignoring or dismissing Nayler's overtures and the advice of his friends.[26]

As a result, Nayler adherents disrupted meetings and sometimes held their own gatherings. "Persons of a loose ranting spirit got up and frequently disturbed our Friends' meetings," one prominent Quaker wrote, "ranting, singing, bawling and reproaching us, crying . . . 'you have lost the power, you have lost the power.'"[27]

Fox himself didn't show any outward anxiety and continued preaching to large and receptive crowds. But the affair had precipitated a sharper understanding of the dangers inherent in a freewheeling belief in the Inner Light. In particular, how could Friends distinguish true from false testimony, which might create dissension, or worse? While he seemed undisturbed by the odium the affair had generated and the disruptions to some Quaker meetings, Fox was thinking about how to reconcile individualism with unity and preserve the Society from schism and possible extinction through the clash of individuals or factions, all devoted to their own interpretation of the Holy Spirit.

It's here that Fox's genius revealed itself. In terms of religion, Fox was an original. He carried the Protestant idea of immediacy in fundamentally new directions. But his breakthrough there was inspirational. A voice spoke to him, he recognized it, and he acted on it. There was no intellectual dimension to what he felt and what he did; he was spurred by revelation, not by reason. The Nayler conflict required something completely different, a high level of strategic thinking and an ability to extrapolate from the problem of the moment to its ramifications for the Society's future. Fox understood that the Nayler phenomenon posed an existential threat to the movement, "a great darknesse in ye nation," as he put it.[28]

He needed a mechanism that would ensure unity without destroying the individualistic essence of the Inner Light experience. He found it in local monthly meetings for business that would oversee conduct, charity, publications, and other activities having to do with the welfare of the whole. Fox established these gatherings first in northern England and then extended them to the entire country, with repeated admonitions about the necessity of keeping order, peace, and unity among Friends. "[It] was his most enduring achievement," Ingle writes, ". . . because it saved Quakerism from going to oblivion."[29] It was, in retrospect, a remarkable transformation, attesting to Fox's judgement and foresight. It allowed the Quakers, this outré sect on the far left wing of the Reformation, to survive when so many other radical Protestant offshoots—Familists, Seekers, Ranters, and Prophetists—did not.

Fox later established quarterly business meetings that encompassed countywide or regional jurisdictions. The Quaker system now included meetings for worship (usually twice a week) and meetings for evangelization, as well as the monthly, quarterly, and then yearly meetings that oversaw conduct as well as counseling and discipline for those considered to be "walking disorderly." As the structure of the Society was regularized, Friends became habituated to order and seemliness in their speech and conduct, a far cry from their earlier incarnation.

By the time Fox died, in 1691, the Quaker movement had become thoroughly institutionalized. When the Benezets became acquainted with them in Wandsworth, the contentiousness and militance of the earlier years were largely gone. Some of the early customs were embedded: the plain dress, the prohibition against taking oaths, the refusal to remove one's hat, the *thees* and *thous*. More important, Fox's core beliefs survived whole, defining the Society of Friends from then until now—nonviolence, equality of all, and, at the center, belief in the Inner Light.

The alacrity with which young Anthony Benezet joined the Quakers in Philadelphia attests to his familiarity with the Society beforehand. It's possible that he was a student at Kuweidt's School at the same time as the French *philosophe* Voltaire, who had been banished from France as an alternative to being imprisoned in the Bastille. Voltaire had chosen to go to England to learn English, and, as it turned out, he found himself living in the midst of Quakers in Wandsworth and applying for English tutoring at Kuweidt's school.

Voltaire was so impressed by the Quakers that he devoted the first four of his twenty-four *Lettres sur les Anglaise* to them. "I was of the opinion that the doctrine and history of so extraordinary a people," he wrote, "were worthy the attention of the curious."[30]

Voltaire was taken by the way the Quakers differentiated themselves so thoroughly from the rest of English society, in their customs and beliefs, the plainness and directness with which they carried themselves, the introspection that marked their worship, their anticlericalism, their pacifism, their fundamental conviction of equality. These were, of course, foundational values that were to define Benezet's own moral character. If Voltaire was picking them up during his time in Wandsworth, Benezet almost assuredly was as well. In a later correspondence Voltaire wrote, "I love the Quakers." If he didn't get so intolerably seasick, he said, "it would be in thy bosom, Oh Pennsylvania, that I should go to finish the rest of my career."[31] By chance, of course, it was Benezet who would spend his entire adult life in Pennsylvania.

Voltaire's famous passage in the *Lettres sur les Anglaise* on meeting "an eminent Quaker" begins with an evocation of Quaker simplicity as opposed to his own French artificiality: "He did not uncover himself when I appeared, and advanced towards me without once stooping his body; but there appeared more politeness in the open, humane air of his countenance, than in the custom of drawing one leg behind the other, and taking that from the head which is made to cover it. 'Friend,' says he to me, 'I perceive thou art a stranger, but if I can do anything for thee, only tell me. . . . Come in, and let us first dine together.'"[32]

The calmness, rationality, and poise of "the eminent Quaker" tell their own story of the Quaker sense of self at the beginning of the eighteenth century. These were the characteristics and spirit Anthony Benezet absorbed as he came of age, the traits that defined his sense of self as the family prepared to embark for Philadelphia.

CHAPTER FOUR

William Penn's "Holy Experiment"

"It was a long and dangerous journey," Jean-Etienne wrote to a friend about the family's Atlantic crossing.[1] Other Huguenot refugees had made that same long and dangerous journey, a few as far back as the 1620s, more than one hundred years before the Benezet family embarked in 1731. They left in November, the worst time of year for a crossing, when the winds picked up, capricious and dangerous. In the late fall fierce gales struck randomly, catching packets in huge seas that could and did swamp boats, overpowering the pumps. That Jean-Etienne and Judith decided to leave then rather than wait for the gentler temperatures and breezes of spring tells its own story of his desire to get shut of England.

Almost all the earlier Huguenot arrivals had settled in New York or South Carolina—New York because the Walloons and French Protestants had been granted permission by the Dutch States General, South Carolina largely in response to promotional pamphlets emphasizing the province's supposedly Eden-like qualities of soil and climate.[2] By the eighteenth century, both provinces had long-established Huguenot communities. But Jean-Etienne decided to uproot his family—for the third time now—and move them to the Quaker province of Pennsylvania, a surprising destination given the general Huguenot scorn for Quakers and their unacceptable theology and odd customs.

But Jean-Etienne almost surely had Quaker business acquaintances and perhaps Quaker friends in England, as well as some familiarity with Quaker religion, so he no doubt had a favorable impression.[3] William Penn's "Holy Experiment" was also attractive because of the state's reputation as a place of tolerance, free of religious controversy and, importantly, of hierarchy. His father, Anthony told the Marquis de Chastellux years later, wasn't happy with the authorities in England; "[wanting] to get out of the way of all hierarchy, he came and settled in this country."[4]

England had given the Huguenot refugees, Jean-Etienne and his family among them, a safe haven from the violence of their homeland, priceless in itself. At the same time, the sclerotic, hierarchical Church of England dominated the country's conflicted, unstable, and in many ways acrimonious religious life. But the Society of Friends had no priests and no hierarchy. And Pennsylvania was more than a confessional community that espoused equality; it was a self-governing province where equality and freedom of worship were foundational principles. "All persons," Penn stipulated in the Frame of Government, "living in this province, who confess and acknowledge the one Almighty and eternal God, to be the Creator, Upholder and Ruler of the world; and that hold themselves obliged in conscience to live peaceably and justly in civil society, shall, in no ways, be molested or prejudiced for their religious persuasion, or practice, in matters of faith and worship, nor shall they be compelled, at any time, to frequent or maintain any religious worship, place or ministry whatever."[5]

No other province, or government, embraced freedom of conscience quite so absolutely—not even Roger Williams's Rhode Island, whose charter preceded Penn's Frame of Government by thirty-nine years and incorporated freedom of religious worship as a "lively experiment." "No person," it stipulated, "within the said colony, at any time hereafter shall be any wise molested, punished, disquieted, or called in question, for any differences in opinion in matters of religion." But this didn't prevent Williams from attacking Quakers as dangerous disturbers of civic order and even, possibly, Satanists.[6]

As far as we know, Jean-Etienne was never molested on account of his religious life in England. Sometimes he attended French churches that adhered to Calvinist forms of worship, sometimes French churches that conformed to the Church of England liturgy; sometimes, it seems certain, he attended Quaker services. He may have looked in on *les Inspirés*—the prophets were from his family's place of origin. But whatever path he might have been following, he was never persecuted. In England he also successfully rebuilt the business he had lost when he fled France. We know he arrived in Pennsylvania with enough money to buy a thousand-acre tract of land and a good brick house.[7] He had done well in England. If he had religious freedom in England and he was flourishing economically, then what moved him to leave for Pennsylvania?[8] Whatever that was, it had to have been compelling.

For entrepreneurial spirits looking for opportunities to dramatically increase their wealth, the American colonies beckoned. Land speculation was rampant, and financial dealings were almost entirely unregulated. Jean-Etienne was a good businessman, but acquisitiveness doesn't seem to have been a primary driver for him; it wasn't likely that he was drawn to Pennsylvania as a place ripe for monetary gain. But he did badly want to get out of England. English civil life obviously was not to his liking, a dislike that must have become increasingly troublesome to him as the years went by. He was fifty years old when he left, a hard age to start over in a new place, but also an age when it may seem more urgent to make significant life changes, especially given the far shorter life expectancy then than now. Benezet may well have felt pressured by a time horizon looming ever closer. By 1731 he had decided the time had come. He wanted fewer disturbances in his life and Pennsylvania, with its Quaker aura of peace and harmony, appeared to offer that potential (years later he wrote to a fellow Huguenot refugee friend back in Holland that Pennsylvania was "a land of peace and tranquility."[9]

But the chief driver was almost certainly religion. Jean-Etienne could have been a Quaker back in England. But Pennsylvania was Quaker in its DNA. It afforded a different kind of spiritual environment. Jean-Etienne was, as Van Ruymbeke says, a man "deeply preoccupied with his spirituality and salvation."[10] He was a seeker after salvation, and by the early 1730s he must have believed that salvation in the Quaker sense applied to him and fulfilled his longing. He could have been a Quaker in England, of course, but Pennsylvania exerted a unique attraction. Nonetheless, whatever Jean-Etienne most valued in his life as a Quaker turned out not to have permanence after all. The Philadelphia Meeting minutes for March 1743 recorded that "Stephen Benezet [he now went by "John Steven"] had been lovingly spoke to respecting his declining to attend our Religious Meetings. . . . He had joined himself to the Society of Moravians."[11]

Jean-Etienne's life as a Quaker wasn't a short-lived affair; his definitive break with the Friends and affiliation with the Moravian Brotherhood only came ten years after he landed in Philadelphia and joined the Philadelphia Meeting. It had taken time, but eventually the kind of assurance implicit in the Quaker Inner Light belief seems to have lost its persuasiveness for him. Whatever disruption followed in the wake of that loss had left him seeking another path to sanctification. At some point he found, or believed he had found, with the Moravians—as he put it in a letter to his friend Prosper Marchand back in Holland—"a precious pearl in comparison to which the largest treasures are only mud."[12] Since this letter was written two years after Jean-Etienne joined the Moravians, his reference to finding the "precious pearl," i.e. salvation, almost certainly refers to his experience with the Brethren.

Moravian spirituality had certain commonalities with Quaker spirituality: nonviolence, the conviction of the equality of all peoples, the quietist style of patiently waiting for inspiration. But its underlying temperament was starkly different. Moravianism was a religion of yearning. Its adherents were, like Jean-Etienne, seekers, striving toward their souls' salvation here and in the life to come. Moravianism laid out pathways to sanctification: intense prayer (Moravians practiced "perpetual prayer," round-the-clock praying by members of the congregation), robust congregational hymn singing, the sacramental power of baptism and communion, the reliance on faith and the dismissal of good works as a factor in salvation, and, overall, a heightened devotion to the suffering of Jesus—to the redeeming efficacy of Jesus's wounds, a leitmotif of eighteenth-century Moravian hymns and sermons.[13]

The Moravian reverence for the physical suffering of Jesus echoes the Catholic adoration of Christ's five wounds that went back to the Middle Ages and earlier, but the Moravian version focused mainly on the lance wound to Jesus's side. The prevalence of this devotion led to a kind of sentimentality that later generations might have found cloying but that was habitual in the Moravians of Jean-Etienne's time. A sense of this is conveyed in a letter from a visitor to the Moravian center in Herrnhaag, Germany, back to his family in Pennsylvania: "We rest in his Side; the Side-hole and the Lambkin fill the exulting heart with flame; and that is all we wish . . . that you and our dear relations may from the womb be brought into the little Side-hole, and there enjoy all the felicity which the Lamb can impart to the justified sinner."[14]

Quakerism, by contrast, was sober, measured, deeply committed to its values but distant from the emotionalism that characterized the Moravian Brothers (and Sisters), as it did so many of the sects built around the belief that salvation was *the* essential necessity in the lives of men and women. If Moravianism was a religion of aspiration, Quakerism was a religion of assurance. Moravianism, too, was structured. Bishops and deacons were consecrated, services conducted according to a liturgy. There was little Quakers disagreed with more decisively than the idea of paid and anointed clergy; their own meetings for worship had no appointed ministers and no formal organization at all.

In England, Jean-Etienne had been acquainted with Peter Boehler, who was appointed bishop of the Moravian churches in America the same year Jean-Etienne committed himself to the Brethren.[15] Jean-Etienne became even more familiar with the sect several years after his arrival in Philadelphia, when he and his family hosted August Spangenberg, a close associate of Moravian founder Count Nikolaus Ludwig Von Zinzendorf. In 1741 Zinzendorf himself visited Philadelphia for a number of months and stayed with the Benezets while a house was being readied for him.[16] With his conversion, Jean-Etienne committed himself wholeheartedly to the Moravians. In 1743, the same year he was admitted as a communicant, he became treasurer to the new Moravian congregation in Bethlehem, a town recently founded north of Philadelphia. At the same time he gave public notice that he was ending his trading business.[17] Anthony's three sisters also joined the Moravians; two of them, Susanna and Judith, married Moravian missionaries.[18]

If one looks at his father's and siblings' religious lives (his three brothers became Anglican), the strength of Anthony Benezet's Quaker spirituality comes into sharper focus. Despite his exposure to Moravian forms of piety and his family's close affiliation with the Brethren, he himself found little to attract him. The church music didn't accord with his notion of worship. Nor did the liturgical service with its readings and sermons. It's also reasonable to speculate that the Moravian dogma of justification ("Justification with all its i's dotted"), which denied any power of good works in the business of salvation, repelled Anthony.[19] Quakers, Protestant though they were, had no time for that way of thinking. "What is faith without good works?" William Penn had written in 1678.[20] Robert Barclay, whose *Apology* was the most complete explanation of Quaker belief, put it this way: "We are not justified because of our good works, yet we are justified by doing them. They are the *sine qua non* or indispensible part of justification. It is contrary to the scriptural testimony to deny this. It has brought great scandal upon Protestantism and it has been the source of rebukes by Catholics."[21]

But beyond the Quaker tenets about good works, Anthony Benezet was a quintessential man of action. The picture of him as a mild, retiring, gentle teacher obscures the underlying lineaments of his character. He was a doer, energetic and creative in everything he undertook. "He ever translated into action what he professed to believe," wrote "the father of Black history," Carter Woodson. [22] His friend Benjamin Rush wrote that Benezet "possessed uncommon industry and activity in everything he undertook. He did everything as if the words of his Savior were perpetually sounding in his ears, 'wist ye not that I must be about my Father's business.'"[23]

Action was Benezet's full-time mode of being, as an educator, a pacifist, and an abolitionist. In contradistinction to his father, he seems to have been utterly secure in his faith and in his existence as a person saved through the Inner Light. As far as we can tell, Anthony Benezet did not yearn or strive for salvation. Like Fox after his life-changing revelation, he doesn't seem much, or at all, concerned with the great question—How shall I be saved?—that tormented so many of his contemporaries. Benezet's sphere of action was in the public space, not in the interior struggle over the fate of his soul.

And that inner peace left him free to devote himself to the kind of good works Moravians dismissed as inconsequential for salvation.

Benezet saw Moravianism close up. In 1739 and 1740 he also witnessed scenes from the most momentous religious movement in American history, known now (though not then) as the Great Awakening. In England, George Whitefield had become a phenomenally successful evangelist, preaching in the open air to gatherings numbering ten, twenty thousand and more. Like the famous New England evangelist Jonathan Edwards, who had initiated the Awakening in his home parish of Northampton, Massachusetts, Whitefield preached fire and brimstone, damnation and salvation. In 1739 he brought his revival meetings to Pennsylvania.

Whitefield's preaching style was as different from Edwards's as it could be. Edwards, one observer said, appeared to be looking at a bell rope in the back of the church when he preached; the calmness of his delivery seemed to magnify the impact of his words. Whitefield, by contrast, wailed, shouted, wept, gesticulated, sang. Edwards's voice was a little weak, when he preached it often seemed strained. Whitefield had a huge voice that could reach throngs. Benjamin Franklin was so taken by its pure power that he calculated experimentally that Whitefield at full volume could be heard by twenty-five thousand people.[24] And Whitefield's histrionics were even more potent than Edwards's blunt simplicity. He regularly left giant audiences weeping and crying for forgiveness. He wept copiously himself, preaching through his own tears. David Garrick, the great British actor, said that Whitefield could throw an audience into paroxysms by pronouncing the word *Mesopotamia*.[25]

Benezet knew Whitefield and liked him. What he thought of his theatrics and the hysteria he triggered among his vast audiences we don't know, although he later wrote that he considered the "enthusiastick Spirit a dangerous Snare . . . which I apprehend very much prevails and often, too often, presents itself amongst the Sons of God, even in otherwise honest hearted ones."[26] It's hard to think that Benezet didn't have Whitefield in mind when he wrote that.

In May 1740 Whitefield preached to crowds estimated at twelve thousand in little villages outside Philadelphia whose entire populations amounted to tiny fractions of that number. His appearances emptied the countryside. In Philadelphia itself he drew possibly two-thirds of the city's population.[27] To modern readers, Whitefield's published sermons can seem bombastic and stiff. But they didn't sound that way to his contemporaries, mesmerized by the preacher's delivery and hanging on exhortations that struck their hearts.

> O wretched man that I am, who shall deliver me from this body of death! O foolish mortal that I was, thus to bring myself into these never-ceasing tortures, for the transitory enjoyment of a few short-lived pleasures, which scarcely afforded me any satisfaction, even when I most indulged myself in them. Alas! Are these the wages, these the effects of sin? O damned apostate! First to delude me with pretended promises of happiness, and after several years drudgery in his [Satan's] service, thus to involve me in eternal woe. O that I had never hearkened to his beguiling insinuations! O that I had rejected his very first suggestions with the utmost detestation and abhorrence! O that I had taken up my cross and followed Christ! O that I had never ridiculed serious godliness. . . . Think, I beseech you by the mercies of God in Christ Jesus, think with yourselves, how racking, how unsupportable the never-dying worm of a self-condemning conscience will hereafter be to you. Think how impossible it will be for you to dwell with everlasting burnings. Come, all ye christians. . . . O think, think with yourselves, how deplorable it will be to lose the enjoyment of heaven, and run into endless torments. O think, think with yourselves, how deplorable it will be to lose the enjoyment of heaven, and run into endless torments, merely because you will be content to be almost, and will not strive to be altogether christians. Consider, I beseech you, consider how you will rave and curse that fatal stupidity which made you believe any thing less than true faith in Jesus.[28]

He preached in Nottingham, Pennsylvania, where "thousands shouted and fainted, some shrieking 'as if they were in the sharpest agonies of death.' Whitefield himself was overcome with emotion and entered a trancelike state, sweetly lying, as he described it, at the 'feet of my Jesus.'"[29]

All this was swirling around Benezet even as he was attending the silent worship of Friends' meetings, where often no one spoke at all. Saint-Jean de Crevecoeur described one such meeting, in Chester, just south of Philadelphia, in his 1782 *Letters from an American Farmer.* De Crevecoeur wrote that he entered a "square white room devoid of any ornament whatsoever," where two hundred or so men and women were assembled. He noted

> a profound silence . . . which lasted about half an hour; everyone had his head reclined and seemed absorbed in profound meditation, when a female Friend arose and declared . . . that the spirit moved her to entertain them on a subject she had chosen. . . . I did not observe one single face turned toward her; never before had I seen a congregation listening with so much attention to a public oration. . . . As soon as she had finished, everyone seemed to return to their former meditation for

> about a quarter of an hour, when they rose up by common consent and after some general conversation departed.[30]

During his tour of America, Whitefield preached up and down the East Coast, south to Georgia, then back north again to New York, Boston, and Edwards's parish of Northampton. Everywhere he went he drew thousands, sparking terror and wringing repentance and conversions throughout the colonies. He was, in the words of religious historian Clarke Garrett, "unquestionably the greatest celebrity the colonies had ever seen."[31]

The Quakers' own days as wild-eyed enthusiasts generating violent visceral reactions in their audiences were long past. George Fox had expelled that temper from the Quaker *corpus religiosus* back in the 1660s. That had been a time of the most impassioned enthusiasm, "a gaudy religious flowering," in Garrett's words.[32] But while George Whitefield might have been a unique phenomenon, he was emblematic of another flowering of religions: Moravians, Anabaptists, New Light Presbyterians, Methodists, ordained and unordained itinerant preachers. Quakers lived in the middle of all this, but it did not touch them. Nor did it touch Anthony Benezet, who sat quietly in meetings for worship, wrapped in silent communion with his God.

Philadelphia's Quakers in the mid-eighteenth century still dominated the city's economic and political spheres, but they had no interest in favoring their beliefs or anyone else's in the city's religious life. "Liberty of conscience," Penn's most recent biographer writes, "had been one of Penn's firm principles since the earliest days of his political activism."[33] Penn was motivated by the persecution Quakers had suffered, but he was clear that the ideal of religious freedom couldn't be limited to Quakers. "We have good will to all men," he declared in a petition to Parliament, "and would have none suffer for a truly sober and conscientious dissent."[34] "Rulers," he argued, "would be well-served to acknowledge the fact of religious diversity."[35] Penn understood that "sober" dissenters had a rightful place in the society he envisioned for his new colony. But one wonders what he would have thought of the kind of massive, church-free upswelling of popular enthusiasm that gripped Pennsylvania a mere thirty years after his death, a grassroots upheaval unattached to any constituted religion and not by any stretch of imagination "sober."

Penn famously described his new colony as a "Holy Experiment," suggesting a new society, organized around Quaker beliefs and along Quaker lines, founded in virgin territory ripe for the implantation of a new way of life. But, in fact, the region Penn encountered when he finally got there was already a society of sorts, diverse and disorderly and not Quaker. A Swedish colony—New Sweden—had been established in 1638. The Dutch were in the region even earlier. The initial European settlements included Germans, Walloons, Welsh, English, Scotch-Irish, and Finns. Historian Bernard Bailyn describes the last group at length, many of them "Forest Finns," whose practices of hunting, gathering, and slash-and-burn agriculture were similar to those of the region's Indigenous peoples and gave them relatively easy access to the native American habitat. "The Finns' inherited culture," Bailyn writes, "became the norm for most Europeans in the Swedish colony."[36]

The amalgam of Finns, Dutch, English, Swedes, and others, not to mention the Indigenous Lenape, did not make for an irenic environment. As Bailyn points out, "The records of the Delaware Valley under the Swedes, and then under the Dutch and English who followed, are filled with references to smuggling, assault, riot, obstruction of justice, tax evasion, rape, ignoring summons, adultery, army desertion, reckless use of firearms, flight to avoid prosecution, sale of liquor to Indians, refusal to take an oath, vandalism, killing a neighbor's livestock, horse theft, prostitution, and insurrection on the part of local Finns and Swedes."[37] Jean Soderlund in her history of the Lenape people, *Lenape Country*, takes a different point of view, describing pre-Pennsylvania society, dominated by the Lenape, as a place of more harmonious coexistence.[38] The two views are not necessarily incompatible. Peaceful collaboration between Europeans and the Lenape (subsequent to the 1632 Lenape massacre of the Dutch settlement of Swaanendael) was carried on at a political and commercial level, but the mix of Dutch, Swedes, English, Finns, and Indigenous people in what was essentially a raw frontier made for an environment ripe with interpersonal and even intercommunal lawlessness and violence.

On this turbulent substratum of previous colonies Penn instituted a constitutionally governed settlement that brought together English norms with a panoply of rights that encouraged an inpouring of new arrivals. But even here the dominant Quakers lived alongside a mushrooming of messianic sects, some of which died relatively quickly and naturally, while others sustained themselves and became ongoing elements in America's religious landscape. "It was in Pennsylvania," Bailyn explains, "that the messianic pietism and the bizarre occultism that swept through the Protestant sects in German states . . . bore the strangest and most plentiful fruit."[39]

Penn's Holy Experiment opened the gates to eccentrics and outliers of all sorts. Directly adjacent to Philadelphia, on the Wissahickon Creek, the mystic Johannes Kelpius established a Rosicrucian group, the Society of the Woman in the Wilderness, where his followers built a substantial log house and individual huts where members prayed, meditated, performed scientific experiments, and awaited the coming of the "Bridegroom." Kelpius himself lived in a cave, still visible in the woods alongside the Wissahickon. Nearby, another displaced German mystic, Johannes Conrad Beissel, created an eccentric offshoot of the Seventh Day Baptists, which attracted converts whom he led to Lancaster County, west of Philadelphia. There he established a vegetarian monastic community he named Ephrata (the ancient name of Bethlehem), which became famous as a center for printing and for its strict asceticism and the otherworldly singing of its choir. The followers of Caspar Schwenckfeld also established themselves in Pennsylvania, as did Zinzendorf's Moravians and the better known, more numerous Mennonite and Amish Anabaptists, both tracing their origins back to the Dutch reformer Menno Simons.

In addition to being home to various ethnic and religious communities, Quaker Pennsylvania was a commonwealth confronted by both internal and external questions, problems and challenges that were utterly foreign to the Friends' reclusive and wary heritage: religious and political conflicts, land disputes, crime, taxation, trade and commerce, foreign relations—the whole gamut of affairs governments need to deal with, but which the Society of Friends had never encountered and had never dreamed of meddling with. Fox supported Penn in his undertaking, but at the same time he saw the danger. "My friends, that are gone," he counseled, "and are going over to plant, and make outward plantations in America, keep your own plantations in your hearts, with the spirit and power of God, that your own vines and lilies be not hurt."[40] In the wake of the Nayler debacle, Fox had seen the existential threat dissension posed, and he had taken measures to assure unity and discipline. He saw danger in worldly engagement too. Quakers entangled in the complex matters of the outside world risked losing their hold on the inward world of the spirit. He saw that Penn's venture posed exactly that risk. He cautioned the Friends not to "medle with ye powers of ye earth" and to "kepe out of all such things . . . [and] kepe out of all vaine Janglinge."[41] "[Keep] out of the world's evil customs, fashions, words, works, manners ordinances and commandments."[42]

The London Yearly Meeting saw it too. In 1789 it advised its members, "Walk wisely and circumspectly towards all men, . . . [giving no] way to any controversies, heats or distractions of this world."[43] In a similar vein, Penn himself warned his fellow Quakers, "Be careful not to mingle with the crowd, lest *their* spirit enter *us* instead of *our* spirit entering *them*."[44]

This wariness was more than simply the common desire of pious sects to seclude themselves from the iniquitous world. Quakers were inclined that way also, but in addition they had suffered decades of brutal treatment by the British government, from Fox's first proselytizing efforts in 1652 until the 1689 Edict of Toleration. Over that period, thirteen to fourteen thousand Quakers had been imprisoned, 338 executed, and many others deported.[45] Jails were rank, dark, infested with vermin, with no heat in the winter, no toilet facilities, no separation of men and women. Sentences were often long and commonly included hard labor. Frequently the condemned were beaten, whipped, and subjected to other cruelties at the hands of jailers. Joseph Besse in his 1753 *A Collection of the Sufferings of the People Called Quakers* noted that Friends endured "beatings, Buffetings, Stonings, Pinchings, Kickings, Dirtings, Pumpings and all Manner of Abuses from the rude and ungoverned Rabble: and from the Magistrates, who should have been their Defenders, they met with Spoiling of Goods, Stockings, Whippings, Imprisonments, Banishments, and even Death itself."[46]

Many Quakers, especially in their earliest days, courted such treatment. They saw it as a mark of faith, a part of Quaker identity, and a demonstration of God's spirit empowering the righteous. Nayler referred to it as "the Lamb's War." Besse believed that "for those who lived in the truth, suffering was easy, sweet, and pleasant unto their souls."[47]

But at the same time, Quakers tried to ameliorate the suffering of their coreligionists. In 1659 Quakers sent a remarkable declaration to Parliament:

> We in Love to our Brethren that lie in Prisons, and Houses of Correction and Dungeons, and many in Fetters and Irons, and have been cruelly beat by the cruel Gaolers, and many have been persecuted to Death, and have died in Prison, and many lie sick and weak in Prison, and on straw. So we in Love to our Brethren do offer up our Bodies and Selves to you, for to put us as Lambs into the same Dungeons and Houses of Correction, and their straw and nasty Holes and Prisons, and do stand ready a Sacrifice for to go into their Places in Love to our Brethren, that they may go forth.[48]

In 1675 the Society established the Meetings for Sufferings, which recorded persecutions and pressed the regime to step back its repression. These meetings were insistent in their various declarations and appeals to Parliament, repeatedly arguing "their brethren's innocuousness, peacefulness, and detachment from national affairs."[49]

In their mostly frustrated efforts to defend themselves, Quakers were involved by necessity with the government, William Penn most conspicuously as the chief Quaker advocate for toleration. But they were walking a fine line. They needed to bring influence to bear, and wherever possible they did. But they also had to guard their separateness, their abstention from involvement in the affairs of government, their "detachment." But in Pennsylvania there was no fine line to walk. There they were fully involved.

Jean-Etienne had written to his friend Marchand in 1758 that Pennsylvania was a "land of peace and tranquility," and it was certainly true that the government was dominated by Quakers and reflected Quaker principles of liberty of conscience, the universal availability of the divine spirit, and the equal right of all to be heard in its egalitarian political structures. But from the beginning there were rifts and tensions, land disputes, discord over political power, commercial conflicts. And though it might not have been foreseen at first, the radical egalitarianism that underlay Pennsylvania's political and spiritual values was challenged by the presence of two culturally and ethnically "alien" peoples, the Indigenous Lenape and enslaved Black people from Africa. For the Quakers the challenges posed by these two groups were to change the course of the Society's life.

As Anthony Benezet integrated himself into the Philadelphia Quaker community, his spiritual life (unlike his father's) seems already to have been largely settled, its values well anchored. But ominous realities lurked beneath the surface of his new home, and these would shape him in ways neither he nor anyone else could have predicted.

CHAPTER FIVE

Links in the Antislavery Chain

Tradition tells us that shortly after William Penn landed at the chosen site for Philadelphia, he entered into a treaty of friendship with the Lenape tribe, the Indigenous people of the Delaware Valley. A painting of the scene executed by Benjamin West almost a hundred years later became an iconic memorialization of the supposed event, cementing Penn's popular image as a peacemaker and fair-minded founder of the Pennsylvania colony, in contrast to the aggressive land grabbing of colonists elsewhere.

Whether the so-called Penn Treaty is fact or legend, it is true that William Penn, whose Quaker principles precluded violence, pursued policies that, generally speaking, recognized Lenape rights and approached land purchases accordingly. For their part, the Lenape engaged with Penn peacefully as well, looking to manage their new neighbors in commercially advantageous ways for themselves. This benign, mutually beneficial relationship dominated colonist/Lenape interactions from Pennsylvania's founding in 1682 until the early 1730s, when friction escalated over white encroachment on tribal land. Lenape unhappiness was aggravated by the 1737 "Walking Purchase," engineered by Penn's sons John and Thomas nearly two decades after Penn's death. As historian Jean Soderlund describes it, the maneuver "defrauded the Delawares [Lenape] out of their last major tract of prime agricultural and hunting land in the Delaware Valley."[1] Lenape anger escalated when the more powerful Iroquois confederation refused to intervene, embittering Lenape-Iroquois relationships, which flamed into violence with the outbreak of the French and Indian War in 1754. The carnage and slave raids that war brought to the Pennsylvania frontier challenged Quaker governance of Pennsylvania in a way that shaped the Society from that point on.

The Benezets arrived in their new home in 1731, just as the earlier colonist/Lenape harmony began to sour. As new arrivals, they would have had little or no notion of the undercurrents that beset what Jean-Etienne later called "a land of peace and tranquility." But just as the French and Indian War profoundly impacted the Friends, it also played a key role in Anthony Benezet's emergence as an antislavery crusader. The war started in 1754, the same year

Benezet published his first demand that slavery among his coreligionists be prohibited. The concatenation of those events was not random, but closely connected as part of a confluence of factors that profoundly changed the course of Benezet's life.

An overriding question about Benezet for biographers is why this dedicated teacher undertook antislavery activism, and why then. At one point, he told a friend that teaching children was his highest aspiration.[2] But something changed his mind about that and gave him an even more consequential calling. The turning point came when Benezet had already entered middle age, almost a quarter century after he stepped off the boat at age eighteen onto Philadelphia's Front Street, with little idea of where his life might lead him or, for that matter, how he might be able to make a living in his new home.

If the Benezets were unlikely to have had any inkling of the festering Indian problem in their newly adopted land, they were also unlikely to have had much if any understanding of the slavery issues facing the colonies, including Pennsylvania. Anthony at eighteen would most probably have heard little if anything about abolitionism in England, which wouldn't get underway until the late 1760s and early 1770s with the Strong and Somerset cases (see chapter 12). Nor would he have known anything about the abolitionist stirrings already beginning to agitate at least some Philadelphia Quakers. His concerns as a young man with few skills and no experience would have had little yet to do with racial equality or humanitarianism more generally; his immediate problem was where to turn for a career, or, at the very least, a job.

We have extremely little information about how Benezet might have supported himself during his first years in Philadelphia. We do know that back in England he had some experience in a "counting house," that is, an accounting firm, very likely arranged by his father. But he didn't feel comfortable there and apprenticed himself to a cooper instead. That didn't work out either. His "frail constitution" wasn't up to the heavy physical work.[3]

Once in Philadelphia, Benezet's younger brothers established themselves as import-export traders; they apparently inherited their father's instinct for business and no doubt benefited from his advice and support. The first we know about Anthony's attempt to develop a career is that some years later he too embarked on a trading enterprise in Wilmington, thirty miles south of Philadelphia. But that failed within months; it seems he just did not have the heart for it. In a letter to one of his trading friends in Nantucket, he wrote, "I find being much amongst the buyer and seller rather a snare to me, as I am of a free, open disposition. I had rather be otherwise employed, and more retired and private."[4]

We might assume that Anthony's inability to find some way of making a living was by then growing worrisome. He was already twenty-six when he moved to Wilmington, well past the time when he should have been supporting himself. And it wasn't only himself he had to think about. He had by then been married for three years to Joyce Marriot, a fellow member of the Philadelphia Meeting, whose Quaker grandfather, Griffeth Owen, had settled in Pennsylvania two years after Penn received his charter. Joyce was herself a confirmed minister, despite her youth, and the fact that the Philadelphia Monthly Meeting approved the marriage indicates that there were no questions about the strength of Anthony's bonds with the Quakers either.

From what we know, the marriage was a good one, but by the time Anthony and Joyce moved to Wilmington they had already been struck by tragedy. A year after their wedding the young Benezets had their first child, a girl they named Mary after Joyce's mother. The baby, though, lived less than a year. A second child, a boy, was born five years later but survived only a week. The extremely high infant mortality rates of those days (Quaker records from the period indicate that one-third of infants died within the first year) did nothing to blunt the sorrow accompanying children's deaths, and given what we know about Anthony and Joyce's tenderheartedness, they must have felt these deaths keenly.

The young couple didn't stay long in Wilmington after Anthony's business failed. That same year, 1739, they moved back to Pennsylvania, to the town of Abington on Philadelphia's northern edge. In terms of a career, Anthony was "still groping through a mist of indecision," as his biographer Brookes put it.[5] But shortly after the move, a teaching position opened at a school in nearby Germantown. It's possible that Anthony's loss of his daughter might have deepened his love of children, which made an offer to teach youngsters especially welcome. Brookes thinks so, and both he and Benezet's early biographer, Roberts Vaux, give the impression that Benezet was harboring his energies just waiting for a career of this sort to come along. But the fact is that we have no knowledge of what might have motivated Benezet to embrace teaching. "In the first instance," one of his friends wrote, "[he] commenced teaching for a subsistence."[6] At the same time, he took on part-time work as a proofreader with a local printer, which gave him additional income and also some familiarity with printing pamphlets and books—good preparation for his future as an antislavery pamphleteer.

Teaching, as it turned out, became not just a job, but a passionate vocation. Benezet discovered in himself a talent for the work and a love for his students. As he said later, if he had any purpose in creation "it [was] the education of children."[7] By a remarkable chance, the Germantown school had an intimate connection with the very earliest expression of Quaker abolitionism through its founder and first headmaster, Francis Daniel Pastorius. As the leader of a group of German and Dutch Quakers and Mennonites, Pastorius had negotiated with William Penn for the ownership of fifteen thousand acres in Philadelphia's northwest in 1684, just two years after Penn established his proprietorship. There Pastorius and his fellow immigrants cleared land, built cabins, and formally established their district, calling it Germantown.

In 1688 Pastorius read aloud in the nearby Dublin Meeting what's thought to be the first colonial protest against slavery. He himself was its author—the original document is in his handwriting—and he signed it, together with three other meeting members. "We are," the letter declared, "against the traffik of men-body. . . . To bring men hither, or to robb and sell them against their will, we stand against."[8] The petition was not in the usual brotherly and gracious format of Quaker epistles sent from one meeting to another. A typical opening might read, for example, "Dear and tender salutation in our Lord Jesus Christ, who is our life and in whom we have fellowship." The Germantown epistle, on the contrary, was blunt, full of outrage and condemnation: "Those who steal or robb men, and those who buy or purchase them, are they not a licke [alike]?" The signers inveighed against the abomination of "separating wifes from their husbands and giving them to others, and some sell the children of these poor Creatures to other men." "Ah! doe consider well this thing, you who do it. . . . Consider well this thing, is it good or bad?"[9]

The Dublin Meeting considered the petition to stop the practice too "weighty" to act on—"[not] expedient for us to meddle with it here," the meeting declared.[10] Instead Dublin passed it up to the Philadelphia Quarterly Meeting, which in turn sent it on to the Philadelphia Yearly Meeting, the colonial senior body. The yearly meeting minutes recorded its receipt: "A paper being here presented by some German Friends Concerning the Lawfulness and Unlawfulness of Buying and keeping Negroes, It was adjudged not to be so proper for this Meeting to give a Positive Judgment in the Case, It having so General a Relation to many other Parts, and therefore at present they forbear it."[11] There is some indication that the Philadelphia Meeting sent it to the London Meeting, which also did nothing.

The Germantown protest never saw the light of day; it was buried. But that didn't mean it died. There had been troubled discussions among the signers and no doubt among many other meeting members. The settlers had come from a place where there were no slaves, and they were appalled by what they found, especially since they themselves had been victims of oppression. We don't hear of any follow-up petitions from the Germantown Quakers, perhaps not surprising given the dismissiveness their first effort met with. But the talk persisted, and the moral disgust did too. Pastorius was passionate in his outrage, and he was the leading public figure in Germantown until his death in 1720. He was bailiff, mayor, Pennsylvania assemblyman, a prominent essayist and poet, and longtime headmaster of the school that now, in 1739, employed Anthony Benezet. Benezet would have known about him. As part of the community Pastorius founded he would have absorbed something, perhaps much, of its moral culture as well. The Germantown Quakers' protest had a "discursive afterlife," the historian Brycchan Carey writes, and was well known "throughout the eighteenth century and beyond."[12]

The Germantown remonstrance might have been deep-sixed by the Philadelphia Meeting, but not only did its arguments live on, it proved a precursor to jeremiads by other, similarly appalled, Quaker antislavery activists. One was Ralph Sandiford, an English sailor who had seen the atrocities of slavery up close in Barbados and had subsequently moved to Philadelphia where he opened a shop on High Street close by the city's slave mart, where he got to see more of it. A sense of injustice and repulsion overtook him to such a degree that he disregarded the usual Quaker deference to meeting oversight of publications and in 1729 published a denunciation of slavery and Quaker complicity in the institution—"this dark Trade creeping in amongst us, to the very Ministry, because of the Profit by it, hath spread over others like a Leprosie."[13] Ben Franklin, in his first years as a printer, was Sandiford's publisher. To get the widest circulation Sandiford distributed copies of *A Brief Examination of the Practice of the Times* at his own expense. A year later he followed up with an expanded version, *The Mystery of Iniquity; in a Brief Examination of the Practice of the Times, by the Foregoing and the Present Dispensation: The Second Edition, with Additions.*

If Sandiford's first version was dripping with vitriol, the second was simply brutal in-your-face aggression, launched not only at the Friends for their complicity but at "all the churches of Christ." "The mystery of iniquity," he wrote, "[is] that the beast and the whore should introduce their merchandize amongst all our churches."[14] God, he says, is a God of justice who "will revenge the Cause of the Oppressed. . . . And What greater injustice can be acted than to rob a man of his liberty, which is more valuable than Life . . . to take a Man from his Native Country, his parents and brethren . . by stealth, or by way of Purchase from them that have no right to sell them, whereby thou receivest the Theft, which is as bad."[15]

This reads as direct condemnation. He's talking to both the Quaker Meeting and other churches. God, he says, will exact vengeance for this injustice, worse than all other injustices. And those who receive these criminally gotten, enslaved people? They are just as evil as those who steal and sell them. Sandiford knew that many wealthy Quaker leaders, so-called Quaker grandees, owned slaves and in some cases engaged in the slave trade, and that their self-interest was a major reason the meeting hadn't taken action against so towering an iniquity. Isaac Norris, for example, clerk of the Philadelphia Yearly Meeting, was a principal importer and sold Africans on commission before he eventually decided against the practice.[16] "Shall we then undertake to remove them, wheresoever Interest may lead us," Sandiford wrote, "to sell them for Slaves, Husband from Wife, and Children from both, like Beasts . . . to the vilest of Men, and their Offspring after them, to all Eternity: Oh! Hard Lot! Oh! Eternal sinking in Iniquity."[17]

This wasn't some abstract discourse about natural law or moral theology; this was personal. Sandiford was raw with the emotion of it, and he wanted his readers to be equally stricken. To that end, he gave a picture he knew would hardly be bearable, although it was true—he'd most likely seen these things himself. After the awful severity of the Atlantic passage, he wrote, "at their first landing in the *West Indies*, . . . the buyer may inspect even their secret parts. . . . The poor creatures are whipped naked to common view, until their secret pores are shamefully extended beyond what may be rehearsed for chaste ears; and also for seeking their liberty [attempting escape], racked and burned to death, as lately in the *West Indies*, which I would leave to the just judgment of God, rather than display the filthiness of the whore; and return to the churches of Philadelphia, who to my greatest wonderment were all defiled with it."[18]

Not only was Sandiford devastated by the memory of it, but he came back to the City of Brotherly Love (slavery gave the lie to that signification, he noted) only to find the same evil rampant there. He is so dismayed he has to fall back on biblical language to convey what he is feeling. "Instruments of Cruelty are in their habitations; O my Soul, come not thou into their Secret nor be united in their Assembly for in their anger they slew a man (but these have slain many), cursed be their anger."[19]

Sandiford published *Mystery* himself (again printed by Ben Franklin), as he had *A Brief Examination*. But sometime after publication he submitted it to the Philadelphia Meeting and asked for publishing approval, which seems gratuitous and illogical. He probably did so to give the book more publicity and exposure but also to poke the overseers in the eye. In any event, he got what he no doubt anticipated: the Quakers disowned him.

Sandiford was in ill health by then, both physically and mentally. For two years after *Mystery* he was subject to incessant hostility, which wore him down.[20] Publication, he said, was "repulsed by the Overseers." The depravity of what he had seen, and was continuing to see, weighed on him "Night and Day." He was "crushed under the burden of it, which so darkened my understanding, that all seemed lost unto me, being Swallowed up in it thro' the violence of the Tempest."[21]

This might sound like emotional hyperbole. It wasn't. Sandiford was extremely sick (he died not long afterward, at age forty), and he attributed his physical deterioration to his immersion in the war he was carrying on against slavery, "which put Nature out of Course." He had written that Quakers should imagine themselves in the same condition as the enslaved. He did that himself, with an empathy that was not simply an attitude of mind but was visceral, "as tho' the Rod [the whip] was on my own Back, I suffered with them in the natural Body."[22] He died, his friend Benjamin Lay said, "in great perplexity. . . . By reason of his sore Affliction of mind, concerning Slave-keeping . . . and Infirmity of Body, he fell into a sort of Delirium."[23]

Sandiford died in Dublin County, not far from where Benezet lived when he taught in Germantown. He had had a cabin built on a friend's farm, thinking that separating himself from all the controversy would help him recover, which, unfortunately, it didn't. His death roughly coincided with the Benezets' arrival in Philadelphia. The brouhaha Sandiford ignited flared up and then subsided seven years before Benezet began teaching. But as with Pastorius's epistle, the aftereffects persisted, influencing others and pushing the Philadelphia Meeting to evolve on the issue.

The transmission threads among early abolitionists—including Sandiford—and various Quaker meetings are tied together by Brycchan Carey in his 2012 book *From Peace to Freedom: Quaker Rhetoric and the Birth of American Antislavery, 1657–1761*. Sandiford's rhetoric, Carey writes, "may not have been without impact."[24] In particular, despite the short shrift he received from the yearly meeting, his fellow Quakers there entertained a serious discussion about the Society's official position on slavery. They considered reports from five quarterly meetings—Chester, Shrewsbury, Gloucester-Salem, Bucks, and Burlington—in addition to their own Philadelphia quarterly. Shrewsbury reported, "The Practice of Buying Negroes is wrong and therefore they Desire Friends may be restricted from purchasing of Them for the Future." Gloucester and Bucks reached the same conclusion. Burlington did too, though less definitively: "It is not agreeable to our Discipline." Friends, they said, should be discouraged from buying or owning slaves. Still, the yearly meeting backed off, issuing the most tepid of directives: "Friends ought to be very Cautious of making any such Purchase [of enslaved persons] for the Future; it being Disagreeable to the Sense of this Meeting."[25] Nonetheless, the meeting was easing away from its unwillingness to confront the issue.

We don't know if Benezet ever saw Sandiford's books. It's likely that a decent, though limited, number were printed, and Sandiford had distributed them gratis. But that was eight years before Benezet and Joyce moved to Germantown; it's impossible to say how many might have been in circulation by that time or whether they were available to him. On the other hand, Benezet certainly knew of Sandiford, whose interaction with the Philadelphia Yearly Meeting had been notorious and who, as Carey argues, influenced ongoing Quaker discussions. Furthermore, Benjamin Lay had befriended Sandiford, whom he considered a soulmate, and Lay and Benezet also became warm friends. In that sense, Sandiford, Lay, and Benezet were "link[s] in [a] chain," to use Maurice Jackson's phrase.[26] It's suggestive, too, that Benezet's antislavery strategy of attacking the dominant British slaving enterprise paralleled Sandiford's. Sandiford addressed *The Mystery of Iniquity* to "the Yearly Meeting of *Friends* assembled in London" as well as to Philadelphia Quakers. He understood that the slave trade had "its original in England," and he urged British readers to "introduce the matter to the helm by which the body is governed, that the ax being laid to the root we may be delivered from the corruption."[27] The text is somewhat ambiguous as to whether "the helm" referred to the leaders of the Quaker meeting or to the British monarch, but since there was no actual Quaker "helm," and because Sandiford identified England as the "original" of the slave trade, it's almost certain he meant the king.

Benezet, for his part, worked long and hard to mobilize British efforts against the slave trade. Along with his initial letter to Quaker contacts in England, he enclosed several copies of one of his tracts, writing "that it was only in England" that "a proper check" could be put on the trade and suggesting that the tract should be reprinted and dispersed among those who had the power "to put a restraint upon the Trade"—namely, "our gracious King, his Counselors, and each Member of both Houses of Parliament."[28] In a later letter to Selina, Countess of Huntingdon, he recounted that his tract *A Caution and Warning to Great Britain and Her Colonies* had been "reprinted in London . . . and delivered to every Member of both Houses of Parliament, and principal Officer in Government that could be found."[29]

Ralph Sandiford was only ten years older than Benezet, but he died early on and while he might well have influenced Benezet we have no direct proof of it. Benjamin Lay, though, was a friend to both, and we do know a good deal about his relationship with Benezet. According to Roberts Vaux, the two shared a "most cordial attachment."[30]

Sandiford was fearless, incensing the Quaker establishment with his scathing denunciations. When Pennsylvania's chief justice warned him not to distribute *A Brief Examination* and threatened him "with severe penalties," he responded by giving the book away for free.[31] Lay was fearless as well. He harbored a sense of rage every bit as furious as Sandiford's, which fueled his writing. Like Sandiford he had seen with his own eyes the most inhuman atrocities that were part of everyday life in Barbados, where he and his wife lived from 1718 to 1720. They saw slaves "Murthered by Working hard, and Starving, Whipping, Racking, hanging, Burning, Scalding, Roasting, and other Hellish Torments."[32] "Oh! My soul mourns in contemplating their miserable, wretched State and Condition that mine Eyes beheld them in then, and it is the same now," he wrote, seventeen years after he and his wife left the island.[33]

Lay fulminated against slaveholding and slaveholders in every Quaker meeting he attended, which often got him ejected, at times forcibly. Looking to escalate his impact, he moved his protests from the meetinghouse and written page to the street. His weapon there was shock. He wanted his audience to *feel* the consequences of their iniquity—at least those among them who owned slaves, or who condoned slavery, or who kept silent about slavery, that is, more or less everyone. His antics could seem bizarre, but his intent was serious. He once stood outside a meeting on a frigid winter day with one bare leg stuck into the snow. As the worshippers entered, many of them urged him not to expose himself like that, it would lead to an illness. According to Vaux, who wrote decades afterward, Lay told them, "You pretend compassion for me, but you do not feel for the poor slaves in your fields, who go through the winter half clad."[34]

Lay was unique, a small man, not much over four feet tall, a hunchback who lived with his wife in a cave-home and practiced vegetarianism, also a relentless agitator and stinging gadfly. He was, in his own words, "a man of strife and contention."[35] Lay spoke out against the evils of tobacco and alcohol, but it was the practice of enslaving fellow human beings that consumed him and stoked his rage. He walked everywhere, and it seemed everyone knew him. He was famous, or notorious, for some of his guerrilla actions. People talked about the bare leg episode. They talked far more and more widely about the time he came to the Philadelphia Yearly Meeting, held that year in Burlington, New Jersey, wearing a large greatcoat over a military coat, under which he had concealed a hollowed-out book with a bladder full of red pokeberry juice inserted between the covers. Strapped at his waist under the greatcoat was a small sword. At what he considered an opportune moment he stood up and threw off the greatcoat, revealing his military getup to the startled meeting of nonviolent Quakers.

According to Roberts Vaux—-who heard the story from a friend, who got it from an eyewitness—Lay began a harangue that went something like this: "All you negro masters contentedly holding your fellow creatures in a state of slavery, especially you who profess 'Do unto all men as ye would they should do unto you'—you might as well throw off your plain coats, as I do. It would be justifiable in the sight of the Almighty if you should thrust a sword through their hearts as I do through this book." He took out the book and ran his sword into it, splattering what looked like blood over those sitting nearby. Then he walked out of the meeting. Vaux doesn't mention whether he was escorted out or just left. It's easy enough to imagine the entire meeting rooted to their seats in astonishment.[36] That was Vaux's description, writing in 1815. Benjamin Rush also described this incident. In his telling—written in 1790, twenty-five years before Vaux composed his account—Lay shouted, "Thus shall God shed the blood of those persons who enslave their fellow creatures." "The terror of this extravagant and unexpected act," Rush wrote, "produced swoonings in several of the women of the congregation."[37] Rush's reproduction of Lay's language sounds more authentic than Vaux's gussied-up version many years later.

Lay perpetrated an even more dramatic demonstration having to do with neighbors of his. A nearby family owned an enslaved girl, and one day Lay decoyed the family's six-year-old into his home and kept him busy there for many hours, "by means of some amusement," says Vaux. It's worthwhile quoting the story Vaux tells to grasp the lengths Lay would go to make his point. In the evening Lay saw the anguished parents coming toward his house. "As they drew near, [Lay] advanced and met them, enquiring in a feeling manner 'what is the matter?'—the afflicted parents, apprehensive that they should never recover their child, replied with anguish, 'Oh Benjamin, Benjamin! Our child is gone, he has been missing all day.' Lay paused, and said, 'Your child is safe in my house, and you may now conceive of the sorrow you inflict upon the parents of the negroe girl you hold in slavery, for she was torn from them by avarice.'"[38]

Benezet was more than likely well-attuned to the atrociousness of slavery before he met Lay, and if he wasn't his friendship with Lay would have definitively clarified the issue for him. But Benezet was neither contentious nor theatrical. Those who talked about him emphasized his benign spirit, his amiability, his generosity, his lack of ego. The idea that Benezet might ever engage in anything like guerilla theater is impossible to imagine. In that regard he was a very different personality type than his friend. But Lay was fifteen years older than Benezet and there were elements in his lifestyle that appealed to the younger man, that jibed with something deep in his own character.

At some point Benezet became a vegetarian. But we know he stopped eating meat much earlier than that. In a letter to John Smith in 1758, he wrote, "I shall scarce ever imbrue my hands in the blood of any creature, having left off eating meat . . . and made a kind of league of amity and peace with the animal creation, looking upon them as the most grateful, as well as the most reasonable part of God's creatures."[39] Rush told the often reiterated story that once Benezet was visiting one of his brothers whose wife invited him to have dinner with them. Poultry was on the menu. "What!" Benezet protested. "Would you have me eat my neighbors?"[40] We don't know when Benezet adopted a vegetarian diet, but his friend Lay's habits might well have served as a model for him.

Vegetarianism was an idiosyncratic choice in mid-eighteenth-century America. Both Lay and Benezet practiced it, and both were enthusiastic gardeners who grew many of their own vegetables. Benezet and Lay shared other lifestyle habits: simplicity in clothing, disdain for ostentation, disregard for wealth. One of Benezet's many friends recalled that in a store "where there was a great display of fine goods and fancy articles," Benezet "pleasantly exclaimed . . . 'What a number of beautiful things are here which I do not want.'"[41] Lay also attributed "the hellish practice of slavery" to avarice and greed, which later became one of Benezet's major themes. Lay's ideas and example, Maurice Jackson writes, influenced both Benezet and Benezet's great abolitionist friend John Woolman.[42]

Lay and Benezet were passionate men whose lives were driven by deep-running emotional currents that gave rise to the values that impelled their actions. For Lay, that intrinsic trait was confrontation; for Benezet, altruism. Lay lived out his life as an agitator and belligerent; he was an inveterate warrior. Benezet's emotions channeled themselves into care for all those who came into his orbit and needed it. That instinct expressed itself in different ways, with homeless Acadians, with defrauded Indians, most consequentially with enslaved Black people. But it started with children.

CHAPTER SIX

Educator

By the time Benezet began teaching, the Quakers had a long, involved history with schooling. Fox himself had a minimal education; he learned to read, possibly at home, possibly during his youthful apprenticeship as a shoemaker. He most likely taught himself to write. His handwriting was execrable, "ofttimes not quite readable," says Larry Ingle, his modern biographer, "and he made up his own spelling rules according to the moment's inspiration."[1] Fox's *Journal* shows his idiosyncrasies not just in writing but in thinking. He's repetitive, ungrammatical, prolix beyond almost all his long-winded contemporaries, at times only semicoherent. The way he expresses himself in writing makes one wonder what his preaching must have sounded like.

In terms of the basic three Rs, handwriting made little difference to him in that era of elegant hands; occasionally one of his followers would copy out his letters before they were sent off. But he read the Bible and other religious texts enthusiastically. Once his soul was illuminated by the Divine Light, learning of any sort seemed secondary. "The Lord," he said, "would teach his people himself."[2]

Fox was notorious for his attack on ministers in their "Steeple Houses." He and his followers disrupted services whenever the spirit moved them, and it moved them often. He inveighed against ministers, "priests" he called them, who took wages for their work. "Who are the hirelings," he wrote, ". . . who seek for their gain . . . who feed themselves with the fat now, and so make a prey of the people? . . . The priests preach for hire, and the prophets prophesy for money."[3] These priestly "antichrists, deceivers and false prophets" received their training in England's universities—an education that, in Fox's view, detracted from and often displaced true enlightenment and spawned insufferable pride. "Lie down all for shame," he wrote, "who are in pride and oppression, and in the steps and places of the Pharisees, and have got a form of the words which the apostles said, and which Christ said, and have got it in three or four languages; the Lord has discovered you now; the Lord God Almighty has discovered you by his prophets and servants."[4]

Quakers believed that only those who had received "true knowledge of things spiritual" by "the light or gift of God" could be authentic preachers of the gospel, whether or not they were ordained by a church—even if they were illiterate. Those who preached for money were "deceivers" and "dissemblers"—"evil beasts," not true ministers of the gospel.[5] Without the light of God, learning was essentially worthless. "I saw," Fox wrote in the introduction to his *Journal*, "that being educated at Oxford or Cambridge did not qualify or fit a man to be a minister of Christ. Knowing that, why would I want to follow people from Oxford or Cambridge?"[6]

Fox was relentless in his attacks. The kind of learning that went on at the universities masked the absence of true knowledge, the knowledge of the heart. He returned to this theme again and again in his *Epistles* and in his lengthy 1659 diatribe against naysayers and critics, *The Great Mystery of the Great Whore Unfolded: The Antichrist's Kingdom Revealed unto Destruction.*[7] It's no wonder the clerical and other students at the universities had little tolerance for him or for the Quakers' disparagement and contempt for their endeavors. But if Fox's polemics could be scurrilous, the reaction at Oxford and Cambridge could be, and often was, barbaric. For example, at Oxford the local Quakers met twice a week in Frewin Hall. The building was originally part of St. Mary's College, but in the seventeenth century it was just opposite the university gate, making the Quakers' presence a regular provocation. "[It] was the constant practice of the scholars there to meet us and act their wickedness," wrote Lawrence Willyer, an Oxford Meeting member.[8] Willyer's description, says Braithwaite, is "too precise in vile detail to be reproduced in full."[9] The description Braithwaite does print is bad enough: the "scholars," Willyer said, engaged in "pulling of Friends' hair off their heads, and beards by the roots, plaiting their hair into knots, pluck[ing] off Friends' hats . . . and then beat[ing] them on the heads." True to their nonviolent principles the Friends apparently didn't resist any of this, but the restraint must have been hard. "They have brought hogs into our meeting," Willyer wrote, "and pulled them about the room to make a noise. . . . They have come into our meetings, whooping and halloing, houghing, scoffing, swearing and cursing and . . . calling Friends rogues and whores, dogs, bitches and toads . . . making a noise like cats and dogs."[10]

The educational ramifications of Quaker Inner Light theology surfaced in the thinking of other Quaker leaders as well as Fox. Growing naturally from the foundational Quaker belief in revelation, the issue generated significant, often heated debate between Friends and their adversaries. The focus for Fox, Robert Barclay, and other Quaker apologists was always on the requirements for true gospel preachers. What kind of education was necessary for that? they asked. The answer was that no education was necessary; in fact, educational accomplishments (they called it "dross") often displaced true spiritual understanding. Even illiterate persons were capable of preaching the truth. But inevitably, the Quakers' enemies embraced the idea that Quaker spirituality was anti-intellectual at its heart and that Quakers denied the value not just of universities but of education generally.

The adversaries didn't have to make up this inference—it seemed clear enough from the Quakers' own words. "If you ponder these things," Barclay wrote in his *Apology*, "then you will say with me that all learning, wisdom and knowledge that are gathered by the aid of man's own nature are but dross and worthless compared with the cross of Christ."[11] Or again: "It would be better to be stripped and naked, and to consider learning as a dross and a drug, and become a fool for Christ's sake."[12] Or: "Many consider us fools and madmen. But we do not ply them with academic and learned argument, but command them to lay aside their wisdom in the name and the power and the authority of the Lord. We urge them to descend from that proud realm of ethereal brain knowledge."[13] And what, then, was one to make of the fact that Barclay himself was a graduate of the University of Paris and wrote his *Apology* originally in Latin?

Barclay was tender about accusations that he was against learning. He says that one of his critics accuses him of "[inveighing] against all human learning. . . . He thinks he has found out our secret design of being against learning and schools of learning, which is neither our affirmation nor our principle, but his own false supposition."[14] But the attack on Quaker ideas about learning went well beyond "he said/he said." Arguments were still going on about Quakers and learning 150 years after Barclay published the *Apology*. When the former Quaker and prominent Presbyterian minister Samuel Hanson Cox said that Quakers had "a characteristic aversion to investigate," he was talking about a predisposition to ignore facts and reasoning, which he couched in traditional Lockean terms. "Knowledge is not innate," he wrote, ". . . that any man is liable to err; that we must make inferences from facts, which theory must follow and not precede, in order to the possession of knowledge; that men come into this world without ideas, ignorant as brutes, and derive all they know by means of sensation and reflection; that we must guard our premises, and make them sure, before we arrive at conclusions; and that one fact is worth a thousand theories, and good against a million: these are the main principles of true reasoning."[15]

Cox was an aggressive adversary. Born into a Quaker family, he was disowned by the Friends when he was twenty for questioning fundamental Quaker tenets of faith. Later he wasn't just skeptical—he came to believe that the Quaker belief in the Inner Light was inimical to Christianity. He thought of Christianity as the ultimate religion of reason, and he hated what he saw as the Quaker disregard for reason and the sect's enthronement of dubious, unprovable inspiration, which, as he saw it, mandated against education.

Cox was a combatant in the clash of two religious mentalities, both driven by faith—one in which faith was framed by tradition, ritual, and interpretive commentary, all of which required learning and reason to understand fully; the other embracing the invisible working of the spirit, which required nothing more than an open heart. Zealots such as Cox could not abide what they saw as the abandonment of reason in exchange for the embrace of something so dubious and illusory as an inner voice.

While Quakers were hardly antipathetic to learning per se, they did, without question, feel the value of education was limited. There was no Quaker ministry that required any kind of advanced education, and almost all occupations were learned through apprenticeships, from mechanical trades up through medicine and law. The three Rs were necessary preparation for apprenticeships, but there was little desire or need for advanced learning. "Higher education in the secular sense," wrote twentieth-century Quaker scholar Howard Brinton, "was for the most part a matter of individual concern."[16] Even the classically educated, erudite William Penn advised his children to "have but few books. . . . Reading many books is but taking off the mind from Meditation."[17] A prominent Quaker contemporary of Benezet wrote that schoolmasters were responsible for imparting practical learning "*tho' within the Bounds of Moderation in a subservient Way*" (emphasis added).[18]

Nonetheless, a few early Pennsylvania Quakers had more expansive ideas. One was Thomas Budd, a Philadelphia merchant and early immigrant from England. His *Good Order Established in Pennsylvania and New Jersey* is a fulsome description of the region's potential in terms of agriculture, industry, and trade. His vision for education was well ahead of its time. Formal education, he believed, should be public and mandatory, under the government's jurisdiction. "It might be well," he wrote, "if a Law were made by the Governours and general Assemblies of Pennsilvania and New-Jersey, that all Persons inhabiting in the said Provinces, do put their Children seven years to the publick School, or longer, if the Parents please." The General Assembly should hire skilled teachers "to teach and instruct Boys and Girls in all the most useful Arts and Sciences that they in their youthful capacities may be capable to understand, as the learning to Read and Write true English, Latine, and other useful Speeches and Languages."[19]

When Benezet got his first teaching job in Germantown, it's unlikely he was thinking about arguments concerning Quaker beliefs on education. He was no doubt pleased to get the job, and his faith was such that he would have been untroubled by the kind of critique Cox articulated. Quakers had been subject to attacks of that nature since their earliest days. Nor was he likely to have questioned the curriculum he was to teach—namely reading, writing, and arithmetic. He was working two jobs at the time—in school and in the print shop—which would have allowed little time to ponder abstract pedagogical matters.

Benezet had been teaching in Germantown for three years when a position opened up at the Philadelphia Public School, "public" in the sense that it was overseen by both Philadelphia's Quaker Yearly Meeting and the Provincial Council. The school had been promulgated in Penn's *Charters of Ye Public School* as a place "where poor Children Might be freely Maintained taught and Educated," since "all Children and servants Male and Female . . . should be taught and instructed[,] the rich at reasonable rates and the poor to be Maintained and Schooled for Nothing."[20]

Penn himself had been educated at Chigwell School then Oxford, where the curriculum included logic, moral philosophy, mathematics, classical languages and literature. He left Oxford (or possibly was expelled) after two years for reasons that are opaque—his dissenting opinions definitely did not fit well in what was at the time a staunchly high church institution, which was true of Oxford generally and Penn's Christ College particularly. Twenty years later when Charles II granted him proprietorship of what would become Pennsylvania, Penn's ideas of an education system for his new colony showed how distant he was from the ideals he had been trained to. "We are in pain to make [children] scholars," he wrote, ". . . to talk rather than to know, which is true canting. . . . We press their memory too soon, and puzzle, strain and load them with words and rules to know grammar and rhetoric; and a strange tongue or two that, it is ten to one, may never be useful to them."[21]

Penn, in fact, had a remarkably progressive approach to teaching children, one that appealed to their innate instinct to learn about the world around them and to their natural playfulness. "Children," he wrote, "had rather be making tools and instruments of play: shaping, drawing, framing and building than getting some rules of propriety and speech by heart."[22] Passages like this can astonish with their modernity. One thinks of John Dewey or even

Maria Montessori. It's one thing to say that Penn repudiated the classical training he himself experienced; it's another to grasp his sensitivity to children and their development. He had the same practical objectives that informed Quaker education generally: if they did nothing else, schools needed to prepare students for productive roles in life. But he was attuned to instincts, to the natural development of children's curiosity and intellect.

All of which is to say that when Benezet began teaching at what would come to be known as the William Penn Charter School, he found himself in a congenial place, one that provided space for his own instinctive empathy and for the astonishing creativity that grew out of it. In his account of Penn Charter's early history, Thomas Woody writes, "With the fourth decade [of the eighteenth century] came a period of real greatness, for in 1742 began the services of Anthony Benezet."[23]

Educational historian Paul Travers describes school in the early eighteenth century as a "grim scene."[24] That was, no doubt, more true in the Massachusetts Bay Colony, with its rigid Puritan approach to both church and school discipline, than in Penn's colony. But throughout colonial America, the teacher's role was primarily to make assignments, hear lessons, and keep order. It was a trying job, since students were responsible for their own progress, or lack of it, which often led to tedium and frustration during the long school days—and, consequently, to unruly behavior. When Benezet started at Penn Charter, school was in session eight hours a day, six days a week. Recitations, copying assignments, taking dictation, and studying texts for so many hours a day no doubt wore the patience of many students, especially younger ones.

Beyond spelling, handwriting, reading, and elementary arithmetic books, which were available in Philadelphia's Quaker schools, religious texts were the common currency of the classroom. "With curricula at all levels rarely suited to children," says Travers, "it is small wonder that children were hard to handle."[25] Whipping, birching, paddling, and pinching were all part of the master's disciplinary repertoire in colonial times. One common method was for the miscreant to be hoisted with his pants lowered onto the back of another student who, leaning forward, afforded the master an easy target. Travers tells us that "punishments were meted out with few reservations" and that "whipping posts were common."[26] "The success of the teacher then," says Brookes, "was measured by his ability to crack the whip of discipline or wield a bundle of well-seasoned rods."[27]

But within that generally harsh environment, masters at the Quaker Public School exercised more latitude in their approach to discipline than was likely the case elsewhere. We don't know a great deal about this subject at Penn Charter, but Woody, who closely examined the school's archives, writes that "there were doubtless two extremes. On the one hand we might take Anthony Benezet as the very personification of mildness, and who ruled by love. On the other hand, there was John Todd who would thrash a boy very severely, and who took great delight in getting his victim to admit the pain that he knew he felt."[28]

The biographies of Benezet by Vaux, Brookes, and Jackson all recount stories of Benezet's indulgent and nurturing relationship with his students. One anecdote recorded by Brookes was originally told by a person acquainted with Benezet who also knew the students involved. The story goes that two boys in Benezet's class captured a mouse in the morning, constructed a tiny pillory of some sort, imprisoned the mouse in it, and placed the assemblage on Benezet's desk with a little verse attached.

> I stand here, my honest friends,
> For stealing cheese and candle ends.

The whole class waited for Benezet to arrive, eagerly looking forward to his reaction. When Benezet came in and saw the mouse, he apparently said, "Poor thing, who put thee here?" Looking over the class, he spotted the two perpetrators by their guilty looks. After freeing the mouse—"Go, poor thing, go"—he turned to the guilty parties. As Brookes told it, "the two boys stood with fear and trembling to hear their fate." It's far more likely that, given their master's well-known gentleness and affection for his students, they were in considerably less danger than if they had been standing before a different judge.[29]

Roberts Vaux was writing thirty-two years after Benezet's death, a time when many of Benezet's former students were still alive and well. A prominent Quaker lawyer, abolitionist, and educator, Vaux helped found Philadelphia's public school system and served as president of its board for fourteen years. So he undoubtedly knew many of these former pupils and consulted them in writing his biography; his book's "List of Authorities" notes "oral information communicated by individuals who were personally acquainted with him."[30]

As someone devoted to education, Vaux was closely attuned to Benezet's unusual attention to individual students' personalities. "[Benezet] investigated the natural dispositions of his pupils," Vaux wrote, "and adapted his management of them, to their various tempers. Persuasion would secure attention and obedience in some, whilst proper excitement to emulation, would animate and encourage others."[31] That approach matches the highest aspirations of the best progressive teachers today, almost 250 years later.

Benezet's attention to his students' patterns of learning made him a critic of the instructional books generally available. He especially disliked the way some texts proceeded quickly to concepts that students couldn't readily grasp. In composing a tutorial for his "accounts" students, which he sent to his friend George Dillwyn to review, he "proceeded . . . in as short a Method as the pupil's understanding & the rules would permit." In the same letter he told Dillwyn that to teach reducing fractions, he used the so-called rule of three, a mathematical formula that makes it easy to solve proportions when three numbers are known and the fourth needs to be calculated. "In the Rule of Three," he explained to Dillwyn, "thou mayest observe I am specially careful that the first sums be very easy, such as the learner may well understand."[32]

Benezet's approach to teaching English grammar is likewise simplified relative to the usual texts, which put English parts of speech and other grammatical forms into a Latin framework. Most grammar books, he told Dillwyn, "dwell tediously upon each of the eight parts of speech loading the learner with needless distinctions, many of which tho' necessary in the latin etc. are not so in the english."[33] He sent this "Essay on Grammar" to Dillwyn in 1780, four years before his death. He'd been thinking about these subjects since he began teaching, forty-one years before, and at age sixty-seven he was still thinking about them.

Even more interesting is the connection he drew between a simple learning model and the Quaker view of higher education, with its supposedly counterproductive effect on faith. He might have been echoing William Penn's thoughts of almost a hundred years earlier, except that Benezet's reflections weren't notional; they derived from a lifetime of experience. "I much wish such a radical [basic, root] knowledge of the English Language was given in our Society," he told Dillwyn, "as may make the use of the learned languages quite unnecessary. Many years experience has shewn me, that a proficiency therein has a natural tendency to wedd to the world; & create an enmity to the cross, I'll allow it recommends to publick employments; helps to make men's way with honour, pleasure & reputation in the world: But certainly a lower a simpler station is safer & more agreeable to divine purity."[34]

Putting aside for a moment Benezet's fundamental piety, his thoughts on pedagogy put him into a modern rather than an eighteenth-century conversation—about teaching math, teaching grammar, teaching reading, and teaching writing. He was, as Carter Woodson wrote, "really a modern teacher, far in advance of his contemporaries."[35] Regarding writing, his advice was what we now call "plain English." Writing about events, desires, etc., he says, "is best expressed simply as we would speak it."[36] Modern specialists on readability such as Rudolf Flesch and Robert Gunning changed the way newspapers, textbooks, work communications, and so on were written, starting in the 1940s, using the same approach. Writing teachers today pursue that surprisingly difficult goal with their students right through college-level courses.

In terms of reading, Benezet noted in a letter to his friend David Barclay, the English Quaker banker and philanthropist, that he had "found a great disadvantage arising from the want of a spelling book and primer, properly adapted." Along with the letter, he sent Barclay a copy of the second edition of his *Pennsylvania Spelling Book*. In this book, used for spelling and reading, he endeavored "to make the spelling more easy, familiar and agreeable than is usual." That conforms to Benezet's overall approach, but it's striking to learn that in his first edition of this book he had "deviated from the common established rules in the division of syllables, rather consulting and favoring the ear, than keeping to the common custom." This was a startling innovation—the idea that students should learn writing and reading by ear—almost as if Benezet had anticipated the modern phonics movement in teaching reading, familiar to anyone with children or grandchildren learning to read and write in the third decade of the twenty-first century. That particular pedagogical advance, he told Barclay, elicited so much confusion from teachers and students "habituated to the common mode of dividing syllables" that he had to give it up in the revised edition.[37]

The import of all this is that Benezet had a unique facility for putting himself inside the mind and intellect of young people. He sensed how they absorbed and processed information and the relation of their intellects to their desire to get satisfaction from learning and enjoy what they were doing. That speaks to his unusually empathetic nature. It's also significant that he carried this exceptional empathic capacity a step further. It wasn't enough for him to understand these things, he was constantly motivated to turn what might be called his interpersonal awareness into action. He wrote essays, primers, and math tutorials that gave concrete form to his understanding and produced results. He was action oriented and results oriented, as a teacher, a humanitarian, and, most important for his place in history, as an abolitionist.

There's probably no better example of Benezet's instinct to engage with and ameliorate others' lives than his undertaking to teach a young woman who was deaf. Vaux reported that "during two years under his tuition, [she acquired] such instruction as to enable her to enjoy an intercourse with society, which had been previously denied to her."[38] In the eighteenth century, handicaps were no longer universally considered to be caused by curses from God or possession by demons, and by 1725, deaf persons in England were presumed capable of comprehension, including in legal proceedings. In both England and France, the 1760s saw significant progress in teaching communication skills to the deaf through the development of sign language.

Unfortunately, Vaux didn't record any of the details of Benezet's efforts, so we don't know when his lessons took place, nor do we know anything about his methods. Did he devise them himself, or was he aware of the work of Thomas Braidwood in England or Charles-Michel, Abbé de L'Epée, in France, both of whom established schools for deaf students during the period when Benezet was teaching? Vaux said that Benezet was the first in Philadelphia and perhaps in America to undertake this kind of instruction, though a few other instances of individuals teaching the deaf are recorded to have taken place at about the same time.[39]

In 1754 Benezet undertook another groundbreaking effort. He had been "much solicited," he told the Quaker school board, to establish a school for girls. After some discussion and apparently no dissent, the board agreed and voted funds for the project, employing Benezet at eighty pounds a year to teach reading, writing, arithmetic, and grammar, to which he added on his own initiative French and elementary Latin.[40]

When Vaux was writing his Benezet biography, he received a letter from a former student at the girls' school. Deborah Logan and her family lived near the Benezets on Chestnut Street, and her mother was a friend of Benezet and his wife, Joyce. The long letter was full of anecdotes and included descriptions of Benezet as a schoolmaster, his innovative work as a teacher of writing, and his insistence on providing time, space, and equipment for the students to exercise. Her memories of him, she said, would be enough for an essay.[41] Brookes believed that Benezet's school was "in all probability the first public school for girls in America."[42]

Benezet initiated the idea of a public school for girls in 1754. The proposal seems not to have been met with any pushback or even any serious debate. The minutes of the board meeting where it was approved read, "After some conversation it was agreed . . ." Given the Friends' egalitarian history, that's no surprise. Women had been regarded as equals from the beginning, quite separately from the common role distinctions of the era. After a hundred years, that value was baked into Quaker DNA. Against this background, the school board, composed mostly of Quakers, embraced Benezet's proposal. There was nothing in it that challenged them.

But for the four years previous to his girls' school initiative, Benezet had been teaching a group of students infinitely more neglected in the colonial educational scene than girls. In 1750 he had started a night school in his own house for Philadelphia's Black children—some free, some enslaved. And despite their egalitarian ideals, for Quakers the idea of Black equality was a fraught subject.

CHAPTER SEVEN

A School for Black Children

Benezet began teaching Black children in 1750, fully understanding what a controversial thing he was doing. In the South, educating Black people was outlawed, punishable by fines or flogging. The South Carolina "Negro Act of 1740," for example, declared, "All and every person or persons whatsoever who shall hereafter teach or cause any slave or slaves to be taught to write . . . shall for every such offense forfeit the sum of one hundred pounds, Current money."[1] In other southern colonies, anyone—white or Black—who dared teach enslaved individuals could be imprisoned, as well as fined and whipped. Educating Black people, especially in the aftermath of the frightening Stono Rebellion of 1739, was seen as a clear and present danger, likely to lead to yet more slave violence.

In the northern colonies there were debates, usually over the desirability of teaching slaves to read so they could know something of the Bible in order to be converted and catechized. But when Benezet initiated his project there were no such schools, for religious or any other kind of instruction.[2] His evening school was very likely the first serious school for Black children in the country. Historians have noted that Benezet initiated a Quaker school for girls and an evening school for Black children, both of them breakthroughs in American educational history. The fatigue that must have been Benezet's daily portion from those exertions can only be imagined. Teaching girls during the day and Black children at night could hardly have left him with much energy for the increasing religious duties he was taking on as a Quaker elder.[3]

The girls' school was public, a formal endeavor of the Society of Friends. The Black school was anything but public. Knowledge of it circulated, but there was no publicity, no public notice. The general opinion in colonial America was that Black people were inferior intellectually, possibly uneducable, very possibly even a different and lower version of humanity—in which case teaching them was not only dangerous, it was a fool's errand.

This common, street-level prejudice was part and parcel of a larger construct that provided an intellectual framework that oriented scientists, philosophers, theologians, and humanists, a presupposition that inhabited the mental background of the era's great thinkers and reached down seamlessly into the minds of ordinary people. This principle, the so-called Great Chain of Being, provided a way of organizing the plenitude of nature—minerals, plants, and animals, including mankind—into a scale according to complexity, reasoning ability, and other criteria. The races of man fit into this continuum as well, best illustrated by Carl Linnaeus's *Systema Naturae*, in which the great taxonomist placed white Europeans at the top of the hierarchy and Black people at the bottom.

The Great Chain of Being as an organizing principle had its origins in Plato and Aristotle, but it was in the eighteenth century, as the intellectual historian A. O. Lovejoy explained, that the concept "attained its widest diffusion and acceptance."[4] Lovejoy characterized the idea as equivalent in its influence on eighteenth-century minds to the theory of evolution that took hold after Darwin. The most fundamental scientific theory of its time, it created a mental atmosphere that nurtured a jaundiced perception of Black people, both enslaved and free. "They were described," writes Roger Bruns, biographer and former National Archives deputy director, "as a people created by nature in the likeness of beasts—a subhuman work force, contemptible in appearance, wretched in manner, lowly in mind, hopelessly incapable of assimilation into American society."[5]

The power and extent of this distorted perception were deep and lasting. While slavery itself was age-old, the New World association of Africans with the institution gave it a racial identification it didn't previously have, along with a need on the part of slaveholders to justify keeping Black people in perpetual servitude. With its steps of gradation, the Chain of Being provided a rationale, in that Enlightenment era of rationales, for explaining how Black people were actually not human in the same way as whites but members of a separate and lower-order species. And since all of animal creation was connected, Black persons weren't just inferior to whites; they were also the link to the lower orders of the kingdom—specifically, to apes, who occupied the next rung down on the ladder. Soame Jenyns, a popular British writer of the period, explained it this way: "Animal life rises from this low beginning in the shell-fish, through innumerable species of insects, fishes, birds, and beasts, to the confines of reason, where, in the dog, the monkey, and the chimpanzee, it unites so closely with the lowest degree of that quality in man, that they cannot easily be distinguished from each other. From the lowest degree in the brutal Hottentot, reason . . . advances, through the various stages of human understanding, which rise above each other, till in a Bacon or Newton it attains the summit."[6]

The idea that Black people constituted a separate and inferior species gave birth to the theory of polygenism, which disputed the biblical description of humankind as a single family descended from one father and mother—Adam and Eve. Polygenism, literally, "many origins," signified that the different races derived from different progenitors. As Josiah Notts, one of the leading advocates of this theory defined it, "There is a Genus, Man, comprising two or more species," each descended from a singular ancestor.[7] Notts's aim was "to cut loose the natural history of mankind from the Bible, and to place each upon its own foundation, where it may remain," as he put it, "without collision or molestation."[8]

Although, as Lovejoy noted, the concept of polygenism first became prominent in the 1700s, the word itself was not used until the nineteenth century. It was in that later era that polygenism emerged as the dominant scientific understanding of racial differences and that scientific racism became the order of the day. Among those who promulgated the idea were leading nineteenth-century biologists Samuel Morton, Charles Pickering, and, most famously, Harvard zoologist Louis Agassiz, who believed that Black people were a "degraded and degenerate race."[9] Agassiz—biologist, zoologist, and geologist—was the most celebrated American scientist of his day, a dogged adversary of Darwin's theory of evolution. His German counterpart, Ernst Haeckel (who originated the term "ontogeny recapitulates phylogeny"), was a staunch evolutionist, yet he too believed that Black people occupied a lower order on the scale of human development. In the nineteenth-century world of science, the racist conception was pervasive.

The poisonous afterlife of this idea still jaundices belief about African Americans today. But the roots of prejudice were well advanced in Benezet's time.[10] Early abolitionists believed as a principle of faith that Black people were as much a part of the human race as white people, equal spiritually if perhaps not in all other ways. The book of Genesis proclaimed humanity's oneness. When that message narrowed among the Jews, St. Paul universalized it. The New Testament proclaimed that Jesus came as the propitiation for sins, "not for ours only but also for the sins of the whole world" (1 John 2:2). A bedrock tenet of the Bible was that humankind was a family. But where, if anywhere, was the *proof* of this Jewish and Christian credo?

We know from Benezet's later life that he was a natural strategic thinker. But it was one thing, wrote Roger Bruns, "for a writer to base an antislavery attack on theological grounds alone or on the cruelty of the institution; it was another to base it on an affirmation of the intellectual and moral equality of the Negro people."[11] Benezet might have begun his school out of compassion for the urchin children of Philadelphia's "Negro people," but it's possible to wonder if, from the very start, he saw a potential argument for Black equality.

But whether he did or not, his enterprise faced strong prevailing headwinds. The opposition to Black education, Benjamin Franklin wrote, "was partly from a prejudice that reading and knowledge in a slave are both useless and dangerous; and partly from an unwillingness in the masters and mistresses of common schools to take black scholars, lest the parents of the white Children should be disgusted and take them away, not chusing to have their Children mix'd with Slaves in Education, Play, &c."[12] By 1750 Benezet was a widely respected, "weighty" Quaker, whom no one in Philadelphia would have considered foolish. But starting a school for Black children, in his own home, free of tuition and without any outside financial support, must have seemed to many not just questionable, but quixotic.

On the other hand, Philadelphia had seen several attempts along these lines before. In 1722 a British immigrant, Samuel Keimer, had advertised that he was offering "his Service to teach poor Brethren the Male Negroes to read the Holy Scriptures, &c. in a very *uncommon, expeditious* and *delightful Manner* without any expense to their respective Masters or Mistresses."[13] It's not clear if Keimer's project ever materialized—he was a mercurial individual who, back in England, had become a devotee of the French Prophets. But it might have; there was apparently some controversy about his efforts several years later, though aside from a sarcastic piece of doggerel about him no other notice of his school has been uncovered.[14]

Even if Keimer succeeded in his plan to instruct enslaved people, it's not likely word of it would have percolated down to Benezet. Keimer fled the country to avoid his debtors in 1729, two years before the Benezets arrived in Philadelphia. But there was another, more promising instructional effort that Benezet was definitely familiar with. In 1740, shortly after Anthony started his first teaching job in Germantown, George Whitefield arrived in Philadelphia and its environs on a revival tour. Benezet and Whitefield had met as youngsters; the Benezet family, Brookes says, was close to Whitefield back in England.[15] Now Anthony, at twenty-seven, had just begun his first real job after years of drifting and indecision, while Whitefield had graduated from Oxford, taken Anglican orders, worked with John and Charles Wesley, the founders of Methodism, and emerged as a sensationally successful preacher, renowned throughout England and America. We do not know at that point what Benezet's thoughts might have been about Black people or slavery, though we might reasonably surmise he was appalled by the institution, if not yet settled on what should be done about it, and certainly not what he himself should do. But Whitefield was already deep into the slavery issue, including slave education. His relationship with the Benezet family was close enough that he sometimes stayed with them on visits to Philadelphia. In Anthony's father, Jean-Etienne, he found a collaborator on a plan to teach Black people.

During his 1740 preaching tour to Philadelphia, Whitefield bought five thousand acres of land seventy-five miles north of the city, on "the forks of the Delaware," intending to build a school for enslaved "Africans" and a religiously oriented town. Franklin's newspaper, the *Pennsylvania Gazette*, ran an ad soliciting money for the project: "All persons who please to contribute to the said school, may pay their Contributions to Mr. Benezet, Merchant, in Philadelphia, Mr. Noble at New-York, Mr. Gilbert Tennent, in New-Brunswick, New Jersey, or to the Printer of this Paper."[16]

Benezet *père* collected money for Whitefield's planned project and served as manager for the venture, which for a variety of reasons never got off the ground and eventually collapsed for lack of funds.[17] Given his father's participation, Anthony was surely familiar with Whitefield's vision for a school, although we can assume the evangelist's motives were not evident to him. Whitefield was no emancipator. On the contrary, he considered that making good, at least minimally educated Christians of the enslaved would not just prepare their souls for salvation in the hereafter but would help them conform better to rule by their masters and discourage disobedience in their lives here on earth.

Education for Whitefield had a two-pronged purpose: on the one hand improving enslaved people's minds so they could better grasp the prospect of salvation, on the other encouraging their docility.[18] In a letter attributed to Whitefield from 1743, the author wrote about the connection between submission to God and slavery:

> And though [God] hath now called you into *his own Family*, to be his *Own Children and Servants*; he doth not call you hereby *from the service of your Masters according to the Flesh*, but to *serve him* in serving them, in obeying all their lawful Commands, and submitting to the *Yoke* his Providence has placed you under. . . . Oh, *take it on you freely* . . . and by your chearful and constant *Obedience, put to silence the ignorance of foolish men* . . . [who] have thought, and said, "That if you, their *poor Slaves*, were brought to *Christianity*, you would be no more *Servants to them*." Oh never let this Calumny be cast upon Christ's Holy Religion, by the disagreeable Behavior of any of you *believing Negroes*.[19]

While Benezet no doubt knew about the proposed school, he would most likely have blanched at Whitefield's thinking about slave education—the exact opposite of his own once he got his thoughts in order. While Whitefield preached the obligation to treat the enslaved humanely, he never came out against slavery itself. Not only was he no abolitionist, his next project was an orphanage in Georgia supported by five hundred acres of crops that needed planting, tending, and harvesting, all of which Whitefield believed required Black labor. "Though liberty is a sweet thing to such as are born free," Whitefield wrote to John Wesley about the orphanage's need for enslaved workers,

> yet to those who never knew the sweets of it slavery, perhaps, may not be so irksome. However this be, it is plain to a demonstration that hot countries cannot be cultivated without Negroes. What a flourishing country might Georgia have been had the use of them been permitted years ago! How many white people have been destroyed for want of them, and how many thousands of pounds spent to no purpose at all! Though it is true that they are brought in a wrong way from their own country and it is a trade not to be approved of, yet, as it will be carried on whether we will or not, I should think myself highly favored if I could purchase a good number of them.[20]

Whitefield went on to say that the orphanage would treat the enslaved persons well and instruct them in the Gospels. To twenty-first-century ears that seems unconvincing as a mitigation of Whitefield's desire for slaves, which he fulfilled after persuading the Georgia legislature to permit slavery in a colony that had previously prohibited it.

Although Whitefield's school for Black students never materialized, his preaching won an unusual convert who did open a school of sorts. Robert Bolton came from Ireland to Philadelphia and opened a dance academy in 1738. For two years, Bolton hosted balls and concerts and was the city's leading dance master, until one day he found himself in a large crowd listening to Whitefield preach and awash in terror for the fate of their souls. Gripped by a wave of guilt for abetting the "devilish diversions" of fellow Philadelphians, Bolton closed his dance studio and opened a school for Black students. He was arraigned before the justices for this apparent violation of the city's Black code, which prohibited any gathering of four or more African Americans coming together for business other than that of their "masters or owners." He seems to have successfully defended himself against the charge and conducted his school, though little appears to have been recorded about his students, curriculum, or teachers. It was, in any event, a short-lived affair. Bolton died "impoverished" in 1742, two years after his evangelization by Whitefield.[21]

Whitefield's attitude toward slavery and education is significant because of his prominence as one of America's spiritual founding fathers. But, in fact, it was not very different from the orientation of many Quakers, who likewise believed the enslaved should be treated humanely and possibly taught to read and write for religious purposes but who had no trouble owning people themselves and benefitting from their labor. Historian Gary Nash points out the general "diffidence of prerevolutionary Philadelphia Quakers to working intimately with slaves and free blacks toward their religious and educational improvement."[22] Some embraced the obligation they felt to provide a degree of religious training and a certain level of education; others were wary of both.

The idea of educating enslaved individuals sufficiently for them to grasp the promises of Christianity had a tenuous pedigree in Quakerism. In 1693 George Keith published *An Exhortation & Caution to Friends Concerning Buying or Keeping of Negroes,* in which he urged Friends to liberate their slaves, and in the meantime "teach them to read and give them a Christian education."[23] But Keith was in the midst of a harsh internal struggle within the Society and was shortly to form a schismatic group he called Christian Quakers. As a renegade, he had lost whatever credibility he might previously have had among mainstream Quakers. Five years later Robert Pile, clerk of the Concord Meeting, presented a paper in front of the Philadelphia Monthly Meeting, in which he argued that "[slaves should] be learned [*sic*] to read english and to put them forward to goe to meetings, and indeavors used to convinc them y^t^ ye witness of god might be reached in them."[24]

Quakers struggled for decades with the notion of Black religious education, going back to George Fox's Barbados sermons in which he admonished Friends to remember that "Christ died for all, both Turks, Barbarians, Tartarians, and Ethiopians."[25] Black people, he declared, were spiritually the same as whites, with the same claim on Christ's saving grace and the same access to the divine presence, which resided within them just as it did in their white masters. Therefore it followed that Friends were obligated to instruct their slaves in the Christian story and the tenets of Christian worship. "Let me see and hear that you are of the faith of Abraham," he wrote to Barbados's Friends when he returned to England, "that you do instruct them in Christianity and in the law of Jesus; and in the circumcision of the spirit, as Abraham did outwardly."[26]

Fox's advice wasn't much followed. Black people might have been spiritually equal, but that didn't necessarily earn them fellowship in the Religious Society of Friends. Quaker masters sometimes took their slaves with them to meetings, but when either enslaved or free Blacks did go they needed to sit on benches set aside for them. In 1756 the Philadelphia Meeting established separate meetings for Black people, which apparently continued until 1805 when they were discontinued for lack of attendance because "they have now several places for worship of their own."[27] Although enslaved people in Philadelphia and elsewhere were often treated with solicitude and care by Quakers whose consciences were troubled by slavery, they were not taken into formal membership. There was no concerted effort by Quakers to attract Black converts, as there was by the Anglicans and later by the Methodists and Baptists. Quakers struggled for many decades to live up to the full meaning of their egalitarian faith, but they never had much enthusiasm for including Black people in their religious lives.

Nor did they concern themselves particularly with the idea of educating Black people, as Fox had intimated they should do when writing to his constituents in Barbados. "Consider, Friends . . . we esteem it a duty incumbent on us to pray with and for those in and belonging to our families . . . and to teach, instruct and admonish them," he reminded the Barbadians. "Now Negroes, Tawnies, and Indians make up a very great part of the families in this island; for whom an account will be required by him who comes to judge both the quick and dead."[28]

Sixty-five years later, Benjamin Lay expanded on this theme in his *All Slave-Keepers That Keep the Innocent in Bondage*, writing, "If our Slave-Keepers had been, or now would be faithful to God, the Truth, and would bring up their Negroes to some Learning, Reading and Writing and endeavor to the utmost of their power in the Sweet Love of Truth to instruct and teach 'em the principles of truth and righteousness and learn them some Honest Trade or Imployment; and then set them free . . ."[29] But Fox's far-off, distant suggestions, Lay's admonishments, and the occasional expressions of others about the obligation to teach enslaved Blacks made little impact on Quaker practice—until 1750, when Benezet opened his home to his first cohort of Black students.

Benezet's evening school for Black students broke through the long-standing neglect of his fellow Quakers. It broke through the near-universal conviction that Black people were incapable of education as well as the underlying fear that education would prime them for violence against their enslavers. His school challenged the hierarchical paradigm that set Africans as the lowest version of humanity on the scale of nature. It disputed what appeared to many to be simply the natural order of things. Benezet's school has been discussed by each of his biographers, but the revolutionary breakthrough it constituted has received little attention in the annals of America's race history. The chances are that Benezet hardly appreciated its full significance himself; he had zero interest in dwelling on his accomplishments or extolling them, not to others and not to himself.

As if to highlight Benezet's school as the radical step it was, shortly after the school opened its doors Benjamin Franklin printed the entire text of Pennsylvania's Black laws in his *Gazette*, at the request of city magistrates who had been getting complaints from citizens about the behavior of the city's Black population. The complainants were concerned that "Negroes and other Blacks, either free or under Pretense of Freedom, have resorted to, and settled in the City, and that slaves . . . have been permitted to wander abroad and seek their own Employment. . . ." These "wandering Negroes" had sometimes rented houses or rooms and entertained "Servants, Slaves, and other idle or vagrant persons," which often caused "Great Disorders," "to the annoyance and Danger of the neighbors."[30]

The Black laws constricted enslaved people's lives in ways large and small. They could not carry weapons. They were prohibited from meeting other Black people in "great Companies or Numbers"—that is, anything above the number four. Free Black persons, the law declared, "are an idle, slothful People," so anyone manumitting them had to put up a thirty-pound assurance to defray expenses they might cause the city. Free Black people couldn't "loiter or misspend their time" or "wander from place to place." Their children could be bound out for service: males till they were twenty-four, females till twenty-one. Free Black individuals couldn't invite other Black, Indigenous, or mixed-race people to their homes unless the prospective guests had permission from their masters. Nor could enslaved persons trade or barter without license, drink in the street, be out after nine in the evening, go with another person more than ten miles from their owner's home without the owner's permission, ramble about, or seek employment for themselves without their owner's permission. The penalty for violations was typically twenty-one lashes or thirty-nine lashes "on the bare back." If slaves were too severely injured from such a whipping to return to their master's or mistress's house, the enslaver had to pay for their transportation.[31] The *Gazette*'s front-page publication reminded those Philadelphians who needed reminding of the racial conditions of life in their city. But meanwhile Anthony Benezet was treating his Black scholars just as he did his white ones—like normal human beings.

Roberts Vaux—the biographer who lived nearest to Benezet's time and the only one with access to those who had known him—wrote that it was in about 1750 when people started noticing that Benezet was "deeply affected by the iniquity of the slave trade."[32] It would be another four years before Benezet wrote anything about slavery, but something had started changing in his thinking about Black enslavement. In 1750 he took Black children under his wing and began talking, if not yet writing, about slavery in ways different than he had before.

If we're looking for an incident that might have precipitated Benezet's new orientation, we aren't likely to find anything. He didn't keep a journal, and as far as we know, none of his acquaintances or correspondents ever mentioned anything of that sort—other than those Vaux no doubt heard from. In this regard, Benezet's evolution as an antislavery activist was different from that of his predecessors, Ralph Sandiford and Benjamin Lay, who witnessed atrocities in Barbados that filled them with a lifetime of rage. Woolman too, Benezet's friend and fellow campaigner, experienced not one but several pivotal moments. Best known is the time his employer directed him to write a bill of sale for an enslaved woman the employer owned. Woolman was troubled by having to write a slavery document, but he was young, he was contracted to his employer, he had been directed to do it. So against his conscience he wrote the bill, "through weakness," he later said. That violation of his conscience "so afflicted him" that later he needed to announce to both his boss and the buyer that he believed slavery was anti-Christian. That relieved his conscience a bit, but the incident stayed with him.[33]

Benezet's turn toward antislavery activism was more likely a process, perhaps driven in the first place by his empathetic nature, which was his primary character trait. We know how that expressed itself in his life as a teacher, his work with his deaf student, the way he initiated a school for girls, his insight into the minds of his students to understand how they thought and how to most effectively teach them, his love for the young people who were his students.

Knowing all that, one can easily believe that his motive for undertaking to teach Black children was his heightened sense of compassion. Vaux called it "his peculiar capacity for being profoundly sensible [sensitive]."[34] Brookes thought he began his school because he saw that Philadelphia's Black children were completely deprived of any sort of education, which affected "his profoundly spiritual nature."[35] His heart, Brookes says, was moved. Later in life, after he had for many years been teaching Black children both in his home and in the school he had persuaded the Society to establish, Benezet himself reflected in *A Short Account of the People Called Quakers* that "having observed the many disadvantages these afflicted people labor under in point of education and otherwise, a tender care has taken place to promote their instruction in school learning, and also their religious and temporal welfare, in order to qualify them for becoming reputable members of society."[36] Characteristically, he didn't claim credit for his own role, and since he composed his book about Quakers primarily for French soldiers who were in Philadelphia at the time, they wouldn't have known that it was his own "tender care" that was behind the schooling of "these afflicted people." "True charity," he wrote to a friend about a different situation, is "to relieve the oppressed and, to the utmost of our power to bind up the broken-hearted."[37] What better way to bind up the brokenhearted than to educate them and by educating them give them a chance to live decent, productive lives?

Benezet lived on Chestnut Street between First and Second, a short walk from Philadelphia's bustling Delaware waterfront, where many Black people, both enslaved and free, worked in the shops and trades that catered to the seagoing traffic; they were day laborers, stevedores, bakers, coopers, caulkers, riggers, and sailmakers.[38] He was often seen spending time with them there, learning about their lives, their origins, hearing their stories. It was characteristic of him, Vaux wrote, to be "surrounded by the sable children of Africa, imparting advice, and deriving information from them concerning the cruelties they had suffered."[39] We can be sure that there, too, he saw Black children, some accompanying their mothers or fathers, some themselves bound to masters, others running through the streets unattended, none of them with any knowledge at all of how to read or write or do sums, and—with no churches for their parents—few of them with any religious training. We can easily imagine how Benezet, with his empathetic soul, his love of children, his devotion to teaching, his spirituality and reverence for Jesus and the promises of Christianity, was, as Brookes put it, "moved with compassion toward them" and how that impelled him to the creation of what came to be known simply as "Benezet's School," which was to have such profound consequences for both himself and for the world order he was soon to challenge.[40]

L'Assemblée surprise (1839–1842), by Karl Girardet, pictures a Camisard prayer meeting surprised by Catholic soldiers. Musée du désert, Mialet.

In the 1738 painting *Noon*, by William Hogarth, dour Huguenots leaving church contrast with carefree English enjoying Sunday pastimes. Metropolitan Museum of Art.

George Fox (1624–1691) established the Religious Society of Friends. Facsimile of portrait drawn on stone by Thomas Fairland, after unknown artist, Library of Congress.

William Penn (1644–1718) founded Pennsylvania as a "Holy Experiment." Portrait, Bibliothèque publique de Neuchâtel.

Benjamin West's painting *Penn's Treaty with the Indians* (1771–1772) helped to cement William Penn's popular image as a peacemaker. Pennsylvania Academy of Fine Arts.

The London Coffee House stood near the Philadelphia market where horses, carriages, and furniture were sold, as well as enslaved humans. *London Coffee House*, New York Public Library.

In this image by an unknown artist, Benezet teaches Black children, as he did for decades. In John Barber and Elizabeth Barber, *Historical, Poetical and Pictorial American Scenes* (Cincinnati: John H. Johnson, 1851).

The colonial Philadelphia waterfront saw a sharp increase in slave ships during the labor shortage caused by the French and Indian War. *Philadelphia in 1753*, artist unknown, Boston Public Library.

The vantage point illustrated in W. L. Breton's *A Monday Morning View of Friends Meeting House and Academy* (1829) would have been familiar to Benezet. Library of Congress.

As depicted in this painting, Quaker meetings were often characterized by long periods of silence, occasionally punctuated by a member offering spiritual testimony. British Museum.

Benjamin Franklin (1706–1790) was a staunch ally of Benezet in the campaign against slavery. Portrait by Joseph Duplessis (ca. 1785), National Portrait Gallery, Washington, D.C.

Even more than the first, the second edition of Ralph Sandiford's *Mystery of Iniquity* (1730) excoriated the Religious Society of Friends, and indeed all Christian churches, for their complicity in slavery. British Museum.

THE

MYSTERY of INIQUITY;

IN A BRIEF

EXAMINATION

OF THE

Practice of the Times,

By the foregoing and the preſent DISPENSATION: Whereby is manifeſted how the *DEVIL* works in the Myſtery, which none can underſtand and get the Victory over but thoſe that are armed with the Light, that diſcovers the Temptation and the Author thereof, and gives Victory over him and his Inſtruments, who are now gone forth, as in the Beginning, from the true Friends of JESUS, having the Form of Godlineſs in Words, but in Deeds deny the Power thereof; from ſuch we are commanded to turn away.

Unto which is added in the *POSTSCRIPT*, the Injury this Trading in Slaves doth the Commonwealth, humbly offer'd to all of a PUBLICK SPIRIT.

The Second Edition, with Additions.

Remember them that are in Bonds, as bound with them; and them that ſuffer Adverſity, as being your ſelves in the Body, Heb. xiii. 3. *If any Man love the World, the Love of the Father is not in him*, 1 John ii. 15. *He that leadeth into Captivity, ſhall go into Captivity*, Rev. xiii. 10.

Printed for the AUTHOR, *Anno* 1730.

Both Ralph Sandiford and Benjamin Lay witnessed the atrocities of slavery in Barbados, which filled them with a lifetime of rage. *Slaves in Barbadoes*, illustration in John Augustine Waller, *Voyage in the West Indies* (London: Sir Richard Phillips, 1820), 21.

Benjamin Lay (1682–1759) was an outspoken opponent of slavery and, in his own words, "a man of strife and contention." Portrait by William Williams (ca. 1750–1758), National Portrait Gallery, Washington, D.C.

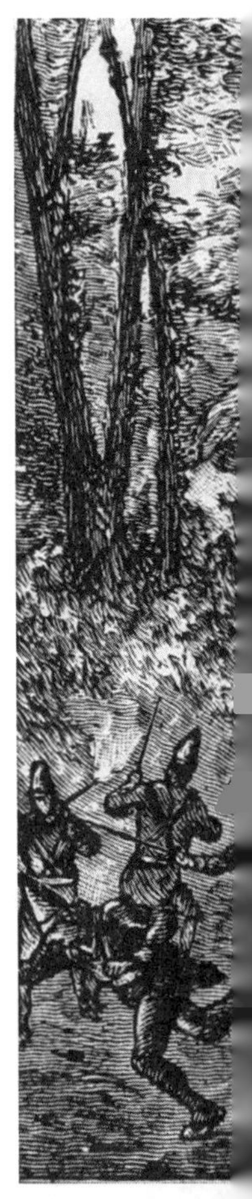

During the French and Indian War, British forces under General Edward Braddock suffered a catastrophic loss at the Battle of the Monongahela. *Braddock's Defeat*, illustration in Henry Davenport Northrop, *Indian Horrors or Massacres of the Red Men* (1891).

Benjamin Rush, a signer of the Declaration of Independence, collaborated with Benezet in the cause of abolition. Portrait by Charles Willson Peale (1818), Independence National Historic Park.

John Woolman (1720–1772) vigorously opposed the slave trade and was the author of the 1762 antislavery tract *Some Considerations on the Keeping of Negroes. John Woolman, Quaker Friend of Thee Negro* (artist and date unknown), New York Public Library.

This image of British abolitionist Granville Sharp appears on the frontispiece of Prince Hoare's *Memoirs of Granville Sharp* (London: Henry Colburn, 1838).

John Wesley (1703–1791), the founder of Methodism, became a high-profile voice for abolishing the slave trade. *John Wesley Preaching in the City Chapel*, engraving by T. Blood (1822), Creative Commons.

Englishman Thomas Clarkson (1760–1846) was so moved by reading Benezet's *Some Historical Account of Guinea* that he devoted the rest of his life to fighting the slave trade. Portrait by Carl Fredrik von Breda (1788), National Portrait Gallery, London.

For nearly two decades, William Wilberforce sponsored parliamentary bills against the slave trade before it was finally outlawed in 1807. Portrait by Anton Hickel (1794), Wilberforce House Museum, Hull, England.

Though it does not bear his name, this plaque—near the spot where his home stood on Chestnut Street, Philadelphia—is one of the few tangible memorials to Benezet.

CHAPTER EIGHT

Equality

Benezet's Most Significant Achievement

His school was the key. To the Black children (and, later, adults) he taught the same subjects he taught his white students. Assessing their progress, Benezet reported, "I can with truth and sincerity declare, that I have found amongst the negroes as great variety of talents, as among the like number of whites, and I am bold to assert, that the notion entertained by some, that the blacks are inferior in their capacities, is a vulgar prejudice, founded on the pride or ignorance of their lordly masters, who have kept their slaves at such a distance as to be unable to form a right judgment of them."[1]

Exactly when Benezet came to that conclusion we don't know, but no doubt it was early on. He was a veteran teacher, an expert, particularly insightful when it came to students' teachability. Experienced teachers develop a working assessment of their students fairly quickly, certainly within months. Benezet must have come to his conclusion during his first period of teaching these neglected, disdained children. They were alert, curious, receptive; they demonstrated a range of talents—the same as his bright and not-so-bright white pupils. In terms of the general belief in Black inferiority, this was a small but potent bombshell.

Black children became his permanent and primary engagement. As Nancy Hornick so insightfully demonstrates, it was a commitment that Benezet came to see as his life's fundamental purpose.[2] "I know of no station in life I should prefer before it," Benezet wrote to his friend Benjamin Franklin a year before his death.[3] The leading Benezet biographers of the modern era—Maurice Jackson, Irv Brendlinger, and others—focus their work on the vast and consequential impact of Benezet's antislavery efforts, which made him the figure of global importance he was. Hornick is unusual among them in concentrating instead on the threads of Benezet's life that allow us to glimpse his intimate personal history.[4]

As the years passed and he began to anticipate the end of life, Benezet reaffirmed his earlier conclusions about Black intelligence and potential in an unusual third-person declaration: "A. Benezet, teacher of a school established by private subscription, in Philadelphia, for the instruction of black children and others of that people, has, for many years, had the opportunity of knowing the temper and genius of the Africans under his tuition, who have been many, of different ages; and he can with Truth and Sincerity declare, that he has found among them as great variety of Talents, equally capable of improvement, as amongst a like number of whites."[5]

He had by then been teaching Black children and adults, enslaved and free, for thirty-three years. No white person, anywhere, had anything like the kind of long-term, close experience with Black people that he had.

Benezet's assessment wasn't his alone. In the early 1750s he and his near neighbor Benjamin Franklin developed a close friendship. Both were dedicated educators, Benezet the longtime classroom teacher and administrator, Franklin the founder in 1749 of the Philadelphia Academy that eventually became the University of Pennsylvania. Given Benezet's breakthrough establishment of his Black school, one of their topics of discussion was almost certainly Black educability.

Franklin was apparently so impressed by Benezet's school and the progress of his students that when he went to London in 1757 as agent for Pennsylvania, he urged the Bray Associates to open their own school for Black students in Philadelphia.[6] The Bray Associates were an Anglican missionary society, one of whose goals was to educate and convert Indigenous and Black people in England's colonies. Up until Franklin's interaction with them, the Bray Associates' efforts in the North America colonies were limited to distributing books and sending out catechists, a mostly unsuccessful endeavor. But at Franklin's urging they decided to fund the Philadelphia school.

In 1758 Bray Associates opened what they thought of as a "trial school," which proved so successful that they subsequently opened three more schools, also at Franklin's urging—in New York, Williamsburg, and Newport. Benezet's school, still a private and unpublicized enterprise, was already, through Franklin, spreading its influence.

Bray Associates, though, was a proselytizing arm of the Anglican church, and as such the Bray schools focused on Bible reading and catechizing, as opposed to the general academic curriculum Benezet was teaching. "We shall be much obliged to You," Bray's secretary wrote to Franklin, "if You will favour Us with Your Sentiments of the . . . conversion of the negroes, & let us know how & what means those poor ignorant people may be most effectually instructed. . . . As the lately Imported Negroes are Strangers to our Language, Little Good I fear can be done with them, but might not the black Children born in the Province be taught to read & instructed in the Principles of Christian Morality?"[7]

It's a bit surprising that Franklin engaged with the Bray Associates in London. He wasn't an Anglican, nor did he seem to have much, if any, religious feeling. In his original proposal for what was to eventually become the University of Pennsylvania, he detailed a curriculum that included practical and higher learning subjects as well as physical education but made no mention at all of any religious studies.[8]

But Franklin was the ultimate pragmatist. No one other than Benezet was teaching Black people anything. In the 1750s they were still very much considered a hopeless cause, inferior and incapable. Benezet was challenging that all-but-universal prejudice. The Bray Associates were ready to do that, too; they had the motivation and the money—even though their motives weren't Benezet's motives, nor were their methods his methods.

In 1770, after twenty years' experience with his Black students Benezet felt it was time, perhaps past time, for the Quakers to formally commit to sponsoring Black education. The success of his private effort argued for it. His two decades of teaching had made progress toward changing minds about Black capability. Given his success, it was hard for anyone to attack the idea of Black schooling as a lost cause. "The evidence," as Hornick put it, "was in."[9] Moreover, Benezet's own standing in the Society gave him leverage and weight. By the early 1750s he had been recognized as an elder and been named as a delegate to the Philadelphia Yearly Meeting. He was a press overseer, one of those responsible for evaluating essays and books for their conformity to Quaker principles. He was a mainstay on the epistle-writing committee of the yearly meeting. In 1756 he was appointed to the new Committee on Sufferings, charged with acting for the Society when the yearly meeting wasn't in session as well as with ameliorating problems encountered by Quakers whose principles put them at odds with province laws, regarding noncompliance, for example, with military or tax requirements. By then, too, along with John Woolman he was establishing himself as a leader in the growing antislavery effort within the Society. Already his was a persuasive voice.[10]

As a result, when in 1770 Benezet submitted a proposal to the Philadelphia Monthly Meeting to formally establish a Black school, there was little argument. It was quickly decided to fund a school for "the instruction of Negro and mulatto children in reading, writing, arithmetic, and other useful learning . . . according to their capacity."[11] With that decision, the "Africans' School" was incorporated as a division of the Friends Public School. At least as far as the Society was concerned, Benezet had proved his point. Black people were not a hopeless subspecies, they were intellectually as well as spiritually on the same plane as their white compeers, members of the same, single human family.

From its founding, the so-called Africans' School, along with Benezet's home school, played an important role in Philadelphia's Black community. Absalom Jones, cofounder of the Free African Society and leading architect of the African Church of Philadelphia, learned to read and write at Benezet's night school.[12] James Forten, a Black sailmaker whose business acumen made him one of Philadelphia's wealthiest citizens, attended the Africans' School. His father, who taught him sailmaking, may well have been a student at Benezet's home school.[13] Jones and Forten were leading abolitionists and—along with Richard Allen, who may have also attended Benezet's school—at the center of organizing and giving shape to Philadelphia's African American community and its emerging institutions. It's well within reason to speculate that not only did these prominent "Africans" learn their school lessons in Benezet's home school and/or in the Quakers' Black school that Benezet fathered later, but that they were also stimulated toward accomplishment in an environment that recognized their humanity and potential.

Another important outcome of the Quakers' Africans' School was, according to the Philadelphia Monthly Meeting Oversight Committee, "the increased appreciation aroused among the Whites for the Blacks. They [whites] were forced to realize that the Negro had talent which might be developed as their own, giving him an insight into greater possibilities that were not beyond his reach."[14] Benezet had set off a slow-moving earthquake, undermining a practically universal preconception about people of color.

Anthony Benezet was what we might call today a late bloomer. He took his time when it came to making a living, and he fell mostly by chance into what turned out to be his calling. He showed a talent, even a genius, for innovation in the classroom in terms of teaching and devising instructional material. He made a breakthrough in normalizing girls' education. His great inventiveness was there, but it manifested in ways that didn't draw widespread attention. But that changed when he decided that Black children needed schooling. That was when he emerged as a still modest yet clearly disruptive figure. He was suddenly doing something no one else had ever done, directly in the face of a pervasive cultural conviction that an effort like his was doomed from the start.

Benezet changed minds about that: first Franklin's, next his Quaker community's. Then he made inroads into the opinions of the larger society, "powerfully . . . recommend[ing] their race," as Vaux observed, "to the notice, and the cause of their suffering to the investigation of many persons of influence, who had previously held both in contempt."[15] "Following Benezet's unequivocal assertions of mental and moral equality of the races," says Hornick, "the subject was intensely discussed in intellectual circles, particularly in the decade following the American Revolution."[16]

The effect of Benezet's convictions only gathered strength after his death. The French revolutionary Brissot de Warville, who visited the Africans' School in Philadelphia in 1788, declared, "I've seen, heard and examined these black children. They read well, repeat from memory, and calculate with rapidity. . . . The black girls, besides reading, writing, and the principles of religion are taught spinning, needlework, &c; and their mistresses assure me, that they discover much ingenuity. . . . It is to Benezet that humanity owes this useful establishment."[17]

Brissot dedicated Letter 19 (in the 1792 Dublin edition of his book) to Benezet and the "School for the Blacks." He extolled Benezet's passion for teaching and his efforts to extirpate slavery.[18] Back in France he publicized Benezet's ideas and strove to incorporate them into the burgeoning French antislavery movement, founding in 1789 the *Société des Amis des Noirs* (the Society of Friends of the Blacks), which attracted Lafayette, Condorcet, and dozens of other leading French progressives. The abolitionist movement in France was another indication of the spread of Benezet's influence, fed in large part by his demonstration of Black equality.

In England Benezet's posthumous impact was even more consequential. The great English abolitionist Thomas Clarkson came across Benezet's *Some Historical Account of Guinea* by chance as he was preparing for an essay contest on slavery at Cambridge University in 1785. Benezet was gone a year by then. "In this precious book," Clarkson wrote, "I found almost all I wanted." But as he prepared for the contest Clarkson became increasingly distraught. "In the day-time I was uneasy," he said. "In the night I had little rest. I sometimes never closed my eye-lids for grief. . . . The subject of it almost wholly engrossed my thoughts." It was as if Benezet had whispered to him from beyond the grave. "It was time some person should see these calamities to their end," Clarkson told himself, and it was Clarkson who partnered with William Wilberforce in Wilberforce's ultimately successful parliamentary campaign to end the British slave trade—using Benezet's arguments and sometimes even his language (see chapter 14).[19]

Benezet's collaborations with and influence on Granville Sharp, John

Wesley, Benjamin Franklin, and Benjamin Rush held their thoughts for years after he was gone. Rush dreamed about him. Benezet's memory would just not let Rush be, says intellectual historian Nina Reid Maroney.[20] James Forten apparently used *Some Historical Account* (the book that so affected Clarkson) to influence William Lloyd Garrison as Garrison was emerging as a fervent abolitionist.[21] Black abolitionists Ottobah Cugoano and Olaudah Equiano made extensive use of Benezet's work in their influential antislavery autobiographies (both men had been kidnapped and sold as children). *Some Historical Account of Guinea* became the standard resource for African studies in the first part of the nineteenth century, with whole sections incorporated into early editions of the *Encyclopedia Britannica*.[22]

Benezet's influence persisted for decades after his passing, until his work and even his name faded out of America's historical consciousness.[23] Yet among a small circle of scholars, his importance continued to be recognized. "Anthony Benezet was the greatest eighteenth century influence on the ending of British slavery and the slave trade,"—writes church historian Irv Brendlinger. "While such names as Wilberforce, Sharp and Clarkson ring with familiarity as champions of the slave, it is Benezet who occupies the position of foundational influence on these men and the entire cause."[24] "The world," biographer George Brookes wrote, "owes Anthony Benezet a Perpetual Memory. . . . He was a Quaker who did more than any other man of his day . . . to quicken the conscience of his own Society of Friends in the matter of slavery and to strike a blow at that inhuman commerce, raising up friends of the enslaved in various parts of the world."[25] Benezet became the key figure in galvanizing the crusade to outlaw Britain's slave trade, which was perhaps *the* signal event in the tectonic shift in the world's view of human slavery. It was, wrote the great scholar of English history and European morality W. E. H. Lecky, "among the three or four most perfectly virtuous acts recorded in the history of nations."

While the small circle of Benezet biographers and commentators have focused very properly on his place in the Atlantic world's campaign against slavery, Benezet's more personal story has been harder to unearth. But that inner story is discernible in the arc of his life that extended from the time he founded his "Black school" in 1750 until his final acts just before he closed his eyes for the last time in 1784. We know about his assessment of Black intellectual potential that was such a breakthrough for him and others—a conclusion he reached not long after he began teaching his new charges. We know, too, that the Africans' School he convinced his fellow Quakers to establish was his constant concern. According to the Oversight Committee's reports, the school fulfilled its educational mission successfully year after year—even though it was often faced with financial difficulties, which led to a frequent change in teachers.[26] When in 1781 the teacher situation seemed unresolvable, Benezet took on the task himself, although he was sixty-eight years old and in deteriorating health. He wrote to his friend Robert Pleasants: "The education of 'the poor blacks' . . . has been so much the object of my consideration that I solicited to be appointed master of the school we have so long maintained for their education. . . . It has been indeed a matter of concern to me."[27] When walking to the school became too taxing, he persuaded the monthly meeting to move the school back to his own house, where he had started it more than thirty years earlier.

By the end of April 1784, Benezet and those around him knew that he was in his last days. During his final illness, he added a codicil to his will specifying that his estate would go to the support of his wife while she lived, with the remainder after her death dedicated to the school he had founded and nurtured. The Oversight Committee recorded after his death that Benezet had made a large bequest—about two thousand pounds—which put the Africans' School on a firm footing after years of financial strain.[28]

He had founded the school and for its first two decades carried it on with no outside support; thirty-four years after he opened its doors, he helped ensure its ongoing survival. Those were the bookends of the journey that was deepest in his sense of himself. The first line of his will read, "Be it remembered That I, Anthony Benezet, a teacher of the Free School for the Black People of Philadelphia . . ."[29] "A teacher for the Black people of Philadelphia" was how he regarded himself; for all he had done in his life, that was his core sense of his own identity.

What he found among his students—namely, that they were full human beings, not only spiritually but in terms of talent, intellect, and temperament—was also the key to his developing engagement with the slave trade—"this enormous evil," "[this] prodigious iniquity," as he called it.[30] Benezet's school was the pivotal event in his personal narrative and the origin of his antislavery efforts.

Contemporaries noticed that Benezet's feelings about the slave trade became more evident, or more insistent, in about 1750. "The impulses of duty"—as Vaux put it—"then for the first time, brought [Benezet] from the retirement of private life before the world, to lift up his voice on behalf of an oppressed and wretched portion of his fellow beings."[31] That is, he began taking greater account of slavery and its consequences at more or less the same time he opened his school for Philadelphia's Black children.

Yet it wasn't until 1754 that he published his first antislavery treatise, *An Epistle of Caution and Advice Concerning the Buying and Keeping of Slaves.* This tells us that his antislavery position, and his decision to go public with it, developed over time. During that period—1750 to 1754—he was increasingly busy with his Quaker responsibilities along with his teaching obligations at the Penn Charter School. But now he was also engaged with the lives of his Black students.

Teaching for Benezet was always a personal matter. He involved himself with the lives of his students, getting to know their mental habits, their aptitudes, their personalities. He got to know their parents as well, sometimes visiting them at their homes to discuss problems and urge the importance of attendance.[32] Given his own gregarious and engaging character, he befriended and was often seen in discussions with Black workers along the bustling waterfront, "imparting advice, and deriving information from them concerning the cruelties they had suffered."[33] Benezet met members of the Black community in the streets and in the marketplace, developing "spontaneous friendships with many of them."[34]

Many of Philadelphia's 1,800 or so enslaved people in 1750 had been brought up from the South or the West Indies, most of them sold to individuals who needed help in shops, businesses, homes, or farms. They often lived with families and worked alongside their owners. As a result, their lives tended to be less closely controlled than they would have been in the far harsher conditions of slavery in Southern colonies or the Caribbean. In the energetic port city of Philadelphia, it was common for Black and white people to mix—easier to strike up conversations and, in Benezet's case, friendships than it might have been elsewhere.

The number of enslaved persons in Philadelphia was relatively stable until the French and Indian War, when the need for forces to meet the raids and fighting on the frontier drew many indentured servants away from their masters, which in turn created a critical labor shortage.[35] The departure of so many white servants in turn precipitated a sharp rise in the demand for enslaved people to fill their places. According to Oregon State professor Darold Wax, "The heavy slave traffic, from about 1755 to 1765 was characterized by . . . a shift in trading patterns which sent local vessels directly to the west coast of Africa in quest of slaves."[36]

A portion of Philadelphia's already resident Black community had come directly from Africa, and now there was a new influx coming ashore on the

Delaware docks straight from the Middle Passage. Benezet heard from enslaved people about their grandparents, their parents, and themselves, now including relatively fresh memories of the horrors of capture in Africa and the dreaded Atlantic crossing.

But what exactly was it that Benezet was hearing in his talks with the Black Philadelphians he had befriended and who trusted him? What was the substance of those conversations between the inquisitive Benezet and these people whose lives were beset with injustice and distress? We can assume they talked to him about family problems, work problems, problems with masters and mistresses, every problem conditioned by the fact of their enslavement. It's also likely that Benezet's interest in these stories was now on a different plane than what it might have been before he had gotten to know his Black students, that is, before he understood the full humanity of these fellow human beings of color. That recognition of equality had been the turning point, allowing him to see Black people in their full humanity, not just equal to whites in God's eyes, but equal to whites period. The anger, pity, and moral outrage he had no doubt felt prior to opening his school was likely now of a different sort. He was talking with individuals in a way he had not done before, who were not just victims of a monumental injustice; they were persons, like himself in every way, whose humanity had been scorned and contemned. And that made him see them with different eyes. It made him see their enslavement through a prism of affiliation. And that may well be the reason his contemporaries began to observe about the year 1750 that he was talking about slavery differently, more publicly, and more personally.

Roberts Vaux, with his access to Benezet's contemporaries, says Benezet listened to stories about "the cruelties they had suffered." Many members of Philadelphia's Black community had suffered hardships on plantations in the South and the Caribbean. Some had been captured in Africa, trafficked from place to place, then transported on a slave ship laden with many hundred others on a barely endurable voyage across the frightening expanse of an ocean they had never imagined—traveling from former homes and lives to perpetual slavery in the Americas.

The most vivid description we have of the Atlantic crossing comes from Olaudah Equiano, an Igbo from what is now Southern Nigeria. Equiano was kidnapped at age eleven and shipped to Barbados and from there sold into Virginia. We know from his autobiography, *The Interesting Narrative of the Life of Olaudah Equiano, or Gustavus Vassa, The African*, the details of how he was captured, sold, and resold by slave traders on a trek of many months from his home to a "factory" on the African coast, where he was loaded aboard a slave ship for the trip across the ocean. Equiano managed to buy his freedom when he was about twenty, learned to read and write, and became fluent in English and educated. His book caused a sensation in England, went through numerous printings, and was published in Holland, Germany, Russia, and the United States. The book, and Equiano himself, played a prominent role in England's abolitionist movement.[37]

The Interesting Narrative was published in 1789. Although Benezet never had a chance to read it, he was likely to have heard from some of his Black friends descriptions of capture and transportation similar to Equiano's descriptions, and these would have moved him to his depths. Equiano described his terror when he first saw the slave ship that was to transport him. Sure he had entered a world of evil spirits and would be eaten, he was "overpowered with horror and anguish [and] fell motionless upon the deck and fainted."[38] He wrote about the pestilential conditions of the hold, the suicides and attempted suicides, the floggings, the confusion and despair that overwhelmed him and his fellow captives as they made the crossing. We know that Benezet heard stories of "the cruelties they had suffered," but to fully understand the effect these stories had on him we have to do our best to imagine or reconstruct what these stories might actually have been. We don't have the documentation for what passed between Benezet and his interlocutors, but we do have reason and plausible surmise.

Meanwhile, the noise and bustle on the Philadelphia waterfront included the sounds of buying and selling at the Front and High Streets market, the largest in colonial America, where commodities of every sort were on offer, from kitchen equipment to agricultural tools to stock animals. Here, too, another commodity was sold—human chattel, newly arrived at the docks in packets and freighters from the South and direct from Africa.

When a new human shipment arrived, a thick wooden board about three feet wide was set atop two barrels, and the captured men, women, and children were displayed, five or six at a time, in front of prospective customers who inspected them, peering into mouths, checking genitals, feeling muscles, making offers. It's stunning to think that Benezet passed that way almost every day. The historian Thomas Drake, former curator of the Haverford College Quaker Collection, wrote that "the public slave block shocked the consciences of many Friends and revolted their sense of propriety."[39] When slaves were on auction there, it no doubt shocked Benezet's conscience too. Two blocks away, at Second and High, stood the public whipping post where passersby could watch as enslaved people guilty of Black law violations were publicly lashed.

Benezet was an inheritor of Ralph Sandiford and Benjamin Lay, men who saw intolerable things and responded with rage so extreme that it likely killed Sandiford and drove Lay toward what some felt was the edge of insanity. Benezet's anger was of a different sort. It was different, too, from that of his friend and fellow antislavery campaigner, the saintly John Woolman. Like Sandiford, Lay, and Benezet, Woolman found human slavery intolerable, but his deep spirituality channeled his response into patient, determined social activism—pastoral and loving, and often persuasive. Woolman is a difficult character to capture, an Old Testament–like prophet who saw himself, and was seen by others, as a model of purity.[40]

Benezet was something altogether different. He had no sense of himself as a model others might aspire to emulate; that kind of self-reflection doesn't seem to have been part of his psychic make-up. Woolman, in contrast, kept a detailed, intimate personal journal. Published in 1774, *The Journal of John Woolman* has never been out of print and continues to have an honored place in the American religious canon. Benezet didn't keep a diary, a journal, or any other documentation of his activities or feelings (other than as they occur in his correspondence); he probably would have considered that kind of thing an egotistical diversion, had he thought about it. His mind worked differently from Woolman's. Woolman was introspective, intensely self-aware, and full of scruples to the point of eccentricity. Benezet was an activist, always thinking about how to give tangible shape to his ideas and make a practical reality out of them. What is it that might move his goal closer to fruition—that was the question that constantly occupied him. "What's the next step?" might have been his motto, had he had one. It was his standard way of thinking, his underlying mindset.

During the final thirty-plus years of his life, Benezet's constant concern was the education of his Black students. He had seen their potential and recognized their claim to full humanity. He had taken that to heart in a way that was revolutionary, challenging what was essentially the universal view of Black inferiority, a prejudice so deep-dyed that it seemed a fact of life. Against the great scope of the international campaign against slavery and the slave trade that Benezet helped galvanize, it's easy enough to simply note, then pass over, this part of his life.

But Nancy Hornick thought differently. "Among the many but relatively little-known achievements of . . . Anthony Benezet," she wrote, "probably the most significant, both in his time and in the two centuries since, was his discovery of the inherent equality of the black and white races."[41] Roger Bruns made essentially the same point, citing the foundational role of Benezet's "affirmation of the intellectual and moral equality of the Negro people."[42]

The two centuries Hornick refers to (she wrote in 1975) have at this present writing become two and a half centuries, and the issue of Black equality with whites is nowhere near being resolved. The question traces through our national history—from slave times to the Civil War and emancipation, to Reconstruction and the Thirteenth, Fourteenth, and Fifteenth Amendments, to the civil rights era and beyond. It is the elephant in the room that casts its shadow over our discussions of race relations today. Forward movement happens, progress toward a recognition of fundamental equality and affiliation of one race with the other. But at the same time racism seems so tenacious that we wonder if it is too much part of human nature to ever be eliminated.

It was Anthony Benezet who first brought this subject into the light of day and insisted that racism was a vulgar prejudice, founded on pride, ignorance, and warped judgment. In history's long view, that may well have been, as Hornick says, his most significant achievement.

CHAPTER NINE

Entering the Antislavery Lists

By the early 1750s, Benezet had had time to digest the significance of his experience with his Black students and their elders. He had also advanced further in his role as a "weighty Friend." He was talking about slavery in a noticeably different way than he had done previously. At some point, he decided it was time to step into the Quaker public space. It was a transition in the way he looked at the world and his role in it, a movement forward in his intellectual and emotional life. From this distance in time that seems an obvious next step, but for Benezet it was a significant marker in the ongoing evolution of his thinking, setting the stage for his emergence as the galvanizing force he was to become.

We can't intuit if perhaps he didn't feel quite ready to write on the slavery issue himself, though that may well have been the case. But now he was a Quaker press overseer, which meant that he shared the authority to approve for publication the works of others.

One leading candidate, which had been circulating in manuscript for seven years, was by his friend John Woolman. Woolman had begun jotting down his thoughts about slavery after walking through Virginia, Maryland, South Carolina, visiting Quaker slaveholders there and observing the harshness of enslaved people's lives in the South compared to what he was used to seeing in Philadelphia and New Jersey.[1] The trips sharpened his thinking and moved him to consider slavery's evils in a more systematic way. Over time he had developed his observations into an essay, which made the rounds privately but which he never submitted for publication, possibly because he thought it unlikely the press overseers would welcome the outright indictment of slavery he was offering.

But in 1752 the situation changed. The old Press Overseer Board had lost several members to age, and the Meeting decided to name a new slate. The five new members were younger people, reformers, more inclined to take a hard line against slavery. Several of the new overseers were friends of Woolman's, including Anthony Benezet.[2] The new board make-up was likely to have persuaded Woolman that the time had come. On Benezet's part, not having written anything of his own, but in a position to publish works that supported his thinking, Woolman's essay, *Some Considerations About Keeping Negroes*, must have seemed ideal for publication.

Woolman's mentality and Benezet's might have differed, but their thinking about slavery was closely aligned. Both men were heirs in that regard of Sandiford and Lay. Woolman's essay was approved for publication in 1753 (though it was not published until 1754). It was, as Carey notes, the first antislavery essay the press overseers had ever allowed to be published.[3] This was a breakthrough, a signal that the rearguard action of the older generation was in retreat.

Benezet, of course, pushed for it. Woolman articulated themes that Benezet in 1753 was apparently still contemplating but that fit perfectly with the direction of his thoughts. In enabling the essay's publication, Benezet was in essence foreshadowing at least some of the principles he himself was to so powerfully to promulgate later on.

The tone of *Some Considerations on the Keeping of Negroes* may have been milder than Benezet would have wanted, but Woolman's nonconfrontational style was actually perfect for the moment. Much of the Quaker leadership was now either against or skeptical of the right to keep slaves, but there were still influential personages, and middling types as well, who benefited from slaves and the trade and who could be counted on to do what they could to delay action. Woolman managed to convey a strong antislavery message in a way that avoided offending those on the other side of the issue. In his introduction, he appeared almost apologetic for bringing the matter up. "What I write on this subject," he said, "is with reluctance, and the hints given are in as general terms as my concern would allow. I know it is a point about which in all its branches men that appear to aim well are not generally agreed, and for that reason I chose to avoid being very particular."[4] What he means is that he's not going to make pointed accusations or indulge in inflammatory overdramatization of the problem. He means only to drop "hints." He knows, he says that "there are various circumstances amongst them that keep Negroes . . . and I doubt not that that there are many well-disposed persons among them."[5]

With that reassuring foreword, he then goes on to convey a message that emphasizes the conviction of equality that was uppermost in Benezet's mind as well as his own. Woolman does this by focusing on two themes. First, he asks his audience to remember that "all nations are of one blood." "The All-wise being," he says, "is Judge and Lord over us all, [which] seems to raise the idea of a general brotherhood and a disposition easy to be touched with a feeling of each other's afflictions."[6] Since we are all (that is to say, Black people, whites, and everybody else) members of one family, we should naturally be able to feel each other's pain. He means, of course, the cruelties Black people are subject to, without, though, actually saying it—as gentle a hint as possible. "To consider mankind," he says, "other than brethren . . . supposes a darkness of understanding."[7] It's not a malicious nature that causes people to ignore the pain of Black people, only a lack of judgment.

Do you think that a "people" (Black people, again) are worse than others? he asks. Please, just "calmly consider their circumstances." Try in your imagination to "make their case ours. Suppose, then, that our ancestors and we have been exposed to constant servitude . . . that we had been destitute of reading and good company; that amongst ourselves we had few wise and pious instructors . . . that while others in ease have plentifully heaped up the fruit of our labor, we have received barely enough to relieve nature, and being wholly at the command of others had generally been treated as a contemptible, ignorant part of mankind. Should we in that case be less abject than they are?"[8]

Reading *Considerations* you have to blink at what Woolman was able to do. *Considerations* is in some ways an ordinary religious tract, adducing biblical stories and texts to support an elucidation of God's love and merciful purposes. It's a gentle sermon. But beneath the surface it has teeth, condemning slave keeping and slave keepers as being outside God's ordinances and violating Jesus's ultimate moral principle, the Golden Rule.

Just as *Some Considerations* was finally making its way toward publication, Benezet and Woolman collaborated on another project, this one arguing against Quaker slaveholders' efforts to slow the momentum toward reform. The original authorship of *An Epistle of Caution and Advice Concerning the Buying and Keeping of Slaves* isn't clear. It may have been Woolman; his most recent biographer, Thomas Slaughter, thinks so, though it was Benezet who presented it to the Philadelphia Monthly Meeting on January 25, 1754.[9] David Crosby in his critical edition of Benezet's antislavery writings attributes it to Benezet. It may have originated in a letter from Woolman that Benezet then expanded.[10] Whatever the origin, it was a frontal challenge to the hesitant, slow-moving Quaker response to slave keeping that had characterized the Society's considerations since the first remonstrance by Germantown Friends back in 1688.

An Epistle was read at a number of monthly and quarterly meetings, then presented to the Philadelphia Yearly Meeting of 1754.[11] That presentation was signed by twelve Friends who had been appointed by the yearly meeting as reviewers, though it's impossible to ascertain what kind of reviewing such an unwieldy committee might have done. Benezet's and Woolman's names were kept off the list, which added to the impression that this was a collective act of the Society. But despite the twelve signatures, *An Epistle of Caution and Advice* was intensely personal. It read as a heartfelt appeal from a senior, authoritative Friend to the Society's most prominent members assembled in meeting.

An Epistle was an exhortation to the writer's fellow Quakers, urging them to live up to their faith as Christians, to their sense of plain justice, and to their feelings as human beings. The author wrote that many weighty Friends had warned Quakers against being "in any respect concerned in promoting the bondage" of fellow humans who had been imported and sold in Philadelphia. Now *An Epistle* was repeating the message, "that none may plead ignorance of our principles therein and also again earnestly to exhort all to avoid, in any manner, encouraging that practice of making *slaves* of our fellow creatures."[12]

The listeners have heard it before; now they're hearing it again, but officially this time, in the yearly meeting, the Society's most authoritative forum. The language was straightforward and eloquent. We know from his journal that Woolman was a moving stylist, and *An Epistle* could be his. But it sounds a little too blunt for him at this stage, too direct. His own inclination, he wrote in *Some Considerations,* was "to persuade, and entreat, and simply give hints of [his] way of thinking."[13] But *An Epistle of Caution and Advice* isn't hinting at anything. It's dignified—nothing like the outraged rebukes of Sandiford or Lay—but it's also uncompromising, explicit, a call to action rather than a humble reminder. This is no committee job, it's personal. Friend to Friends.

This is likely the first taste we have of Benezet's public style, and it's impressive. The writing manages to be at the same time commanding and imploring. Unlike previous admonitions to avoid buying imported slaves, *An Epistle* exhorts Friends to "avoid *in any manner* [emphasis added] encouraging that practice of making *slaves* of our fellow creatures."[14] For the first time in a publication authorized by the yearly meeting, the moral imperative of the Golden Rule was invoked. (This was before Woolman published *Some Considerations.*) "Remember our blessed redeemer's positive command," *An Epistle* continued, "to *do unto others as we would have them do unto us*, and that *with what measure we mete, it shall be measured to us again.*" Then a more ominous biblical reminder, from Exodus 21:16: "He that stealeth a man, and selleth him, or if he be found in his hand, he shall surely be put to death." This, he says, is the only theft violation in Mosaic law punishable by death.[15] There's a warning here that the Society may be moving toward a stronger enforcement regime concerning those who persist in owning human beings.

Most striking is *An Epistle*'s declaration that for slaves to answer "the end of their creation and God be glorified and honored by them as well as by us . . . [you] *should think it your duty to set them free*."[16] The language here was convoluted, as if the author was struggling to explain under exactly what circumstances enslaved people ought to be set free. But difficult language aside, here we are far beyond "Don't buy slaves brought into the province." Instead, we are listening to a motion that Quakers who believe the "spirit of grace applies to all" should consider it an obligation to set their slaves free. That has the air of a demand, but it's followed directly by an intensely moving emotional plea to the same end: "Finally brethren," the author says to his fellow Quakers, "we entreat you in the bowels of gospel love seriously to weigh the cause of detaining them in bondage."[17]

In many ways *An Epistle of Caution* recapitulates the Germantown remonstrance of sixty-six years before, which also invoked the Golden Rule and asked freedom for the enslaved. "Being now this is not done in the manner we would be done at therefore we contradict and are against this traffic of men-body. . . . And such men ought to be delivered out of ye hands of ye robbers, and set free."[18] The Germantown letter was passed along from the monthly meeting to the quarterly and ultimately to the Philadelphia Yearly Meeting, which shunted it aside as "not to be so proper for this Meeting to give a Positive Judgment . . . It having so General a Relation to many other Parts."[19] *An Epistle of Caution*, on the other hand, was a powerful, direct denunciation of slave keeping that was now the official position of the yearly meeting and was printed and distributed through the various quarterly meetings, "ensuring that prominent Friends through the region had access to the text and would get the message, that as far as the Yearly Meeting was concerned, the debate had finally been settled."[20] It had taken two-thirds of a century for Philadelphia's Quakers to get to this point, but the question about the legitimacy of slave keeping was finally crystal clear. Quakers were against it.

Yet despite the yearly meeting's adoption of *An Epistle of Caution*, the Society issued no order to free slaves and developed neither an enforcement mechanism nor penalties for keeping human beings in bondage. Important as *An Epistle* was, manumission hardly became universal, among Quakers or anyone else. Indeed, from the point of view of the reformers, the effect was modest at best.

Worse, after 1754 the demand for slaves jumped precipitously with the onset of the French and Indian War. As Pennsylvania's western regions were assailed by increasingly violent raids by France's Algonquin, Lenape, and other Indigenous allies, the need for soldiers escalated. "Beginning in the fall of 1755, English commanders in the colonies began recruiting indentured servants in order to bolster the strength of British units, which were reeling under the attacks of the French and their Indian allies on the western frontier. About two thousand indentured servants had been recruited by the end of 1755."[21] The result was a severe labor shortage as Philadelphia's merchants, artisans, farmers, and householders lost essential white workers and began replacing them with enslaved Africans.

The French and Indian War was the North American theater of the clash between the British and French empires. In America the immediate cause was French expansion from Canada into the Ohio River Valley, which threatened to cut off the British colonies from an outlet for westward growth. The war's early period was marked by British disasters. Virginia militia forces under their young major George Washington were surrounded and cut off. Washington was captured and paroled, then joined British general Edward Braddock for a large-scale attack on the French, which led to the British catastrophe in the Battle of the Monongahela. Pennsylvania's frontier areas were aflame, as France's Indigenous allies swept down on farms and settlements, killing and abducting colonists, selling some off into slavery and ransoming others, forcing still others into servitude or adoption by the tribes that had captured or bought them. Over two thousand Pennsylvania frontier people were abducted, triggering rage and dismay in Philadelphia and throughout the region.

To stir up even more war fury and stimulate recruitment, in the spring of 1756 frontiersmen from one of the raided villages hauled a wagon loaded with the bodies of several bloodied settler victims through the streets around the new Quaker meetinghouse at Second and High Streets. A mob of infuriated Philadelphians followed behind, cursing Indians and Quakers, whose nonviolent principles were obstructing war and self-defense efforts in the colonial assembly. The frontiersmen's grim display coincided with a Quaker meeting of ministers and elders. John Churchman, a minister from Chester, watched it. "What will become of Pennsylvania?" he thought. "This land is polluted with blood. . . . How can this calamity be?"[22]

It's likely Churchman wasn't the only Quaker who watched in shock as the wagon with its massacred corpses rumbled past the meetinghouse. We don't know if Benezet witnessed the grim spectacle, but he may well have. If not, he certainly would have heard about it. The demonstration undoubtedly caused tremendous distress among the assembled Quaker leaders. As Churchman said, "It was very afflicting."[23] Benezet's feelings can be imagined. One wonders if this vivid picture might not have been in his mind as he contemplated his own next steps.

It's no exaggeration to say that the French and Indian War spelled the end of William Penn's dream of a Quaker Holy Experiment. Pennsylvania's assembly raised troops for the frontier war and imposed taxes to pay for them. When Quakers, faithful to their peace testimony, refused to pay, the government seized and sold off Quaker property. Quaker assemblymen still dominated the legislature, but the tension they faced was unresolvable. George Fox had declared back in 1660, "We utterly deny all outward wars and strife and fighting with outward weapons for any end or under any pretense whatever; this is our testimony to the whole world."[24] The peace testimony was an unbreakable Quaker article of faith. Unable to conscientiously participate in war making, most Quaker lawmakers quit the assembly.

Some historically minded Friends may have recalled Fox's admonition from the founding era to "kepe out of all such things . . . kepe out of all vaine Janglinge." "[Keep] out of the world's evil customs, fashions, words, works, manners ordinances and commandments."[25] Or even Penn's warning not to mingle with the crowd, "lest *their* spirit enter *us* instead of *our* spirit entering *them*."[26] The utopian idea that a Quaker society could address the hard problems of a state entity without forfeiting its core values fell victim to the realities of this war. Churchman, staring at the wagon with its bloody corpses and hearing the angry mob, understood it instantly. "What will become of Pennsylvania . . . polluted with blood?" The wonder of it was that Penn's vision had sustained itself for three-quarters of a century.

To Benezet's mind, Friends relinquishing their role in government was long overdue. Participating in government, in his opinion, was a deplorable diversion, a conflict of interest that inevitably compromised purity of the heart. "Many of our Friends," he wrote to his English friend Jonah Thompson,

> begin to rouse from that Lethargy in which they have too long been plunged, thro' a love of this World, an endeavor to reconcile those two contrarities the World & Heaven; many addresses haveing been presented to the Assembly & Govr. & Epistles wrote to Friends declaring our disunity with the warlike measures that have been & and are now

> gone into Friends begin to see, what they might long ago have seen, if the God of this World, the deceitfulness of wealth and Honour had not blinded their eyes viz. the impossibility for us, as a People, with true Honour and integrity of Heart, in times of War, of Conquests & Bloodshed to maintain the Governmt. & be honest & true to that noble, evangelike Testimony which God has given us to bear as a People.[27]

Meanwhile, Woolman and Benezet were on the front lines of another existential test of the Society's core values: African slavery. If the war challenged the Quakers' peace testimony, slavery challenged the Society's essential belief in the universal availability of the divine Inner Light—that is, in the fundamental equality of all God's children. The decision to remain faithful to the peace testimony was hard; it straddled two conflicting values: nonviolence and responsibility for the lives of others. But that was, in a sense, a clean choice: either give up part, or all, of your Quaker identity, or stay faithful to the Inner Light of Christ as you and your fellowship understand and believe in it.

But there was nothing simple about choosing to end slavery. That had been a hard, uphill progression ever since Fox's visit to Barbados in 1661. Benezet's 1754 *Epistle of Caution* was an officially approved declaration for liberation. Woolman's *Some Considerations*, published the same year, was a reiteration of that call. And yet because of the war, many more enslaved people were arriving at the city's waterfront wharves, and Quakers were as willing to purchase them as non-Quakers, maybe even more so.[28] By 1757 there was widespread frustration over the recalcitrance of Quakers who held slaves and ignored the declarations and pleas of 1754. And as eloquent as Benezet and Woolman were, their essays, while officially approved, amounted to admonishment rather than enforceable requirements. By 1758 the vexed question of what further steps the Society should take was referred to that year's Philadelphia Yearly Meeting.

After Woolman's *Some Considerations* and especially after Benezet's *An Epistle of Caution and Advice*, with its direct appeal to Quakers to consider it a "duty to set [enslaved people] free," some of the Philadelphia area's monthly meetings began taking action against slaveholding members. But there were questions about how far their disciplinary measures could go. The yearly meeting had expressed its firm opinion about slave keeping but had not made any definitive declaration on enforcement. In 1758, that question was on the table.

The reform leaders—Benezet, Woolman, and others—were prepared, but so were Quakers on the other side, who owned slaves and were not eager to give them up. From their point of view, the enslaved people had cost money, they were good workers, their masters treated them well; no abuse was involved. Some gave their slaves religious instruction, perhaps even teaching them to read and write. It was hard for them to see the urgency of setting them free. At the same time, the old justifications for slave owning—arguments from the Bible, or the idea that people brought to the colonies as slaves were better off than they had been in "savage" Africa—had lost whatever force they might once have had, at least among Quakers. Over the years of struggle, Quaker culture had emerged as largely abolitionist, whatever the absence of official constraints.

But that didn't mean that no arguments were available. During the debate the slaveholders' objective was to temporize, make plausible excuses, and delay any final determination. They made the point that any definitive conclusion against slave keeping would "give uneasiness to many brethren." Disunity, they argued, was always antithetical to the well-being of the Society. That ingrained conviction went back to the existential threat of the James Nayler episode in 1656, which spurred Fox to remake the Society's organization. No action was necessary now, the proslavers maintained: "If Friends patiently continued under the exercise, the Lord in time to come might open a way for the deliverance of these people."[29]

On the slaveholders' part, there may also have been an unspoken (at least in public) sense that they were ordinary people beset by eccentrics obsessed with their own purity. Many of those who owned slaves were shopkeepers, artisans, and farmers who may have acquired a slave to help with work. Quakers, but intent on making a living and not necessarily preoccupied with the purity of their souls. Woolman, meanwhile, perhaps their chief antagonist, considered himself a prophet on the order of Ezekiel.[30] In his later years he took to wearing only white clothes to symbolize purity. He knew that at least some people "carried shy" of him and thought he affected "singularity."[31] Benezet also had some singular habits, although his personality was engaging rather than off-putting.

For several days prior to the meeting, Woolman was deep in prayer. Like the Old Testament's King David, he said, "tears were my meat night and day." The case of slaveholding "lay heavy" on him.[32] It was four years since he had published *Some Considerations on the Keeping of Negroes*—eleven years since he wrote it—and the interval since then had been filled with bloodshed as the war ground on with no letup. With British forces on the defensive, western settlements were still being battered, frontier people who hadn't fled were still living through horrors, victims were still being abducted and herded north into slavery.

When Woolman looked around in 1757 and early 1758, the scene wasn't heartening. The number of enslaved Africans in Philadelphia was still rising.[33] Over ten percent of the city's Quaker *leadership* still owned slaves.[34] Resistance to manumission maintained its hold on many. The movement toward prohibition continued to make headway, but there was no official action. The 1758 meeting loomed large for the Friends—reformers and slaveholders alike—and for no one more than the preoccupied John Woolman.

The six-day meeting dealt with other issues first, chiefly on the war and prohibitions against Friends contributing to it in any fashion. When the slavery question finally came to the floor, it precipitated a "spirited debate."[35] Woolman was encouraged when several Friends "spoke weightily" about slaveholding and the need for action. That "comforted" him, but still "feeling a concern," he took the opportunity to "cast in his mite," as he put it.[36]

This was not the John Woolman of *Some Considerations*. In the interval of years, with all the carnage, with the increase in slave numbers, with the continued recalcitrance of many, Woolman had hardened. He had for years been resolute, but now he was ready to express his resolution in unvarnished terms. When he spoke now there was nothing at all of the apologetic tone of 1754, nothing about dropping "hints" or speaking with "reluctance." In particular, he was not ready to brook the speciousness, as he saw it, of slaveholders' arguments about discomfiting many of the brethren or waiting for God to resolve the issue in his own time. All these arguments, he told them, were nothing but self-interest:

> In the difficulties attending us in this life, nothing is more precious than the mind of Truth inwardly manifested, and it is my earnest desire in this weighty matter we may be so truly humbled as to be favored with a clear understanding of the mind of Truth and follow it. . . . The case is difficult for some who have them [slaves], but if such set aside all self-interest and come to be weaned from the desire of getting estates, or even from holding them together when Truth requires the contrary, I believe way will be open that they will know how to steer through these difficulties. . . . Should we now . . . neglect to do our duty in firmness and constancy, still waiting for some extraordinary means to bring about their deliverance, it may be that by terrible things in righteousness God may answer us in this matter.[37]

You have a choice, he tells slaveholders. Give up your self-aggrandizement, your financial interests. Give them up and you'll find a way to liberate these oppressed people. "It is not a time for delay," he tells them.

When some slaveholding Friends suggested that the meeting should make a rule "to deal with such Friends as offenders who buy slaves *in the future*," the answer was that the "the root of this evil" would be eradicated only when a "thorough search" was made into current slaveholders' motives for keeping slaves.[38] Then several reformers declared that "a visit might be made to such Friends who kept slaves," that "liberty was the Negro's right," at which point several Friends volunteered to undertake such visits.[39] Whoever suggested sanctioning only future violators probably wished he hadn't.

Woolman says that in the end "the love of Truth in a good degree prevailed,"[40] which suggests that to some degree it did not. But Benezet's biographers George Brookes, following Vaux, read the meeting's conclusion differently. When, after a long, drawn-out debate, it looked as if the meeting might defeat a motion to repudiate slavery and enforce restrictions, Benezet stood up and walked to the front, weeping ("like Hosea for the sins of his people," said Brookes). He had been silent during the debate. Now he recited from Psalm 68: "Ethiopia shall soon stretch forth her hands unto God." The emotional force of Benezet's plea for justice "carried the day," says Jackson. With this vote, the essential corner was finally turned. "If there is a single moment when the beginning of a new period in the fight against slavery was catalyzed," Jackson writes, this was it.[41]

But why had Benezet been silent during what was a long and grueling debate on this issue to which he was so committed? And what accounted for his weeping? As usual, we have no comment or explanation of his feelings from him, but we do have two highly unusual letters Benezet wrote to his friend Samuel Fothergill toward the end of 1757. Fothergill was an English Quaker minister who had spent several years in America, much of it in and around Philadelphia, during which time he and Benezet had become warm friends. To Fothergill Benezet wrote:

> Nothing but the deepest sense of inward poverty could have so long prevented my writing to thee, my near and dear friend. But thus it hath been, that I have not dared to meddle with religious things [i.e., with commenting on religious subjects]. . . . That my love is as entire to thee as so low a creature is capable of, is fixed and certain. But what shall I say. O my leanness, my leanness—it is beyond expression, and so sensibly felt by me, that I dare not as it were extend any further, lest I should

> defile God's jewels [Christian truths]. . . . Why is it so with me?—if thou hast any comfort or counsel to communicate, do it I beseech thee. May the God of all consolation be with thee.
>
> From thy afflicted friend,
> Anthony Benezet[42]

Benezet usually has no trouble at all commenting on Quaker and other Christian truths; it's an ordinary mode of discourse with him. But now he's afraid he'll *defile* God's words. "Why is it so with me?" He can't say what's wrong with him, but something is, apparently desperately. He needs comfort, counsel. He is "afflicted."

Benezet writes on occasion of what he considers his insufficiencies, usually in terms of ego as opposed to the perfect humility he strives for but cannot reach. "O!" he writes to a friend, "that a true gospel nothingness may prevail in my heart, is my most sincere desire."[43] But this is different, not a meditation on humility and self-abnegation (Thomas à Kempis's *Imitation of Christ* was in his library). These lines to Fothergill are full of obvious personal pain.

Two weeks later Benezet wrote to Fothergill again. "Painful in many, very many respects, is our situation, particularly mine, under an uncommon sense of poverty & desertion the weakness, the instability, the Self, the remains of subtle Pride that hangs about human nature. . . . I hope I am cured from any more dependence & expectation from man. May I steadily seek comfort & Establishment in God alone, by retirement, Silence and Prayer."[44]

The depression evident in his former letter is redoubled here. He speaks of "poverty" again. He feels "deserted." The inner strength that has always sustained his determination and optimism has somehow vanished. He needs to be "cured from expectations of man." Those expectations that have been fueled by the belief in the goodness at the heart of each person, even those who have not yet recognized the indwelling Light—that belief has deserted him.

We know of nothing in his personal life that might have triggered this dark mood. But the world around him was overflowing with examples of man's inhumanity to man. In western Pennsylvania the bloodshed was ongoing. In 1755, as part of that war, the British expelled—we might say "ethnically cleansed"—the French population of Nova Scotia and Prince Edward Island, sending them to various points in the colonies, few of which wanted them. Almost five hundred were transported to Philadelphia and were for a time kept aboard their ships anchored in the Delaware, where they were decimated by smallpox. Benezet volunteered to help alleviate the desperate circumstances of these countrymen of his. In 1757 he was still petitioning the colonial assembly for their relief. Then there were the hard-core Quaker slaveowners, some of them seemingly immune to appeals from religious truth, reason, or the heart ("the bowels") of gospel love. If Benezet was temporarily overwhelmed by these grim realities, it would have been only human.

His reticence at the 1758 Philadelphia Yearly Meeting doesn't prove that his depressed state of mind persisted that long, but the silence, the weeping, and what sounds like a *cri de coeur* suggest that he was still, at the least, emotionally wrought, and that he found the prospect of losing the motion on slavery simply intolerable.

The 1758 Yearly Meeting was a watershed moment, the culmination of seventy years of frustration and struggle, from Pastorius to Sandiford to Lay to Benezet, Woolman, and a few other equally appalled and determined antislavery pioneers. The 1758 meeting invoked the Golden Rule, which would "induce [those] who have any slaves to set them at liberty, making a Christian provision for them according to their Ages &cetera." This meeting advisement went out to all slaveholding Friends. It was a warning. Slaveholders would be visited to ascertain their reasons for owning slaves, their treatment of enslaved individuals, and their intentions for them. "And if after the sense and judgement of this Meeting now given against any Branch of this Practice any professing with us should persist to vindicate it and be concerned with importing Selling or Purchasing Slaves, the respective Monthly Meeting to which they belong should manifest their disunion with such persons."[45] Slaveowners who could satisfactorily explain why they had slaves and who seemed to treat their slaves well were not yet sanctioned. But buying and selling were proscribed. Disciplinary procedures were established and carried out. The antislavery activists got a good part of what they had been striving for. And everyone understood: a total prohibition on slaveholding would be coming before too much more time had passed.

CHAPTER TEN

A New Antislavery Language

The minutes of the 1758 Philadelphia Yearly Meeting emphasized the "desolating calamities of War and bloodshed, so that many of our fellow Subjects are now suffering in Captivity."[1] The minutes were not the place to convey a picture of the trials abducted settlers were undergoing on their long marches back to French-controlled Quebec, often after seeing loved ones slaughtered in front of them. "Prisoners were taken by force," writes historian Elaine Letki. "All captives endured an agonizing life and death journey; some were bound, starved, tortured, mutilated and brutally killed. All of them were separated from kin. The fortunate were redeemed by family members or others once they reached Canada. Many were sold, adopted, forced to relinquish their name, religion, language and heritage, sold as animals in the public square, or pedaled door to door."[2]

Until ransomed survivors began returning home, people in Philadelphia didn't have direct news about these events, but they did have a general idea of what the captives were going through. Abductions were a feature of life on the frontier going back to the seventeenth century and the various conflicts between Indigenous people and colonists. Pennsylvanians had been largely spared from such terrors due to William Penn's peaceful and fair approach to the Lenape (and theirs to him). But they knew. The famous Deerfield Massacre had happened only fifty years earlier, with more than forty people killed and over a hundred abducted. The Reverend John Norton, one of the captives, wrote about it once he was redeemed, as did John Williams, another Deerfield victim. Other books by survivors were in circulation: *A Narrative of the Captivity of Nehemiah How*, *A Narrative of the Sufferings and Surprizing Deliverances of William and Elizabeth Fleming*, *A Faithful Narrative, of the Many Dangers and Sufferings as Well as Wonderful Deliverances of Robert Eastburn*.[3] The books were read and talked about. The idea of Indian captivity haunted the minds of settlers and potential settlers. Nothing worse could happen to you if you were drawn to the frontier.

The 1758 meeting saw the "desolating calamities" of the war in terms of God's "judgments," a powerful admonition to Quaker slave owners "to set them at liberty." A terrible reciprocity seemed to be unfolding, with the unspoken threat of more in the offing. The meeting lamented, "We are not yet capable of informing you of a prospect appearing of the Sword which hath been drawn in these and adjacent Provinces being speedily sheathed."[4]

The meeting failed to note, perhaps few of its members recalled, that twenty-one years earlier the Quakers' so-called Walking Purchase had defrauded the Lenape of their last Delaware Valley hunting grounds. Since then the tribe had been pushed westward step by step, and by the time of the French and Indian War most Lenape had settled in the Ohio territory, now being fought over by French and British forces and their Indigenous allies. In this conflict Lenape war bands and raiding parties fought alongside the French; the memory of their forced migration was painfully current to them, if not to the meeting. So although the meeting didn't register it, there was another level of retributive justice at work here.

Slavery was the final agenda item of the 1758 Philadelphia Yearly Meeting. The lead-in was the war; the text and subtext were the Golden Rule. Four years earlier, Benezet's *Epistle of Caution* had been the first approved publication to cite Jesus's pronouncement from the Sermon on the Mount. Woolman had used it as well in his *Considerations*. It was a touchstone for reformers as they pressed their arguments in the meeting. "Do unto others as you would have them do unto you" perfectly encapsulated the essence of Jesus's moral teaching—the "Royal Law," Benezet called it—with such obvious (and powerful) pertinence for slave owning. There wasn't anyone who hadn't imbibed the expression, more or less with their mother's milk. It rolled off tongues, a commonplace, which at the same time embodied the underlying requirement of Christian morality—the rock reformers relied on in the face of self-interest, whether large scale avarice or just the common everyday desire to make more money.

An Epistle had been Benezet's entry into the antislavery lists. He had from 1750 on recognized the full humanity of Black individuals, free and enslaved. He had been instrumental in approving Woolman's *Considerations*, which embraced that same underlying conviction of the equality, the essential sameness of the two races. In the *Epistle* Benezet had drawn the obvious conclusion. Friends simply had no business holding people in bondage. They "should think it [their] duty to set them free," he wrote there. For the Friends to publish such a declaration, after many decades of willful disregard, was a landmark, a signal change of direction.

It was also a stage in Benezet's own understanding of what he himself should be doing—namely, everything he was capable of in terms of impacting his Quaker community with the truth, as he saw it, of the fellow humanity of the two races. As Roger Bruns pointed out, "He would offer to the antislavery argument an unequivocal assertion of the moral and intellectual equality of the black race. . . ." "[Benezet] was grounded on the assumption of Negro intellectual, spiritual and moral equality."[5]

In Benezet's 1754 *Epistle of Caution* he told Quakers that they should emancipate their enslaved people. He had said this forcefully, but intelligently, strategically, and his effort had been approved and promulgated by the Society. But his argument there had been less than effective. Quakers were still slave keepers, and even the 1758 Philadelphia Yearly Meeting hadn't declared a binding judgment on the issue. At the same time, the frontier war that was rearranging Quakers' conception of their place in the world was also absorbing much of Benezet's time and energy. In peace overtures, letters, and pamphlets, Benezet put himself in the middle of efforts to stem the violence.[6]

But the ongoing war didn't just trigger Benezet's peacemaking impulses, it also opened his mind to what became the next phase in filling out the picture of Black and white affinity. The 1758 meeting had expressed the conviction that the suffering of the settlers was visited on them by a just God angry at the cruel treatment of enslaved Black people. Benezet picked that theme up in his next antislavery tract, *Observations on the Enslaving, Importing, and Purchasing of Negroes.*

Observations began with a look back at "ancient times," when many nations had the custom of selling into slavery people they captured in warfare. It's our "sad experience," he wrote, to find that native people in America did this also. "In the present war how many of our poor countrymen are dragged to bondage and sold for slaves?" he asked. "How many mourn a husband, a wife, a child, a parent or some near relation taken from them? And were we to follow them a little farther and see them exposed to sale and bought up to be made a gain of, what heart so hard would not melt with sympathy and sorrow?"[7]

But these evils "do not arise out of dust," he says. "Let us give some serious consideration to a practice . . . to which we as a nation are deeply engaged. . . . I mean the slave trade, . . . purchas[ing] and bringing the poor Negroes from their native land and subjecting them to a state of perpetual bondage, and that often the most cruel and oppressive."[8] He continues, "Will not the just judge of all the earth visit for all of this? Or dare we say that this very practice is not one cause of the calamities we at present suffer, and that the captivity of our people is not to teach us to feel for others and to induce us to discourage a trade by which many thousands are yearly captivated. . . . When a people offend as a nation, or in a public capacity, . . . the justice of His moral government requires that as a nation they be punished."[9]

The writing here is packed with emotion. Benezet is moving to a place well beyond simply telling his fellow Quakers to give up their slaves. His vision is enlarging from what it had been. You feel it not just in what he says but in the pace, rhythm, and power of his prose.

The initial version of *Observations on the Enslaving, Importing, and Purchasing of Negroes* was published in 1759. It was not immediately approved for publication, perhaps because it was considered too radical for the moment. But the reception was enthusiastic enough that he immediately planned and published a second version.[10] The updated edition was similar to the first, except that Benezet added a two-paragraph introduction taken from Woolman's *Some Considerations on the Keeping of Negroes*. Our duty in life, Woolman wrote there, is "to seek the kingdom of God and his righteousness." The means to doing this, he says, is "to love the Lord our God with all our heart and our neighbor as ourself, so as never to do to another that which in like circumstances we would not have done to us." These are momentous points, Benezet says, "worthy of our most serious consideration."[11]

Observations on the Enslaving, Importing, and Purchasing of Negroes is an essay on the Golden Rule that unpacks the saying beyond its obvious meaning to bring out the underlying theme of mutuality.

Here Benezet is making a further exploration of his seminal discovery: the fellow humanity of Black and white people. In that regard *Observations* marks the ongoing expansion of a mind wholly engrossed by the great moral issue of his time. In the midst of all the extraordinary political, scientific, philosophical, and cultural ferment of the mid-eighteenth century, Benezet was focused like a laser on one issue—what we would call "racism." The word itself wouldn't be invented for another 150 years, but even without its own descriptive term the reality was a ubiquitous feature of life in Pennsylvania and every other American colony. For Benezet, *racism* meant Black slavery and the perception of Black inferiority—the first a barbaric atrocity, the second a vulgar prejudice.

Although the American Civil War eliminated slavery in the United States 160 years ago, the notion of Black inferiority is still very much with us. It casts its shadow on all of our ongoing national conversations (and conflicts) about equality and equity. It's arguable that today's focus on racial inequities was originally precipitated by Benezet in his two earliest antislavery works: the 1754 *Epistle* and the 1759 *Observations*, both of them radical departures from near-universal assumptions about Black incapability.

The text of the Golden Rule provides a precept for moral behavior. The subtext it rests on is an assertion of reciprocity or "mutuality." The saying brings together "we" and "they": Do unto others as *we* would have *them* do unto us. Woolman's introduction presents the negative version: "Never do unto another what we would not have done to us." The saying links others and ourselves in a relation of reciprocal morality. This subtext of the Golden Rule is obvious rather than hidden, although it is not discussed as often as it perhaps should be.

The connection of Benezet's themes to our modern world is sometimes eye-opening. Montague Cobb, a globally renowned medical anthropologist and professor of anatomy at Howard University, often was invited to lecture at mainstream universities and medical schools—this was in the 1950s and 1960s, a time when typically there were neither Black faculty at these schools nor visiting Black scientists. Cobb, an African American, always opened his presentations with the greeting: "Good morning [or afternoon or evening], my fellow humans." It was a greeting that extended a welcome to his listeners, whom Cobb recognized as his "fellow humans," and simultaneously invited them to recognize him as their fellow human. The white audiences were often a little startled to be called on in this way. It was exactly that recognition of mutual humanity the Golden Rule embodied, directly alongside its ethical teaching.[12]

In adducing the Golden Rule, Benezet was not talking about "equality." Quakers had recognized the equality of Black and white people, at least in a spiritual sense, from the Society's founding. Equality connotes parallelism, with one element or individual on the same plane as another. After opening his Black school, Benezet had expanded that idea to recognize first that African Americans had the same talents and intelligence as whites and then to acknowledge their character and humanity.[13]

In *Observations,* he was moving toward the "mutuality" embodied in the Golden Rule, another step in the recognition of communality between white and Black. "Benezet," says Jean Soderlund, "was one of the very few eighteenth century figures who believed that Blacks were as capable of learning as whites."[14] In fact, Benezet's recognition of Black intelligence had taken him far beyond the question of educability. It had led him to the realization not just of equality but of affiliation, and here he stood on new moral ground.

We know that Benezet had friends and acquaintances who were people of color, including James Forten and his aunt, Anne Elizabeth Fortune. Such relationships were not at all common, even among abolitionists.[15] We know there were sexual connections between Blacks and whites; Philadelphia's mixed-race children were proof of that. It's likely a few of these were not exploitative but true romantic partnerships. But ordinary friendships would have raised eyebrows in a place where all "Africans" were looked on with disdain and suspicion. The idea that white and Black people could be social equals was radical for that time and place, when even the idea of *spiritual* equality was not common. In friendship, it wasn't just equality Benezet had risen to; it was mutuality, or affiliation. And with affiliation, morality takes on another level of meaning.

Modern thinkers have explored the relation between affiliation and moral behavior. Neuroscientists such as Donald Pfaff talk about affiliation and empathy, which "[require] an emotional and cognitive connection," the closing of emotional distance between one person and another. "The image of that [other] person," as Pfaff explains, "blurs with that of oneself. This step is crucial as it provides the basis for treating the other person like oneself."[16] This is how the brain is wired, Pfaff says. It's the neurological basis of the Golden Rule. Pfaff doesn't note the connection, but his theory has classical roots. Aristotle in his *Nicomachean Ethics* discussed friendship as "the bond of social communities." The highest level of friendship, he maintained, is the reciprocal relationship of equals.[17]

Ralph Sandiford experienced this closing of emotional distance to the extent that it felt visceral, "as tho' the Rod was on my own back. I suffered with them," he said, "in the natural Body." Benjamin Lay wanted his fellow Quakers to *feel* what enslaved people felt: the cold of winter on their poorly clothed bodies, the anguish of separation from a beloved child.

For Sandiford and Lay, the affinity they felt with the suffering slaves manifested in dramatic ways. Benezet's response furthered his already heightened sense of empathy, which, according to Pfaff, provides the surest basis for moral interaction, what might be called "reciprocal morality."

Observations on the Enslaving, Importing, and Purchasing of Negroes puts a spotlight on the Golden Rule—which had never appeared in a Quaker-approved publication prior to 1754, almost certainly because the Society's former leadership was not eager to underline their tacit approval of slave keeping. In *Observations* Benezet, spurred by the suffering in Pennsylvania's west, focused on God's just wrath for the province's participation in slavery, in heinous violation of the Golden Rule. In *An Epistle* he had linked Jesus's teaching in the Sermon on the Mount ("Remember our blessed Redeemer's positive command to do unto others as we would have them do unto us") with his continuation of that teaching ("With what measure we mete, it shall be meted to us again").[18] *Observations* was a dramatic rendering of "with what measures we mete"—a recital of the barbarism perpetrated by enslavers on Africans and consequently the guilt of everyone implicated—by which he meant his Quaker community.

Here Benezet spelled out the reverse side of the Golden Rule: If this is what we do to others, this is what God does to us, usually "by war, famine, or pestilence."[19] If we violate Christ's Golden Rule teaching by harming our brothers and sisters, we suffer dreadful consequences.[20] Benezet may well have been thinking of Jeremiah, a significant prophet in early Quaker tradition whose warning was relevant to Benezet's purpose here: "Behold, I will visit upon you the evil of your doings" (Jeremiah 23:2).[21]

Observations broke new ground. Brief as it was (the original was eleven pages), its theme served as the basis for Benezet's evolving recognition of Black people as his fellow humans. The pamphlet, as various commentators have shown, also broke ground in terms of its rhetoric. In the 1754 *Epistle* Benezet had written, "What dreadful scenes of murder and cruelty those barbarous ravages must occasion in these unhappy people's country *are too obvious to mention* [emphasis added]."[22] Now, five years later, he had realized that actually depicting these scenes of murder and cruelty could be persuasive in a way that appeals to faith, logic, and sympathy could not. In *Observations*, he announced, "That [purchasers of slaves] may see what a deep dye the guilt is of, I beg leave to quote some extracts from the writings of persons of note, who have been long employed in the African trade and whose situation and office in the factories will not admit any to question the truth of what they relate."[23]

What followed was a vivid portrait of murder, kidnapping, rapine, and carnage driven by the demand for enslaved labor in the plantations, mines, sugar operations, and households of the Americas. "Without purchasers," he wrote, "there would be no trade; and consequently every purchaser, as he encourages the trade, becomes partaker of it."[24] Benezet found material in the various travel narratives that by this time had become available, including *A Collection of Voyages and Travels*, gathered by the brothers Awnsham and John Churchill, and the *New General Collection of Voyages and Travels*, published by Thomas Astley.[25]

No one had ever presented these vivid descriptions as a means of antislavery argument, and doing so established a formidable means of persuasion for

Benezet's subsequent writing and for the later work of his abolitionist colleagues and followers. Benezet, says David Crosby, "virtually invented [this] rhetorical style. . . . [His] use of evidence [from travel literature] is unique to him and sets him apart from all earlier anti-slavery polemicists."[26] We can see the power these descriptions give to Benezet's writing, and it's not hard to imagine the impact they had on readers never previously exposed to the naked ferocity that marked chattel slavery.

Here was yet another manifestation of Benezet's intrinsic creativity, which we've seen at work from his early days as a schoolteacher, to his work with girls and with Black children, both almost surely firsts in American educational history. And now, with *An Epistle of Caution* and *Observations* we see him grappling to fill out his understanding of the character of Black people—who still seemed to most whites in the 1750s and 1760s almost a subhuman species. At the same time he is thinking strategically, developing an approach that will soon galvanize an audience across the Atlantic world.[27]

We know from the work of David Crosby, Brycchan Carey, and others how significant Benezet's innovations in persuasive language were. They caught the spirit of the times and moved an audience that had been left unmoved by appeals to sympathy, brotherhood, or even the most heartfelt demands of faith. He used narratives of slaving expeditions and slaving voyages by participants, often detailed, about the cruelties of capture and transportation. Collections like those published by Thomas Astley provided first-person accounts that Benezet mined for descriptions that, as he wrote, "didn't admit any to question the truth of what they relate."[28] He mobilized a new weapon for the antislavery campaign he, Woolman, and others were waging.[29]

But what was behind the rhetoric he brought to bear in *Observations*? Where did he get the idea to use visualizations in his writing? The form itself is ordinarily described as a breakthrough use of rhetoric, which is true. It's less often seen as an organic outgrowth of Benezet's early engagements with his Black students and their elders.

Unlike Woolman, who traveled through most of the colonies observing and preaching, Benezet never ventured beyond Philadelphia and its immediate environs. Woolman was an eyewitness to the harshness of slaves' lives in the South, which gave rise to his essay *Some Considerations on the Keeping of Negroes*. Benezet had no such experience, but there were vivid enough scenes to make lasting impressions on him right there in Philadelphia. He had, of course, witnessed slave buying and selling outside the London Coffee House. He had heard the stories of his Black friends and acquaintances about their experiences being captured and trafficked in Africa, then subjected to the trauma of the Atlantic crossing and the "seasoning" process in the West Indies or the South. He had not personally seen these things, but the stories undoubtedly conjured up indelible pictures in his mind. A scene he most likely did witness was the wagon with its bloody corpses rumbling along the street opposite the Quaker meetinghouse, followed by a mob of angry Philadelphians shouting curses at the Quakers for their obstruction of military preparations in the assembly. Perhaps seeing such a real-life tableau and the reaction to it started him thinking about the power of dramatic scenes to evoke emotional responses. Generalizations and abstract arguments would not do that, but graphic images could elicit raw responses. What if he incorporated scenes of that sort into his antislavery writing?

This is what he does in his 1759 *Observations on the Enslaving, Importing and Purchasing of Negroes*. His sources were so-called travel narratives written mostly by individuals who had significant experience in the slave trade, including André Brüe, the French governor for Senegal in the early eighteenth century, whose book was included in Thomas Astley's four-volume *A New General Collection of Voyages and Travels*. Brüe described what happened when a trading vessel arrived off the African coast: "The king of the country sends a troop of guards to some village, which they surround; then seizing as many as they have orders for, they bind them and send them away to the ship, where, the ship's mark being put upon them [each captive was branded], they are heard of no more. They usually carry the infants in sacks, and gag the men and women for fear they should alarm the villages through which they are carried."[30]

Another source was Willem Bosman, the chief merchant for the Dutch African Company, who spent fourteen years on the Gold and Slave Coasts, first as an apprentice, eventually rising to vice chairman of the company's Africa operations. Bosman's 1702 book, *New and Accurate Description of the Coast of Guinea*, was a detailed description of the region. Also included in Astley's *New Collection of Voyages*, it was one of the most popular "travelogues" of its time.[31] Bosman's descriptions amplified Brüe's: "When vessels arrive, if they have no stock of slaves, the factors trust the inhabitant with goods with the value of one or two hundred slaves, which they send into the inland country in order to buy slaves at all markets, even sometimes two hundred miles deep in the country, where markets of men were kept in the same manner as those of beasts with us."[32]

Most of the narratives Benezet quoted described the way European traders incited African tribes and kingdoms to war on their neighbors in order to procure captives. In *Observations* Benezet makes sure these are on prominent display. The Quaker peace testimony had created a crisis in the Society during the French and Indian War, which was just then coming to a conclusion. Involvement in war—in any way— was, and still is, a defining Quaker issue. In *Observations,* Benezet took pains to demonstrate the causal connection of slave owning to warfare.

Philadelphia surgeon William Chancellor had sailed to Africa on a slaving voyage as a ship's doctor, tasked with checking the health of captured Africans on purchase and doing what he could to keep them alive during the crossing. Chancellor and Benezet were contemporaries. They apparently knew each other, and Benezet had access to the diary Chancellor kept of his time as ship's surgeon, an excerpt of which Benezet included in *Observations*:[33]

> Being on that coast, at a place called Basalia, the commander of the vessel according to custom sent a person on shore with a present to the king of the country, acquainting him with their arrival, and letting him know that they wanted a cargo of slaves: the king promised to furnish them with slaves, and in order to do it, set out to go to war against his enemies, designing also to surprise some town and take all the people prisoners. Sometime after, the king sent them word he had not yet met with the desired success, having been twice repulsed in attempting to break up two towns, but that he still hoped to procure a number of slaves for them; and in this design he persisted till he met his enemies in the field, where a battle was fought which lasted three days, during which time the engagement was so bloody that 4,500 were slain on the spot. Think what a pitiable sight it was to see the widows weeping over their lost hus-bands, and orphans deploring the loss of their fathers, etc.[34]

America's Quakers had never before seen the relationship between owning slaves and the instigation and conduct of brutal wars. They had never been presented with impossible-to-ignore descriptions of the awful details of slaving, the children in sacks, the adults branded with hot irons, the prisons, the slave marts where humans were sold like beasts. Benezet's pious anger, always present, at least in undertones, was now intensified, as if he had been further inflamed by his own reading and writing. "I hope," he wrote, "what is already said will be sufficient to prevent any considerate Christian from being, in any degree, defiled with a gain so full of horrors, and so palpably inconsistent with the gospel of our blessed Lord and savior Jesus Christ,"[35] evoking even the belligerent polemics of his old friend Benjamin Lay. He ends *Observations* with the biblical pronouncement that man stealing is punishable by death. But the power of *Observations* is not in the Christian outrage—it's in the pictures that make their lasting impression on the minds and imaginations of his readers.

In his essay on the transformation of Benezet's antislavery rhetoric, David Crosby points out that while Benezet arrived at this new form of argument on his own, some of the period's leading philosophers were elaborating on the power of rhetoric from the same perspective. Instead of the classical deductive form of argument, moving from general principles to particulars, John Locke and his followers, such as the Scottish thinkers David Hume and Francis Hutcheson, set out empiricist principles—that is, arguing from the particular to the general. In terms of rhetoric, that meant that to be effective, the arguer (the "rhetor") needed to present vivid pictures that would strike the senses, then the imagination, then the beliefs of the audience. "Since ideas," they argued, "come originally only through sensation, which is the source of all knowledge of fact and human affairs, the force of ideas comes from the vivacity of our perceptions of matters of fact."[36]

The highly influential Lord Kames (another Scotsman), for example, wrote in his *Elements of Criticism*, "The power of language to raise emotions, depends entirely on the raising such lively and distinct images. . . . The readers' passions are never sensibly moved, till he be thrown into a kind of reverie; in which state, forgetting that he is reading, he conceives every incident as passing in his presence, precisely as if he were an eye-witness."[37]

Benezet had looked at his own experiences, thought them through, and come to the same conclusion. But he was still operating in the insular Quaker world, while Hume, Kames, and their colleagues were establishing patterns of thought that were molding universal—or at least Western—views of knowledge, language, psychology, science, politics, and much more. In 1759, when Benezet published *Observations,* he had not yet entered this world of Enlightenment thinking. But that was soon to change. In *Observations* he had, says Crosby, "[sounded] the prophetic note of divine retribution for the sins of the people, [making] slavery, for the first time, a pressing public issue rather than a matter of private conscience and inner enlightenment."[38] He was soon to make it an issue for the public beyond the narrow confines of Quakerdom.

At the same time Benezet had set his own stage for yet a further phase in his progressively fuller effort to comprehend what it meant to be a Black person and what that meant for the white world Black people were living in. The message of equal humanity vibrated in his mind (in Peter Moore's words) and drove his thinking. With his next book, *A Short Account of That Part of Africa Inhabited by the Negroes*, he established the parameters for the transatlantic campaign that was to change the world's idea of slavery—an idea that had been ingrained for so much of human history that it was regarded simply as a normal part of life.

CHAPTER ELEVEN

Two Streams of Morality

The Quaker Board of Overseers funded the first edition of Benezet's 1759 *Observations on the Enslaving, Importing, and Purchasing of Negroes*, but they took their time about it; they were hesitant, possibly even reluctant, to formally approve it. After all, even the critical 1758 yearly meeting had not issued a firm edict against owning slaves (that didn't happen until the mid-1770s), and in *Observations* Benezet was demanding manumission. That was the meaning of "Do unto others as you would have them do unto you." "Oh ye cruel taskmasters," he had called enslavers, "Ye hard-hearted oppressors! Will not God hear their cry; and *what shall ye do when God riseth up and when he visiteth*."[1] If that wasn't damning enough, he had concluded the tract with a reminder from Mosaic law that "man-stealing," or selling or even keeping "stolen" human beings, merited the death sentence.[2] Not that the nonviolent Benezet (or any other faithful Quaker) would actually impose a death penalty on anyone, but he wanted Quaker slaveowners to understand the utter depths of the enormity they were practicing.

The overseers might have been against slavery—Benezet sat on the board, as did Woolman—but the majority apparently felt *Observations* went too far, and they declined to approve the second edition. Benezet published it himself, with the help of Pietist printer Christopher Sower. Publishing it independently was a telling deviation from Quaker directives, suggesting that in his developing antislavery campaign Benezet was looking beyond the borders of his Quaker base.

In 1762 Benezet followed up *Observations* with *A Short Account of That Part of Africa Inhabited by the Negroes*, a far more fully developed tract that used the rhetorical innovations he had pioneered in *Observations* and went beyond even those. The overseers didn't approve this pamphlet either, so Benezet again published it himself—but this time he did so anonymously, which suggests he wasn't completely comfortable operating outside Quaker guidelines. Since the overseers hadn't approved the second edition of *Observations*, Benezet no doubt understood they wouldn't want their imprimatur on *A Short Account*, which took the stark revelations of *Observations* to an even more damning level. "No one," he wrote in *A Short Account*, "can be a silent and innocent spectator."[3]

The opening paragraphs of *A Short Account* indicate that Benezet intended it for the larger, non-Quaker audience as well as for his fellow Friends. He reiterated the conviction that the corruption in people's hearts could be addressed only "through the efficacy of the blood of Jesus Christ," and he blamed "selfish avarice" for "[giving] life to this complicated wickedness."[4] Europeans, he declared, "have made all other considerations give way to an insatiable desire for gain."[5]

The language was especially powerful, but the themes were those Benezet had expressed before, a strong indication he had a new audience in mind, people who might not have read him previously. He even restated the certainty that God would unleash his wrath on "everyone who is in any respect concerned in this wicked traffic," those who "must upon a serious recollection be impressed with surprise and terror from a sense that there is a righteous God and a state of retribution that will last forever."[6]

Until now Benezet had been assiduous to show that Black people are fully human in the same way white people are, "restoring humanity to the Africans," as Maurice Jackson put it.[7] That was Benezet's overarching theme in the *Epistle* and *Observations*. But in those works he always made the assertions himself, in his own voice. In *A Short Account* he advances the argument by adducing the opinions of others whose long association with Africans in their native countries makes them convincing witnesses.

He had written that Black people possessed intelligence, talent, temperament, character, and morality, just as white people did. But these characteristics were difficult to see in a population as suppressed as enslaved Black people were, with no access to the modes of living that white people enjoyed: education, rights, control over their persons, their labor, the common customs of individual, family, social, and civil life. To illuminate the scope of Black humanity, it would be necessary to provide a picture of African people living under normal circumstances, not possible anywhere in the Americas, where even free Black people faced debilitating restrictions. But the authors of the narratives in Astley's and other collections had often spent many years living alongside Africans pursuing normal lives in their home surroundings. These writers became sources from which Benezet could convey an authentic picture of "normal" Black life.

Here again Benezet broke new ground. No abolitionist had ever presented this kind of picture. It was imaginative and eye-opening; Benezet clearly understood its polemical potential. David Crosby has written that "each of [Benezet's] major publications threw the net a little wider, incorporating larger and larger chunks of eyewitness testimony."[8] Benezet had first used the rhetorical technique in *Observations*. In *A Short Account of That Part of Africa*, he was already demonstrating how to wield it most effectively. He was soon to add yet another dimension to his antislavery offensive, but the slavery narrators—Brüe, Bosman, and others—were a rich and permanent resource for him as he went about depicting the manners, customs, and dispositions of native Africans.

From these witnesses, Benezet wrote, "it will appear that the *Negroes* are generally a sensible, humane, and sociable people, and that their capacity is as good and as capable of improvement as that of the whites."[9] Benezet had been making this case in one way or another since the early 1750s, but the shock value was no doubt still considerable, given the persistent view of Africans as dull, slothful, and dissolute. For white people who had encountered Black people only as illiterate, subservient laborers or impoverished menials, the idea that they were actually sensible, humane, sociable beings must have been disorienting.

That he was laboring to change a deeply embedded preconception is one reason that Benezet's tracts, starting with *A Short Account*, tended to include an accumulation of citations. He knew he was battering at long-closed mental gates that required multiple assaults. For example, Benezet quoted Bosman, the Dutch chief merchant for the Gold Coast, who wrote that the Africans he dealt with were "generally friendly with strangers, of a mild conversation, courteous, affable, and easy to be overcome with reason; in conversation they discover a great quickness of parts and understanding. . . . some Negroes who have had an agreeable education, have manifested a brightness of understanding equal to any of us."[10] William Smith, whose account Benezet also found in the Astley collection, recounted that the Africans he got to know were "civil, good natured people, industrious to the last degree. . . . It is easy to perceive . . . how great progress they would make in the sciences in case their genius was cultivated with study." He is, he says, speaking about the upper classes, though "peasants, workmen and shepherds are as ignorant in these parts as elsewhere."[11] André Brüe, the French governor for Senegal, had, like Bosman, previously appeared as a witness in *Observations*. Here Benezet quotes him describing the people of Benin, "generally good natured and civil, and may be brought to anything by fair and soft means. If you make them presents they will recompense them double. If you want anything of them and ask it, they seldom deny it, even though they had occasion for it themselves. But to treat them harshly or think to gain anything of them by force is to dispute with the moon."[12] Benezet did not deny that Africans had flaws, that they warred with each other prior to the arrival of Europeans, or that African kings were as greed driven as the Europeans they dealt with. But in *A Short Account* his main concern was to bring out the human qualities, social and personal, of ordinary Africans—normal people who had been transformed by enslavement in the Americas into an ignorant class, exhausted by hard labor and drained by psychological stress.

In *Observations,* Benezet had for the first time portrayed some of the horrors of the slave trade as seen through the eyes of the slavers themselves. The visions of children transported in sacks and slave markets where human beings were kept and sold like animals were vivid and no doubt shocking. In *A Short Account,* the pictures were more detailed, more vivid, and even more shocking because more complete. Here's the Dutch factor Bosman describing what happens to prisoners taken as booty:

> They are all brought out together in a large plain, where by our surgeons they are carefully examined—and naked too—both men and women without the least distinction or modesty. Those which are approved as good are set on one side; in the meanwhile a burning iron with the arms or name of the companies lies in the fire, with which ours are marked on the breast. When we have agreed with the owners of the slaves, they are returned to their prisons, where from that time forward they are kept at our charge, [and it] cost us two-pence a day a slave, which serves to subsist them like our criminals on bread and water; so that, to save charges, we send them aboard our ships the very first opportunity; before which their masters strip them of all they have on their backs so that they come on board stark naked, as well women as men: in which condition they are obliged to continue, if the master of the ship is not charitable (which he commonly is) as to bestow something on them to cover their nakedness. . . . Six or seven hundred are sometimes put on board a vessel, where they lie as close together as possible for them to be crowded.[13]

This machinery of enslavement, Benezet wrote, was "the most iniquitous and cruelest act of violence and rapine . . . that to our knowledge is perpetrated in any part of the world."[14]

Benezet's tract had no illustrations. It relied on the power of words to evoke images, strike imaginations, and impact beliefs, in just the way Lord Kames and his rhetorician colleagues prescribed.[15] *A Short Account* showed that Benezet was already a master rhetorician, able to conjure up dramatic pictures in the minds of his readers. Printed images and graphics became important in the antislavery campaign waged by Benezet's successors, but only after he had passed from the scene. Film and video media lay far in the future. But we can imagine what Steven Spielberg, who made *Schindler's List*, might have done with Willem Bosman's description of a large plain crowded with naked men and women being examined and branded—a twenty-first-century equivalent to the mental pictures Benezet hoped to set off and did set off.

Another of Benezet's rhetorical advances had to do with storytelling. In *Observations* he had related through witness accounts illustrations of scenes from the slaving enterprise. In *A Short Account* he reprinted what amounted to short stories, which engaged the reader on a different level. One of these was from John Atkins, a slave ship surgeon who described his experiences traveling from Ghana and Sierra Leone to Brazil and the West Indies. Atkins wrote about a village chief named Tomba, who was captured and sold and whom Atkins saw being whipped mercilessly on the beach at Sierra Leone for refusing to be examined. At sea, Atkins's ship encountered another slaver on its way to the Americas with a cargo that included Tomba. From the master of this vessel, Atkins heard that Tomba had led a shipboard revolt.

> This Tomba had combined with three of his stoutest country men and a woman to destroy the white men in order to get their freedom; that one night he went upon deck to put his design into execution, being accompanied by one man and the woman, who were all he could engage to follow him; where finding three sailors on the forecastle, he presently dispatched two by single strokes on the temples (with a hammer the woman had given him); the other man rousing with the noise, his companions seized and Tomba killed him in the same manner. But two other sailors taking the alarm, stood upon their defense, which soon awakened the master underneath, who, running up, took a handspike, and felling Tomba with it, secured them all in irons. The reader, says Atkins, may be curious to know their punishment: why [the captain], weighing the stoutness and worth of the two slaves . . . did whip and scarify them only; while three other abettors . . . he sentenced to cruel deaths, making them first eat the heart and liver of one of them he killed. The woman he hoisted by her thumbs, whipped and slashed her with knives, before the other slaves till she died.[16]

The ferocity of this account sounds as if it might be exaggerated. But it wasn't. Numerous witnesses recorded by abolitionists who came after

Benezet gave similar and even more appalling testimonies. This is raw reading today. In 1762 the bloodthirstiness of it forced the nonviolent Quakers to grapple with the full horrors of the slave trade as they rarely had before.[17]

In *A Short Account of That Part of Africa*, Benezet not only highlighted disturbing stories and concrete images; he also cited authors, works, and even page numbers, confirming the authenticity of his material. That kind of footnoting was unusual, possibly unique, in antislavery polemics of the period. It had the effect of further situating Benezet as an empiricist, as distinct from his native Christ-centered mindset. It's not that he changed. He was still a man of faith, but other elements from contemporary philosophy, or at least epistemology, had crept into his writing. In *A Short Account* his mental horizon had expanded; the voice of contemporary thought began to be heard alongside the Christian themes of sin, guilt, retribution, and the possibility of repentance.

In *A Short Account* Benezet provided numbers of enslaved people transported to the Americas on British shipping, also a new addition to his polemics.[18] He cited statistics from an essay by the pseudonymous J. Philmore, noting that in 1725 the yearly number was about fifty thousand, but by a more conservative estimate, "we will suppose that the number . . . , one year with another, are no more than thirty-five thousand."[19] He wasn't far off the mark. According to modern estimates, approximately forty-two thousand enslaved human beings were shipped from Africa's west coast each year during this period of Benezet's activism.[20] Taking into account other reports, Benezet estimated that "at least a tenth part of them die on the voyage."[21] Recent studies put the Middle Passage death rate at ten to fifteen percent.[22] In addition, the mortality rate during the so-called seasoning process was atrocious. Seasoning was how enslavers referred to the process that began with disembarkation and might continue for a year or two, during which enslaved individuals were subjected to an adjustment regime of low food intake, hard labor, and psychological conditioning. Those who acclimated successfully were expected to perform better and last longer; consequently their market price was set higher.

Benezet estimated that twelve thousand African captives each year died on the crossing and during seasoning. (The real number was probably considerably higher, especially if the many deaths that occurred during trafficking in Africa are added.) "What a sad and dreadful affair is this man-trade," he wrote, "whereby so many thousands of our fellow rational creatures lose their lives, are, truly and properly speaking, murdered every year. I do not think there is an instance of so great barbarity and cruelty carried on in any part of the world as this, year after year. It is enough to make one tremble to think what a load of guilt lies upon this nation on this account, and that the blood of thousands of poor innocent creatures, murdered every year, in carrying on this cursed trade, cry aloud to heaven for vengeance."[23]

Much of this material is included in the long excerpt (seventeen pages in the Crosby edition) from an anonymous publication printed in London and entitled *Two Dialogues on the Man-Trade*. Couched as a dialogue between an abolitionist and a slavery advocate, it is an obscure tract whose author has never been definitively identified. "Philmore" (clearly a pseudonym for the author) was also the abolitionist in the dialogue; "Allcraft," the slavery advocate. Unlike Benezet, Philmore was a classical scholar who peppered his arguments with Latin references. But he was so close to Benezet in his thinking and values that he might be considered an alter ego. The fictional Philmore of the *Two Dialogues* even uses real travel narratives to illustrate and drive home his points. In incorporating *Two Dialogues* into *A Short Account*, Benezet cut out the dialogue and presented Philmore's arguments as a continuous narrative.

According to Crosby, Benezet edited some of the *Two Dialogues* text so it would conform better to his own writing style.[24] In fact, it's often difficult to tell the difference. Here's the beginning of the excerpt (which Benezet referred to as an "Extract"):

> The African blacks are as properly and truly men as the European whites; they are both of the same species, and are originally descended from the same parents. . . . They have the same rational powers as we have; they are free moral agents, as we are, and many of them have as good natural genius, as good and as brave a spirit, as any of those to whom they have been made slaves. To trade in blacks, then, is to trade in men; the black-skinned and the white-skinned being all of the same species, all of the human race, are by nature upon an equality.[25]

A few paragraphs later, the author condemned slavers and slave keepers in words that echoed Benezet's and made his points much as he did himself: "[Do] they [enslavers] think and consider that these [Black people] have rational immortal souls, that they are made after the image of God, as well as themselves, and that, being in the same body, they have the same passions, and senses, and feelings, as they have, and are as susceptible of pain, and grief, and upon the same occasions, as they[?]"[26] The point here was not reiteration; Benezet was merely presenting confirming witnesses to establish his case.

For many years the author of *Two Dialogues* was unknown, though the names of the London printers appeared on the title page. In 2022, John Coffey, a history professor at the University of Leicester, undertook a comprehensive investigation that included slave ship databases, stylistic analyses, and considerable biographical sleuthing.[27] Coffey's surprising conclusion is that the anonymous author was none other than John Newton, who wrote "Amazing Grace," the best known of all British and American hymns. Newton was a former slave ship captain who later in life was ordained and became an important abolitionist, famous penitent, and sometime advisor to the antislavery politician William Wilberforce. Coffey further speculates that Benezet was in contact with the publishers of *Two Dialogues*, which was how he learned about the piece. "Our investigation," Coffey writes, "has highlighted the trans-Atlantic connection between Dissenting publishers in London and the Quaker abolitionist in Pennsylvania."[28]

That conclusion may or may not hold up. Benezet's connection with English publishers at that period is not otherwise attested. Coffey also speculates that the publication of *Two Dialogues* suggests a collaboration among Newton, John Wesley, Benezet, and other abolitionists, which would constitute "a prefiguration of the Quaker-Evangelical-Methodist-Dissenter alliance that would drive the British abolitionist movement from the 1780s to the 1830s."[29] If that were so, it would open a new avenue of exploration regarding Benezet's earliest contacts with British abolitionists. Unfortunately, all the evidence we have militates against this possibility. But the subject does bring up another unanswered question regarding Benezet's access to his sources—not about who wrote the little-known and soon forgotten *Two Dialogues*, but about how it made its way into Benezet's hands in the first place. Crosby notes that for Benezet to have included the tract in *A Short Account*, he must have received a copy in late 1761 or early 1762.[30] But neither Crosby nor anyone else seems to know who sent it or from whom Benezet received it.

That mystery brings up a connected but much larger question. In his earlier work, *Observations on the Enslaving, Importing, and Purchasing of Negroes*, Benezet adduced travelers' reports to illustrate the horrors of the slave trade. In *A Short Account of That Part of Africa* he expanded this breakthrough in rhetoric, bringing to bear far more (and even more graphic) first-person witness reports. At the same time, he made another innovation: incorporating works by the Enlightenment thinkers George Wallace, James Foster, and Francis Hutcheson. But an enduring question is: What made him broaden his reasoning to include these secular thinkers? Benezet had regularly argued the injustice and inhumanity of slavery, alongside his heartfelt and often anguished Christian exhortations, aimed at Quakers first and the larger Christian community second. But allying himself with secular philosophers was another matter; it changed the scope and feel of his writing. Their presence in his work has always been regarded by commentators as a significant new phase of Benezet's thinking that initiated his appeal to a wider audience.

Most commentators don't address the question of how Benezet became knowledgeable about Wallace, Foster, and Hutcheson, whom Jackson categorizes as "Scottish Moral Philosophers."[31] Benezet mined the writings of these three for their comments on slavery, but it's not at all clear how he came across their works or to what extent he at this point grasped the underlying harmony between Quaker Inner Light belief and Enlightenment principles of liberty and natural rights, which played a significant role in his thinking and writing later on. In other words, was their inclusion in *A Short Account* simply a strategic innovation intended to widen his audience, or did Benezet, as early as 1762, see a vital connection between his Quaker faith and the Enlightenment's outburst of liberal thought? If we knew how he accessed these works, we would have a better understanding of his evolution as a thinker and activist.

Jackson notes that works of Wallace, Foster, and Hutcheson were largely or completely unavailable in Philadelphia when Benezet wrote *A Short Account of That Part of Africa*.[32] There were also no books by or about the philosophers in Benezet's own extensive library.[33] Benezet owned quite a few volumes on health and medical science (his health was often fragile). He also had books on gardening—he was a vegetarian and kept a large garden, where he raised his own vegetables. These were joined on his shelves by many books on religious and spiritual subjects. But there was nothing at all on contemporary philosophy.

As it's a mystery how Benezet learned about *Two Dialogues on the Man-Trade*, it's also surprising that he ever alighted on George Wallace's (Benezet spells the name "Wallis") "massive" tome on Scottish jurisprudence, *System of the Principles of the Law of Scotland*. The principles of Scottish law would have had limited appeal to an American audience, and the book seems not to have made any headway in the colonies. Wallace himself, though a student of Montesquieu's *L'esprit des lois*, was less an Enlightenment figure than a scholar of Scottish legal history who wrote two other books in addition to *System of the Principles*: one on the origin of feudal tenures in Scotland and another on ancient Scottish peerages. His connections with Enlightenment thinking came through his section on slavery, which was entered into Denis Diderot's *Encyclopédie* in 1765 in a plagiarized version by Louis de Jaucourt, three years after the publication of *A Short Account of That Part of Africa*.

According to David Brion Davis, Wallace was "a curiously obscure figure."[34] T. H. F. Fletcher, a historian who wrote about Montesquieu, says Wallace, while brilliant, "was forgotten almost as soon as he was remembered. . . . His plea for humanity [i.e., his antislavery discussion] would have been more effective had it been read; but it was hidden away in a massive and expensive volume laden with abstractions, charged with erudition."[35] It's not likely that Benezet would have just come across Wallace's antislavery digression while thumbing through a large tome on Scottish law.

James Foster, an English dissenting minister and controversialist, was likewise little known in the colonies. His polemics were largely anti-Trinitarian, and he is regarded as an early British Unitarian. Unitarian belief didn't take hold in America until later in the eighteenth century, well after the publication of *A Short Account of That Part of Africa*, and the controversies between Trinitarians and Unitarians were of negligible interest to Benezet.[36] In his 1783 *Short Account of the People Called Quakers*, Benezet described Quaker positions on baptism, worship, prayer, and communion—but never alluded to the Trinity, an indication of his relative indifference to the subject. Which is to say that there was little that might have drawn Benezet to read Foster, except that he somehow learned of Foster's discussion of slavery in his *Discourses on Natural Religion and Social Virtue*.

The third writer Benezet included in *A Short Account of That Part of Africa* was Francis Hutcheson, who, unlike Wallace and Foster, did have a strong presence in America during Benezet's time, as well as in the history of philosophy afterward. Hutcheson was one of the originators of the Scottish Enlightenment. His students at the University of Glasgow, where he held the chair of moral philosophy, included the philosopher and economist Adam Smith, who utilized some of Hutcheson's teaching in his landmark *The Wealth of Nations*.

Hutcheson is regarded as an originator of moral sense philosophy, the idea that human beings are born with a number of innate "senses," including a sense that enables moral judgment. The moral sense concept comes close in various ways to the primary Quaker tenet of the Inner Light, also present at the core of each individual. Benezet did not pursue this parallel in *A Short*

Account of That Part of Africa, although it can be seen as a hinge connecting the Quaker belief in the spirit of God dwelling in every person with the Enlightenment's emphasis on the moral and social competence of each individual human being.

Benezet does not explore the parallel in *A Short Account* overtly, although it's there in essence. Instead, he has realized that it's advantageous for him to bring in the secular world of thinkers who have their own commitment and approach to antislavery. Doing that, he saw, would broaden his audience and provide him with an extra dimension of firepower at a time when Enlightenment thought was striking lightning in the minds of men and the principles of democratic political theory, with Locke and Montesquieu, were gathering adherents in Europe and the American colonies. Benezet may not have immersed himself in Enlightenment thought in any meaningful way; in fact, slave trade scholar Roger Anstey writes that though Benezet's marshaling of moral philosophy was important and original, "the choice of quotations, and spelling variations, e.g., Wallis for Wallace, Hutchinson for Hutcheson, make one doubt that Benezet had first hand acquaintance with the authors in question."[37] But to whatever extent Benezet might or might not have been conversant with Wallace, Foster, and Hutcheson in 1762, he was sufficiently attuned to the period's revolutionary advances in thought to tap into them strategically.

While the excerpts he quoted from his three exemplars incorporated various reasons to oppose slavery—its cruelty, its avariciousness, its economic destructiveness, its assault on the common feelings of humanity—the primary arguments of all three were legal. Wallace, the juridical scholar, wrote, "Kings, princes, governors, are not proprietors of those who are subject to their authority. . . . Of course they have not a right to dispose of their liberty and to sell them for slaves. Besides, no man has the right to acquire or to purchase them; men and their liberty are not (in Commercio), they are not either saleable or purchaseable. [A slave] never lost his liberty. He could not lose it; his prince had no power to dispose of him. Of course the sale was *ipse jure* void."[38]

Hutcheson similarly declared that "each man is the original proprietor of his own liberty." He eviscerated the proslavery argument that slaves taken prisoner in wars would be killed as a matter of course; therefore buying them from their prospective murderers as slaves was an act of kindness. What then, he asked, about surgeons and midwives and physicians who save lives or bring new lives into the world? "One who was the means of preserving a man's life is not therefore entitled to make him a slave, and sell him as a piece of goods," said Hutcheson. "Strange that in any nation where a sense of liberty prevails, where the Christian religion is professed, custom and high prospects of gain can so stupefy the conscience of men and all sense of natural justice that they can hear such computations made about the value of their fellow men, and their liberty, without abhorrence and indignation."[39]

Foster reinforced Wallace's and Hutcheson's arguments. Slavery, he declared, was "a criminal and outrageous violation of the natural right of mankind."[40] Foster's *Discourses on Natural Religion and Social Virtue* was published in 1749. Twenty-seven years later, Thomas Jefferson wrote in the famously deleted clause of the Declaration of Independence, "[King George] has waged cruel war against human nature itself, violating its most sacred rights of life and liberty in the persons of a distant people who never offended him."[41] The emphasis here is on legal and natural rights. Hutcheson and Wallace speak of individuals possessing liberty as something they own, that is inherent in them and isn't capable of being alienated. Foster speaks of "the natural right of mankind." These are new arguments Benezet is bringing forward. Proprietorship of oneself is a Quaker tenet in the sense that a person's conscience belongs to no one except its possessor—that is, a person's core self is not subservient to any external force or jurisdiction, not to priests, not to kings, not to parliaments. Quakers did not take their hats off to anybody. Proprietorship of oneself in the age of Enlightenment was also an increasingly accepted secular conviction. The right of liberty, Wallace said, "[man] carries about with him."[42]

As he drew in Wallace, Hutcheson, and Foster from the secular world, Benezet adopted their arguments as his own. "It is," says Roger Anstey, "in his writing that we find a rounded case against slavery, of which the inspiration is Quaker but, being directed to the non-Quaker world, also brings into service the moral philosophy and the sentiments of the age."[43] Protestantism had always been, in one form or another, a religion of interiority, and Quakers were on the far left end of that spectrum. In *A Short Account of That Part of Africa,* that defining religious vision converged with the secular conception of liberty as a natural and fundamental right. In other words, the profound shift in the Reformation's definition of the self here met with the secular expression of that same profound shift.

Anstey asserts that Benezet's "recourse to moral philosophy" "was a novel line of argument."[44] That is true, but it was a great deal more than that. Bringing together the religious and secular arguments was, in fact, a convergence of monumental importance, and that convergence gave Benezet's campaign its great appeal to the British people and Parliament. The joining of these two streams of morality can be seen as the decisive factor in the eventual triumph of Wilberforce's parliamentary campaign to put an end to Great Britain's Atlantic slave trade.

In the eight years from the 1754 publication of *An Epistle* to the appearance in 1762 of *A Short Account of That Part of Africa*, Benezet expanded on his theme of Black and white equality, bringing out a progressively more complete picture of Black humanity. *A Short Account* seems a culmination of this truly revolutionary endeavor that broke through the deep-seated racist prejudice that defined the Atlantic world's perception of African people. According to Jonathan Sassi, it was this tract that showed Benezet had reached his "intellectual maturity."[45] Roger Bruns, quoting Quaker historian Frederick Tolles, notes that in Benezet's writing, the "'radical social ethics implicit in the Quaker faith' [met] the . . . Enlightenment ideas of natural law and the natural rights of man."[46] Benezet was to develop that convergence further in the larger books that were to come. But in *A Short Account of That Part of Africa,* his quest to establish the truth of Black humanity has linked with the Enlightenment invention of a larger identity for all men, Black and white. *A Short Account* may appear to be a culmination of sorts, but in 1762 Benezet's restless mind was still hard at work.

CHAPTER TWELVE

A Shift to England

"At a time when the general rights and liberties of mankind and the preservation of those valuable privileges transmitted to us by our ancestors are become so much the subject of universal consideration, can it be an enquiry indifferent to any, how many of those who distinguish themselves as the advocates of liberty remain insensible and inattentive to the treatment of thousands and tens of thousands of our fellow-men . . . who are at this very time kept in the most deplorable state of slavery in many parts of the British dominions?"[1]

So begins Benezet's tract *A Caution and a Warning to Great Britain and Her Colonies*, published in 1766, four years after *A Short Account of That Part of Africa*. It's telling that the earlier work began with a declaration about "the efficacy of the blood of Jesus Christ." "Till this divine help is embraced," Benezet lamented, "the heart of man will remain corrupt."[2] Four years later, he was no longer appealing to Christ's blood but to the "rights and liberties . . . transmitted to us by our ancestors." By which he does not mean his actual Huguenot ancestors, but his adopted British ancestors. Benezet had become a British subject thirty-one years before; here he's addressing his fellow subjects and claiming his, and their, British heritage of rights, liberties, and privileges, so heinously violated by the slave trade.

Despite his embrace of such liberal values, Benezet hadn't become a wholehearted convert to Enlightenment political theory in the interim between *A Short Account* and *A Caution and a Warning*. But in those four years his perspective had shifted and sharpened. Somewhere in that period he set his sights squarely on a different audience: neither Quakers nor Christians more generally, but the English people writ large and their ruling elites, their king, their peers, their representatives in Commons. Back in 1730, Ralph Sandiford had the same idea when he wrote in *The Mystery of Iniquity* that the slave trade "hath its original in England" and urged his British readers to "introduce the matter to the helm [the king] by which the body is governed, that the ax being laid to the root we may be delivered from the corruption."[3] Sandiford's plea was a nebulous hope. Benezet's appeal was calculated and strategic.

At some point in those four years, Benezet read the *Liverpool Memorandum Book*, a listing of ships sailing out of Liverpool, the hub of the British slaving fleet. Meant as a tool for businessmen, the *Memorandum Book* also specified cargoes. Benezet had gotten hold of a copy from 1753, which showed more than thirty thousand captured Africans had been transported by Liverpool-based ships that year. Looking at the numbers of slaving vessels sailing out of London, Bristol, and elsewhere, Benezet calculated, "We may with some degree of certainty conclude there are at least one hundred thousand Negroes purchased and brought on board our ships yearly from the coast of Africa."[4] His calculations were confirmed by another trading book he read, Anderson's *History of Trade and Commerce*.[5]

Benezet's dawning understanding of the vast extent of Great Britain's involvement awakened him to the reality that if anything were to be done about the slave trade, it needed to go through England's lawmakers and the ordinary people whose opinions could swell a tide of public opinion. For the larger British audience he was now aiming at, invoking long-established, dearly held rights and liberties was likely to at least stir emotions and to do so more effectively than the most impassioned calls on Christian faith. That recognition may have dismayed the deeply pious Benezet, but if it did, he never mentioned it, as he so infrequently ever mentioned anything personal.

The fact was that Benezet had been thinking about the British public and especially its elites for several years. As far back as 1763 he had written to Joseph Phipps, a prominent English Quaker, that if the slave trade ever "receives a proper Check [it] must come from amongst you."[6] Along with the letter Benezet had sent Phipps several copies of *A Short Account of That Part of Africa*, explaining, "If the Treatize [*sic*] was reprinted amongst you, with such amendment as might be thought necessary, & dispersed among those in whose power it is to put a restraint upon the Trade &c particularly of our gracious King, his Councelors, and each member of both Houses of Parliament had one put in their hands, might it not with divine Assistance, answer some good end; surely they are not so void of feeling . . . that some would endeavor the suppression of this enormous Evil."[7]

Now, with *A Caution and a Warning*—whose subtitle declared that the tract was "submitted to the Serious Consideration of All, more especially of Those in Power"—he was making a direct assault on Great Britain's slave trade, its supporters, and its perpetrators, using the common-law heritage of rights and liberties as a wedge to muster opinion to his side and condemn the slaving industry and sugar interests whose "insatiable desire for gain" perpetuated the enormity.[8] *A Caution and a Warning* was approved by the Philadelphia Meeting for Sufferings, the press overseers, and the Philadelphia Yearly Meeting. Two thousand copies were printed and sent out to Pennsylvania's quarterly meetings and Quaker meetings in other colonies. The Philadelphia Meeting also asked the London Meeting to print another 1,500 copies, at Philadelphia's expense, and "have them delivered at the dwellings of the Members of both houses of Parliament in and about London & Westminster."[9] Benezet was a member of the Meeting for Sufferings, a press overseer, and a yearly meeting member. He was likely an active participant in the decision to distribute his tract to English as well as American Friends. Since 1754 Benezet had been working relentlessly to sway Quaker opinion on slaveholding. Twelve years later, he himself had a seat in the Society's principal institutions, each of which was mobilizing behind him. It must have seemed to him a good start along the road he had now clearly marked out for himself.

When the Philadelphia Meeting's message reached London, abolitionism had not yet taken root in England. Black people were a presence in the capital, as menials or servants, but they amounted to only a small portion of London's population, perhaps five or seven thousand in a city of almost three-quarters of a million.[10] Though some of London's Africans were free people, the majority were enslaved, and London had active slave marts, the largest at the city's Royal Exchange. But aside from the London Quaker Meeting, in England there was little agitation over slavery and little discussion of abolition.

But that was due to change. At almost the same moment Benezet was writing his essay invoking England's constitutionally established rights, one Englishman was thinking along the same lines, and doing something about it too.

Granville Sharp was not an abolitionist. He was a mid-level bureaucrat at the government ordnance office located in the Tower of London, where he spent his days monitoring cadet violations of the military code of behavior and looking over saltpeter supplies (for gunpowder production) and storage facilities for cannons and muskets.[11] To allay the boredom of his work, he delved into theological studies and thought up plans of a religious nature—he was a devout Anglican, grandson of an archbishop and son of Thomas Sharp, the archdeacon of Northumberland. He was also a virtuoso flutist capable of playing two flutes simultaneously in the famous Sharp family band, where his surgeon brother was organist, his ironmonger brother played the jointed serpent, one sister played the lute and another sister the harpsichord, while his sister Frances was the group's singer. When Granville Sharp's head wasn't filled with religious schemes, he thought about music: the family's evening rehearsals, the next concert or weekend session with other musicians and an audience including some of London's most prominent people, how to teach music to children—he was writing a book on that. He saw Black people on the street, or dressed in silken liveries as servants to the rich. But London's Black population and their plight, and the plight of tens of thousands of their enslaved brothers and sisters laboring and dying in the West Indies and American colonies, were not a noticeable presence in his crowded brain and imagination—that is, until the day he met Jonathan Strong outside his brother William's clinic for London's poor, sick, and debilitated.

As usual, there was a line of people in medical straits outside William's door, but one young man looked near the verge, barely able to stand, his head swollen, his face a mask of blood. Sharp brought him instantly to see his brother William, and while William administered first aid the brothers listened to his story. Jonathan Strong was enslaved to a vicious master who beat him regularly, this time clubbing him with his pistol until it broke. Then, seeing that he was almost dead, his enraged owner had thrown him out on the street as worthless goods. But instead of dying, Jonathan had managed to get up and stagger to the surgeon's house, where he joined the long line of other unfortunates.

After making some minor repairs to Strong's wounds, William had him admitted to St. Bartholomew's Hospital, where it took Strong four months to recover at least enough to function on the outside. On his release, the Sharps got Strong a job as a delivery person for a pharmacist. But two years later, Strong had the bad luck to be spotted by his former owner as he was attending the pharmacist's wife as a footman. What the former owner, David Lisle, saw was a healthy, valuable piece of property, which, in his view, he still owned. With the market for slaves in the West Indies booming, Lisle sold Strong to a Jamaican planter, which meant Lisle first had to repossess him. Tracking his former property to a pub, Lisle paid two strongarms to grab Strong and take him to the Poultry Compter prison, where he could be kept as a captured runaway until the ship captain Lisle contracted with could take possession and transport him to his new owner's Jamaican plantation.

In prison, the distraught Strong managed to get a message to his old savior, Granville Sharp. Outraged, Sharp demanded that Strong not be released to any outside party until his case could be heard by the lord mayor.

Curiously, the jailer agreed, probably because Sharp threatened him with legal action, and Strong's case went to the lord mayor over the objections of Lisle and the ship captain. When the lord mayor ruled that since Strong hadn't broken any laws he was free to go, Lisle became furious. When the lord mayor left the room, Lisle and the captain laid hold of Strong and started to take him away, at which point Sharp shouted, "I charge you in the name of the king with an assault upon the person of Jonathan Strong."[12] Intimidated, Lisle and the captain unhanded Strong, who walked away with Sharp, a free man.

That wasn't the end, though. Lisle brought suit against Sharp for kidnapping and deprivation of property. When he lost the suit, he challenged Sharp to a duel, which Sharp declined, telling Lisle that since Lisle was a lawyer as well as a planter he should be satisfied with the remedies provided by the law. The trial was a limited victory. It indicated nothing about the legality of slavery in any fundamental way, only that Jonathan Strong himself was a free man and could not be considered someone's property.

When these events began, Granville Sharp knew nothing about either slavery or the law. But he was shocked by the idea that British common law might allow human beings in England to be owned as chattel. He hadn't given any thought to it before; he refused to believe it. So he put himself to work researching legal history. As he did he by chance found in a bookstore a copy of Benezet's *Short Account of That Part of Africa Inhabited by Negroes.*

Sharp finding *A Short Account* was one of those improbable accidents of history that prove to have huge consequences. The fact that Benezet's tract was in a bookstore was itself almost a miracle. Benezet had sent several copies to Joseph Phipps, along with his letter, three years earlier. He had at the same time sent an identical letter to Dr. John Fothergill, a royal physician and, like Phipps, a leading figure among British Friends.[13] It's almost certain that he sent *Short Account* booklets to Fothergill too. He was in the habit of including articles and tracts on slavery to any of his correspondents if he thought they might bring some benefit. It's possible he sent copies to other British Friends as well, although we don't have evidence of that. In any event, there could not have been more than a few copies of the booklet in circulation in 1765 when Sharp began his education about Black slavery and England's complicity in it.

In *A Short Account* Sharp understood immediately that he had something in hand that could help with his case. He didn't know who Benezet was, and without waiting to find out or receive permission he reprinted the pamphlet, added his own conclusion, and distributed it to bookstores.[14] It didn't sell well, he reported later, but the tract's impact on Sharp himself was far more significant than a few extra sales might have been. "The tract helped Sharp form his arguments," says Maurice Jackson, "especially about the humanity of the Africans, because *A Short Account* gave Sharp vital empirical information about Africa and tied the antislavery cause to the ideas of some of the philosophers of the Scottish Enlightenment."[15]

Sharp was eventually to become England's leading abolitionist, but during the Strong case he was just at the beginning of his learning curve. There were, in fact, no other books or tracts available that could have provided the array of information and arguments that he found in *A Short Account*. Benezet had spent years striving to educate Quakers and other Americans about the equal humanity of Africans and the vileness of the trade in human bodies. But he never had a more consequential student than Granville Sharp.

Once started, Sharp became obsessive. A quick learner, he also had a penchant for in-depth research. As a young man he had learned Greek and Hebrew so he could dispute with a Christian adversary about the New Testament and with a Jewish adversary about the Talmud. For all his eccentricity (which might have led some to underestimate him), Sharp possessed a serious intellect. In 1769 he published *A Representation of the Injustice and Dangerous Tendency of Tolerating Slavery, or Admitting the Least Claim of Private Property in the Persons of Men in England*, in which he declared, "By the English laws, no man, of what condition soever, to be imprisoned, or any way deprived of his LIBERTY without a legal process." "God be thanked," Sharp wrote, "there is neither law nor even a precedent, (at least I have not been able to find one) of a legal determination to justify a master in claiming or detaining any person whatsoever as a slave in England, who has not voluntarily bound himself as such by a contract in writing."[16]

The Strong case drew attention. A Black man owned by a white man given his freedom by the lord mayor was hardly believable. The decision put a spotlight on the person responsible, Granville Sharp, the semi-famous flute virtuoso for the Sharp family band. Meanwhile, as he made himself an expert on the common law, Sharp launched himself into a nonstop one-man campaign to set England straight regarding its own heritage of personal freedom, applied in particular to the disgrace of Black slavery. He wrote to William Blackstone, the Vinerian Professor of Law at Oxford; he wrote to the archbishop of Canterbury; he wrote to the lord chancellor; he wrote to Lord North, the prime minister; he wrote to anyone who came onto his radar screen as someone who should be written to. Along with his letters he sometimes sent a copy of his tract, *A Representation of the Injustice*. Sometimes he sent clips of reward notices for runaway slaves or advertisements for slave sales: "To be sold, a Black Girl . . . eleven years of age"—as a means of illustrating his points or embarrassing the recipients.[17] He was becoming, in Simon Schama's words, "a tireless public nuisance," but also someone who could be applied to for help when an egregious kidnapping or slave capture took place.[18]

As he became more practiced in these matters, he kept a sharp eye out for a case that would unequivocally test the right to own slaves in Great Britain. The Strong decision had been made on narrow grounds; it applied only to Strong himself. Another well-publicized case he took on and won was decided because there was no valid sales contract. What he wanted was a pure and clean situation that put the question of the right to enslave on the block.

In 1772 he found such a case in the person of James Somerset, an enslaved man who had been brought by his master from Massachusetts to England and was now being shipped by his owner for sale in Jamaica after being recaptured as a runaway. Somerset had, though, been baptized in England, and his godparents applied for a writ of *habeas corpus*, which was granted. The chief justice of the King's Bench, Lord Mansfield, set the trial for February 1772 with himself presiding. Would Somerset by law be returned to his master for sale in Jamaica, or would he be considered free and his own man?

One of Sharp's acquaintances, Dr. John Fothergill, it turned out, was also a friend of the heretofore unknown author, Anthony Benezet, the same John Fothergill to whom Benezet had sent copies of *A Short Account of That Part of Africa* in 1762. John Fothergill's brother Samuel was even closer to Benezet; it was to Samuel that the depressed Benezet had written in 1758 about needing counsel and comfort in his low state of "inward poverty" (see chapter 9). From the Fothergills Benezet had received a copy of Sharp's *Representation of the Injustice*. In that book Benezet recognized a comrade in the war against slavery, and he wrote to Sharp, initiating a yearslong partnership that wedded the American and English efforts and played a key role in eventually shutting down Great Britain's participation in "the accursed thing"—which Sharp lived to see, though Benezet did not.

The exchange of letters between the two began while the Somerset case was underway. To defend Somerset, Sharp engaged a team of four lawyers, including serjeants-at-law William Davy and John Glynn, both famous courtroom performers. They argued that England's common law nowhere recognized slavery, nor had Parliament ever passed a positive law permitting it; therefore, slavery in England proper was illegal, regardless of its status in other lands, the North America colonies, for example, Barbados or Jamaica. On behalf of James Somerset's owner, the opposing lawyers maintained that

England's property laws covered people held in bondage despite the absence of specific legal mention in either common or statutory law. Beyond that, they argued, freeing all slaves in England (perhaps fourteen or fifteen thousand of them throughout the country) would wreak havoc on the economy and disrupt the nation's social order.

Lord Mansfield was a renowned legal scholar and an acute observer of political as well as social and economic behavior. He hated this case because of its potential for setting off an earthquake in England's settled social customs and business practices, and he tried various ways of rerouting it, including urging one of Somerset's godparents to simply buy and manumit him, an overture that went nowhere. Mansfield had faced the same dilemma in several other cases brought by Sharp and had always found ways to decide them without setting an intolerable precedent. He was firmly on the side of stability and was widely expected to decide that the law was on the side of Somerset's owner. But Sharp also knew about Mansfield's unusual domestic situation. Lord and Lady Mansfield were guardians of a Black girl who was the daughter of their nephew, a naval captain who had "rescued" the girl's mother from a Spanish ship he had captured. Mansfield was raising his Black great niece together with a white great niece for whom he was also guardian. The two girls had a close, sisterly relationship, and Mansfield's Black ward was considered part of the family. To what extent that relationship might influence the thoroughly conservative chief justice was a matter of speculation.[19]

In the 1765 Strong case, Sharp had made use of Benezet's *A Short Account of That Part of Africa*. Seven years later, when the potentially more momentous Somerset case came to docket, another Benezet book fell into his hands. At that opportune moment, John Fothergill presented Sharp with a number of copies of Benezet's recently published major opus, *Some Historical Account of Guinea*. Sharp later wrote to Benezet, "I was able to immediately dispose of six: one to Lord Mansfield, the Chief Justice, one to Lord North, first lord commissioner of the Treasury; and four to the learned Counsel who had generously undertaken to plead gratis for Somerset."[20] The book gave serjeants Davy and Glynn and the junior barristers in-depth information about Black slavery and the nefarious trade; it made them experts and provided ammunition. No doubt it stoked their emotions about the cause they were arguing for. Mansfield received the book and may or may not have read some of it. Sharp was an increasingly painful thorn in his side, and getting this lengthy Benezet polemic from him couldn't have improved his disposition.

Mansfield handed down his decision in Westminster Hall on June 22, 1772. "The cause returned," he declared to a hushed audience,

> is, the slave absented himself, and departed from his master's service, and refused to return and serve him during his stay in England; whereupon by his master's orders, he was put on board the ship by force, and there destined in secure custody, to be carried out of the kingdom and sold. So high an act of dominion must derive its authority, if any such it has, from the law of the kingdom where executed. A foreigner cannot be imprisoned here on the authority of any law existing in his own country. . . . The power claimed by this *return* [the claim of Somerset's owner for the right to sell his slave] was never in use here; no master ever was allowed here to take a slave by force to be sold abroad because he had deserted from his service, or for any other reason whatever. . . . *Therefore the black must be discharged* [emphasis added].[21]

When Mansfield and the associate judges left the hall, the Black people in the audience bowed to them in reverence for a decision that seemed to restore their rights as human beings. Then they celebrated. They and many other observers believed that Mansfield had ruled slavery illegal in England. But he hadn't. He had ruled only that England had no laws pertaining to slavery and that those who been enslaved in another country who came to England could not be unwillingly sold abroad. Sharp got something, but not what he wanted. Mansfield had escaped his clutches again. Still, the decision attracted wide attention; it was covered in all the newspapers and was discussed and debated in every coffeehouse. It triggered a wave of thought about abolition where previously the subject had hardly been noticed.

Sharp informed Benezet of Mansfield's decision in an August 1772 letter. Benezet may already have known; the Somerset case had been covered in American as well as British newspapers. He most likely took the news with a measure of calm. He understood all too well how easy it was for people to do nothing about slavery, despite knowing about its horrors—because that's precisely what happened after the publication of *A Caution and a Warning*.

In 1766, the Philadelphia Meeting had printed and distributed two thousand copies of *A Caution and a Warning* and paid for another 1,500 to be printed in Great Britain. More were produced later and sent out. It was by far Benezet's most widely disseminated work.[22] He undoubtedly had great hopes the tract would generate not only support but action. In that optimistic mood he wrote letters and sent books to increase the momentum such a large distribution was likely to produce. *A Caution* coupled secular arguments from Hutcheson, Wallace, and Foster with Benezet's fervent evocation of "gospel truths"; it combined logic with faith, appeals to natural rights and revealed religion. The writing was lucid, powerful, moving. Despite his innate humility, Benezet almost surely was satisfied with this effort. His mission enveloped him, and this was a significant opportunity to expand his reach, to consequential people especially.

The Society for the Propagation of the Gospel was near the top of Benezet's correspondence list. The SPG was the Church of England's missionary arm, organized initially by Thomas Bray, the clergyman who lent his name to the Bray Associates (see chapter 8). The SPG was chartered to send priests and teachers to the North American colonies and the West Indies; their remit included enslaved Africans and Indigenous people. In addition to preaching the gospel, the SPG owned and ran the Codrington Sugar Plantation in Barbados, which like other West Indies sugar plantations was a place of brutal labor and early death. Its absentee board of governors included the Regius Professors of Divinity at Oxford and Cambridge and the archbishop of Canterbury. The archbishop, noticing the high death rate and the need to continually replenish the slave population, wondered at some point if there wasn't some "defect of humanity" at work or "even [of] good (business) policy," apparently deciding, though, that "we must take things as they are at present."[23]

The SPG, which was highly connected in England, was starting to discuss treating slaves more humanely, and Benezet must have anticipated that it would be responsive to an appeal. "Gentlemen," he wrote, "I make bold hereby, respectfully to salute you, and let you know that I have, with much satisfaction, observed, by the last years printed acct. of the Transactions of your Society, that the unjust Captivity and Grievious Sufferings of the Negroes, in the British Plantations are become the objects of your Consideration."[24]

Readers today might wonder if this was too undiplomatic a greeting, considering that the SPG itself operated a plantation. But Benezet continued, "I herewith transmit to your Society a number of treatises published here, viz. *A Caution to Great Britain and her Colonies* with respect to the Negro Trade, which contains a particular acct. of the corrupt motives & wicked means by which that infamous Trafick of our fellow Creatures, (free by Nature and as well as we the Objects of redeeming Grace) are annually brought to a miserable and untimely End." The slave trade, he told the SPG, "is the biggest impediment to the promulgation of the Gospel of Jesus Christ."[25] Benezet most likely did not know that the Codrington Plantation typically bought thirty slaves a year to replace those who had expired, though he certainly knew about the deadly conditions that prevailed on sugar plantations generally.[26] Codrington existed, as did all the West Indies sugar operations, precisely *because* the "infamous Trafick of our fellow Creatures" made their operations possible.

Benezet's objective in this letter was hardly to point out the SPG's hypocrisy. He simply believed that Christians couldn't fail to help confront such a sinful violation of everything Christ embodied and taught—if only they understood that correctly. "Permit me, Gentlemen," he wrote, "respectfully, and yet earnestly, to request that you would seriously consider whether the necessity of at least endeavoring to put a Stop to this infamous Traffick, is not an Object peculiarly worthy the attention & labor of a Society appointed for the Propagation of the Gospel—whether by your appointment, you are not more particularly those from whom it's expected an effectual alarm will be sounded on such an occasion, where-in the Cause of Christianity & and the Welfare of the Nation are so deeply concern'd."[27]

This must have been an extremely difficult letter for Benezet to compose. He wanted to enlist the SPG in his fight against the slave trade, yet the SPG was benefiting from the trade. He must have given a good deal of thought to how to couch this missive. How could he ask these people to help "raise the attention and inform the judgment" of king and Parliament ("those whose Business & Duty it is to put a stop to the Trade") without alienating them by reference to the evils of the trade?[28] Could that circle be squared, at least in an introductory letter?

It couldn't, of course. Even if he could have written a judicious and respectful letter, the whole purpose was to get them to read the enclosed *A Caution and a Warning*, which was as blunt as you could get. It would be fascinating to know how he felt when he received their response.

Benezet wrote to the SPG on April 26, 1767. The response from the group's secretary, Daniel Burton, is dated February 3, 1768, more than nine months later. The SPG board clearly didn't feel a strong sense of urgency about the issue.

> Sir:
> Your letter to the society for Propagating the Gospel in foreign parts of the 26th of April last, hath been considered by them with all due attention, & I am directed to assure you, that they have great esteem for you, on account of the tenderness & humanity which you have expressed for the Negro Slaves, & are extremely desirous that they should be treated with the utmost care & kindness, both with regard to Temporals and Spirituals.[29]

Burton assured Benezet that the SPG's slaves had always been treated with great care and that the board (made up of absentee owners) had sent inquiries and instructions to make sure the humane treatment was continuing. Further, the board members hoped their example would influence other slave owners. "*But*," Burton wrote,

> they [the SPG] cannot condemn the practice of keeping Slaves as unlawful, finding the contrary very plainly implied in the precept, given by the Apostles. Both to Masters & Servants; which last were for the most part Slaves: And if the doctrine of unlawfulness of Slavery should be taught in our Colonies, the Society apprehend that Masters, instead of being convinced of it, will grow more suspicious and cruel, and much more unwilling to let their slaves learn Christianity; and that the poor Creatures themselves if they come to look on this doctrine, will be most strongly tempted by it to rebel against their Masters, that the most dreadful consequences to both will be likely to follow; And therefore, tho' the Society is fully satisfied that your intention in this matter is perfectly good, Yet they most earnestly beg you not to go further in publishing your Notions, but rather to retract them, if you shall see cause, which they hope you may, on further consideration.
>
> I am, with great regard, & esteem Your affectionate & humble servt.
> D. Burton[30]

Not only would the SPG not support Benezet in his endeavors to stop the slave trade, they urged him to retract his *notions* in that regard. Benezet had thought a major reason for apathy about the trade was that people weren't conscious of the reality of its evils. Some years back he had even written to the archbishop of Canterbury, Thomas Secker: "How an evil of so deep a dye, has so long, not only passed unnoticed, but has even had the countenance of the government, and been supported by law, is surprising, it must be because many worthy men in power, both of the laity and clergy, have been unacquainted with the horrible wickedness with which the trade is carried on."[31]

His job, then, was to educate them. If he could do that effectively, how could they not be persuaded? The SPG's response no doubt went some way toward disabusing him of that theory.

The response from the parliamentary recipients of *A Caution and a Warning* wasn't encouraging either. Perhaps eight hundred copies of the book reached the hands of parliamentarians and other policymakers. But from them there was no action either. Some years before, Benezet had expressed the conviction to Joseph Phipps that lawmakers could not be "so void of feeling" that they would allow the "enormous Evil" of slavery to continue. But he was wrong.

That apathy must have been frustrating, but perhaps not as troubling as what he learned when he sent *A Caution and a Warning* to his old friend Sophie Hume with a request that she distribute it. Hume was a Quaker minister from South Carolina who lived in London for many years but had come back to visit her former home. She responded that she "encountered strong resistance from Carolinians who refused to accept Benezet's antislavery literature."[32] Indifference from a legislature was one thing. Benezet was nothing if not a persistent man. He might have been severely disappointed, but he wasn't going to be deterred by that. Hardcore resistance from ordinary citizens was another matter. That was, as he wrote back to Hume, "grevious, very grevious."[33]

In the words of historian Jonathan Sassi, "After such rejections Anthony Benezet must have realized that slavery would not come tumbling down just because he had blown his trumpet, if indeed he had ever been so naively optimistic."[34] The rebuffs were sobering. They no doubt attuned Benezet further to the hardness of heart that he was increasingly to identify with humanity's incessant demand for more acquisitions and greater wealth—that "insatiable desire for gain," as he put it in *A Short Account*.[35]

The callousness and hypocrisy Benezet met with in the aftermath of *A Caution and a Warning* might have daunted him. We know that while he wasn't prone to depression, neither was he invulnerable to it. He had nearly given in to despair back in 1757 when he wrote to his close friend Samuel Fothergill about his "deepest sense of inward poverty," his unaccountable feelings of "weakness," "desertion," and "instability." But those didn't last. We hear no reflection about that; no meditation on depression came out of it. He wasn't given to self-display, and he continually found the strength and energy to get on with what he saw as his purpose in life. Less than a year before his death, when his health was failing, Benezet wrote, "Prayer, watching & contemplation, could I reach it, seems the most earnest longing of my mind; nevertheless necessary action seems continually pressing, which I dare not refuse."[36] When assessing Benezet, with his generous spirit and unfailing altruism, it's easy to overlook the iron will that sustained and drove him over decades of uphill, often disheartening battle.

Whatever the depth of his disappointment over the lack of tangible effect *A Caution and a Warning* produced (despite the more than 5,500 copies eventually in print), in the years after its publication Benezet spun together a transatlantic network of prominent allies, including Benjamin Franklin, John

Wesley, Benjamin Rush, the Abbé de Raynal, and the redoubtable Granville Sharp, each of whom brought his own influence to bear. He also wrote his longest, most detailed, and by far best organized book: *Some Historical Account of Guinea.* That book powered abolitionists and abolitionism during the rest of Benezet's life and well after he passed.

CHAPTER THIRTEEN

Going Public

Despite its wide distribution, *A Caution and a Warning* did not have anything like the effect Benezet had hoped for. Almost every parliamentarian received the book, as did George III and his councillors. But the response was mainly silence, at best a cursory acknowledgment. For fifteen years he had been speaking, writing, accosting his fellow Philadelphians with solicitations, pamphlets, and petitions. "It's tiresome," one of his friends said, "to hear Anthony always saying the same thing."[1] But he was relentless, and the anger evident in his earliest writing had become increasingly pronounced. In *A Caution and a Warning*, it was white-hot.

By the time he began writing *A Caution*, the slave trade, its inhuman cruelties, its vast number of murders had simply become intolerable to him. An excerpt from *Two Dialogues on the Man-Trade*, which he had incorporated into the earlier *Short Account*, he used again here; it served to articulate his rage. What a "load of blood-guiltiness . . . now lies upon your souls," the author told enslavers. "What crime that is more heinous can you name than that in the habitual, deliberate practice of which you now live? How can you lift up your guilty eyes to heaven? How can you pray for mercy . . . to think what calamities, what havoc and destruction . . . you have been the authors of for filthy lucre's sake."[2] If the author of *Two Dialogues* actually was the former slave ship captain and now penitent priest John Newton, this passage revealed the lasting torment of the guilty soul.

A Caution and a Warning combined religious admonishments with arguments from natural and civil law. The Golden Rule is here. So is the certainty of divine retribution and final judgment ("What will you do in the end," the author asks the perpetrators, ". . . under all that load of blood guiltiness that now lies upon your souls?")[3] This is Benezet's voice if not his hand. The tract embodied Enlightenment arguments of rights and liberties from Hutcheson, Wallace, and Foster. Montesquieu, author of *L'esprit des lois*, makes an appearance. There's also an emphasis on English traditions of legal justice: "Since our English law is so truly valuable for its justice, how can they overlook these barbarous deaths of the unhappy Africans without trial or due proof of their being guilty of crimes adequate to their punishment. Why are those masters of vessels . . . thus suffered to be the sovereign arbiters of the lives of the miserable Negroes, and allowed with impunity thus to destroy (may I not properly say, to murder) their fellow creatures . . . ?"[4]

Benezet had brought it all to bear using the rhetorical methods he had pioneered, the graphic scenes with their indelible images, the empiricism of detail and proof, the unimpeachable witnesses, and the most compelling language he was capable of. And yet his objective seemed as distant as ever. He, along with John Woolman and a few others, had indeed convinced the Philadelphia Friends. He had made serious inroads in the attitude of other Philadelphians and Pennsylvanians (in 1773, Benjamin Rush wrote to Granville Sharp, "Anthony Benezet stood alone a few years ago, in opposing Negro slavery in Philadelphia; and now three fourths of the province, as well as the city, cry out against it").[5] *A Caution and a Warning* had gone out to the right people in England. But despite these successes there was still no real progress in stopping "the accursed thing," which had its own terrible momentum.

Sometime—most likely in 1770, three and a half years after the publication of *A Caution and a Warning*—Benezet began researching and writing what was to be his magnum opus, *Some Historical Account of Guinea*.[6] By then, copies of *A Caution and a Warning* were "becoming scarce," and one can assume that he felt an increasing urgency to get something else in print. "Time," he wrote to his close friend Sam Fothergill, "has given an opportunity of a farther insight in the progress & and consequence thereof . . . to make some additions, in order to set the Origine & Nature of the Trade &c in a more regular order."[7]

By "some additions," he meant some additions to *A Caution and a Warning*, and in *Some Historical Account,* he did make use of substantial material from his earlier tract. But the new book turned out to be a different animal, and it raised Benezet from an impassioned polemicist to someone much larger and more consequential.

Granville Sharp had written to Benjamin Rush—Benezet had introduced them—that sales of *A Caution and a Warning* were so dismal that "when I reprinted Mr. Benezet's acco't. of Africa in 1768, so few Copies were sold that I gave away, by degrees, almost the whole impression being determined to make it as publick as I could." The meager sales Sharp blamed in the same letter on the fact that books *not* on entertaining subjects didn't sell because of the "Depravity of the generality of Readers."[8]

The weak response to *A Caution* must have moved Benezet to ask himself what in the world *would* work. He had put everything he had into the tract. The anecdotes and stories were enough to break your heart with their unspeakable violence and violation of human decency. If they couldn't stoke rage—and action—what could? What new take on the subject or new way of expressing it could he muster that would draw readers and rally people to the cause?

Benezet was in a classic dead end, with nowhere to go. His initial thought was to add some additional excerpts, stories, statistics, or other information that would reinforce what he had said before. But he also asked a few of his close collaborators for editorial comments or fresh ideas; he was in the habit of sending works in progress to friends and requesting feedback. One of these requests, to Samuel Allinson, is intriguing. Allinson was a leading attorney in New Jersey, a Quaker, clerk of the Burlington Meeting, and no doubt a competent writer; he had been selected by New Jersey's legislature to prepare the *Laws of New Jersey* for the printer. Benezet wrote to Allinson while he was composing *Some Historical Account*, "When I have proceeded a little farther . . . I shall earnestly request a little of thy time seriously to peruse and candidly to make thy remarks and such addition as may occur thereon; for which purpose I leave a blank leaf facing each written one."[9] Providing a full facing page for each written page suggests that Benezet was hoping for a large number of possibly extensive suggestions.

In the end, his ever-creative mind gave him what he believed was the answer to his dead-end problem. He needed something more convincing, much harder to deny or ignore. He chose first to enlarge the book substantially, using many of the same arguments and admonishments but with more descriptions and witnesses and greater detail. Second, he decided to organize the book so it could be used easily, to set the facts "in a more regular order than had yet been done."[10] "He wanted it," David Crosby writes, "to be a resource to other like-minded activists who might draw from it the rhetorical ammunition needed to fight the guns, bullets, and bribes of the slave traders."[11]

Both of his aims are evident at a glance. The book is impressively larger. *A Caution and a Warning* counted forty-six pages; the new *Some Historical Account* came in at 144. The earlier "book" was really a largish pamphlet. The new effort looked and felt like a real book. Readers' expectations were partly set by this kind of difference. A pamphlet bore the aspect of a relatively brief polemic, which is how it tended to be read. A book was likely to be much more serious; it required a more serious attention.

The text's organization was likewise far different from what had gone before. *Some Historical Account* included front matter: a formal table of contents, followed by an introduction, where Benezet noted that the book was "for the satisfaction of the serious enquirer."[12] The table of contents informed readers concisely but clearly of each chapter's subject matter. The first three chapters, for example, described the three primary geographic regions that furnished the bulk of captives: the climate, which "agrees well with the natives, but extremely unhealthful to the Europeans"; the soil ("rich, deep, amazingly fertile"); the produce from the different regions ("rice, millet, yams, potatoes, Indian corn, all sorts of trees, fruits, roots and herbs"); the great rivers, the Senegal and Gambia, and the peoples in these regions—Mandingoes, Jolofs, Fulis—and their dispositions, characteristics, and ways of life. Chapters 4 and 5 related the history of these places, from older times to the slaving present. Chapter 10 described how African governments functioned. The book was an accessible, substantial encyclopedia of the slave trade rather than simply a hit-or-miss, condemnatory broadside.

In composing it this way Benezet did not just provide a large amount of information in usable form; he considerably elevated his own stature. Prior to *Some Historical Account* it was easy for general readers to regard him as an angry, one-horse polemicist. With this new book he took on a different aspect. He was every bit as moral and implacable, but now he could be seen as a scholar, with a scholar's breadth of knowledge as well as a moralist's passion. "[He] became," Nancy Hornick writes, "the leading humanitarian reformer and social critic of late eighteenth century America."[13]

As different as *Some Historical Account* was, Benezet didn't have high hopes for it. The sales experience of *A Caution and a Warning* warned against optimism. "I have but small expectation of the service this publication may be of," he wrote to English Friends John and Henry Gurney, "considering the selfishness that so much prevails among all orders of men; but however I shall have the satisfaction of having done what I could to set this weighty matter in a true point of view." That rang a note of resignation. "How unfeeling for the sufferings of others," he laments, "how languid [we are] in our endeavors for their relief."[14]

But if Benezet allowed himself some sneaking underground pessimism, his actions displayed only his usual vigorous pursuit of allies and objectives. The Gurney brothers were widely influential bankers and industrialists whom Benezet did not know personally but was actively trying to recruit. In the same long letter where he expressed his doubts, his main purpose was to get the Gurneys to bring their influence to bear. "Can we be innocent and yet spectators of this mighty infringement of every human and sacred right?" he asked them. "Is it not the duty of everyone who knows these things, to do all in their power . . . to bring this matter before king and parliament? Will any thing short of this excuse us to God . . . ?"[15]

At about the same time, he sent copies of *Some Historical Account* to other prominent London Friends, including John Fothergill and the banker David Barclay, suggesting that it was the duty of the London Meeting or at least some group of Friends there "to lay the iniquity & dreadful consequences of the Slave Trade before the Parliament, desiring a stop may be put to it."[16] Five years earlier, copies of *A Caution and a Warning* had been distributed to nearly every parliamentarian, which had failed to generate any measurable enthusiasm. Now Benezet was assaulting Parliament again, urging friends and others to use their influence and lay the case before the MPs and Lords. This was not a man easily stymied by frustration. It's hard to think he was optimistic about the prospect, but he was going to apply pressure any way he could, and keep applying it. Maybe some effort or another would break through the dam of apathy and indifference. We don't hear of this overture to the Friends generating a response, but Benezet could at least assume he was planting seeds.

In fact, Fothergill did get back to him, with affirmations of friendship and warm regards, if not with any news of action on the Friends' part. Benezet responded, telling Fothergill that the Pennsylvania assembly would send a proposal to king and Parliament to impose a twenty-pound duty on each slave transaction, which would effectively end the trade in the province. He asked Fothergill to be ready to support the proposal if the opportunity came up and included a copy of his letter to Benjamin Franklin, in London as Pennsylvania's agent, likewise urging his support. The best they could do, he told Fothergill, was to "draw the notice of governments."[17]

Franklin was a longtime friend, "a fellow pilgrim on a dangerous and heavy road," as Benezet called him in a letter written the day before his missive to Fothergill. In it he urged Franklin to keep the cause "precious in thy eyes" and asked him to think whether there might be at least something in his power that he could do—though he warned that Franklin could expect a good deal of "disagreeable opposition" from those who "laugh at human nature & compassion and defy all religion [except] that of getting money." Nevertheless, he says, the "testimony of a good conscience" brings a good deal of comfort on a "winter's evening."[18]

These undertones of doubt and resignation suggest how hard the struggle had become for Benezet. He was troubled by fluttering intimations of failure, but at the same time he was doing everything he could to press his case. His major work had just been published; he was rallying friends and allies and making connections one to another. Beneath it all ran an unshakable religious faith that sustained him through frustration and disappointment. "Nothing of this kind," he told Franklin, "is so difficult but, thro' the divine blessing it may succeed."[19]

Meanwhile, Benezet introduced Franklin to Sharp. "I am glad to understand," he wrote to Sharp, "that you have commenced an acquaintance, and that he expects in future to act in concert with thee in the affair of slavery."[20] At Benezet's urging, Franklin had written a short piece for the *London Chronicle* on the James Somerset case that Sharp had precipitated. Taking his numbers from Benezet, Franklin wrote that "there are now about eight hundred and fifty thousand Negroes in the English Islands and Colonies; and . . . the yearly importation is about one hundred thousand, of which number about one third perish by the gaol distemper on the passage, and in the sickness called the *seasoning* before they are set to labour." "So much misery [is] produced among our fellow creatures, and such a constant butchery of the human species by this pestilential detestable traffic in the bodies and souls of men."[21] The campaign to influence public sentiment was now underway, paralleling Benezet's focus on Parliament and the potential for legislative action.

Shortly after Franklin and Sharp became acquainted, Benjamin Rush approached Sharp, also at Benezet's urging. Benezet had persuaded the young Dr. Rush to write his own antislavery tract, which he did after some coaxing, entitling it *An Address to the Inhabitants of the British Settlements in America, upon Slave-keeping*. He wrote it, Rush told Franklin, "at the particular request of a worthy citizen [Benezet] to accompany a Petition to the Assembly of Pennsylvania to procure an increase of the Duty upon Negro Slaves imported into the province."[22] Rush used his pamphlet as an entrée to Sharp, writing, "From the amiable character which I have received of you from my worthy friend Mr. Anthony Benezet I have taken the liberty of introducing myself to your correspondence by sending you a pamphlet."[23] It was the beginning of a lifelong correspondence between the two.

Rush and Benezet were fellow Philadelphians, though a generation apart; they had met in 1769 after Rush established his medical practice in the city. Though only twenty-six at the time, Rush already had a reputation as a person of unusual ability. He had showed signs of brilliance early: he graduated from the College of New Jersey (later renamed Princeton) at age fourteen and apprenticed himself to a prominent Philadelphia doctor for a number of years before leaving for Scotland to study medicine formally at the University of Edinburgh. According to historian Donald D'Elia, when Rush debarked in Liverpool, the sight of that city's large slaving fleet enraged him and set him off on his career as a leading abolitionist.[24] Jackson, though, says, "Rush first came to his opposition to slavery through reading, above all Benezet's writings, and then developed his social and moral stance in part as a reaction to his family's and his own ownership of slaves."[25] Rush was an avid Son of Liberty and a signer of the Declaration of Independence. "Do you recollect the pensive and awful silence which pervaded the house," he wrote to John Adams many years later, "when we were called up, one after another . . . to subscribe to what was believed by many at the time to be our own death warrants?"[26] During the Revolution he served as Washington's surgeon general and afterward was appointed professor of medical theory and clinical practice at the University of Pennsylvania. Along with Franklin and Jefferson, he was prominent among American Enlightenment figures.

Benezet wrote to Sharp and Franklin about Pennsylvania's resolution placing a twenty-pound prohibitive tax on slave transactions. He wanted them to be ready with whatever support they could muster when it came before Parliament. In fact, the Pennsylvania assembly had passed the tax resolution under pressure from a Benezet-organized petition drive buttressed by the distribution of Rush's *Address to the Inhabitants of the British Settlements.*[27]

Petitioning was a new front Benezet had opened in his campaign. Sharp was all in favor. Petitions could influence Parliament with their message that the public was turning against slavery. "You mention," Sharp wrote to Benezet, "the information you have received from a person who has spent some time in Maryland and Virginia that he thinks 10 or 20 thousand people would freely join in a Petition to Parliament against the further importation of Negroes. Such a petition would retrieve in some respects the reputation of those colonies."[28] In organizing these multipronged attacks, Benezet was displaying his mature talents as a strategist. Some commentators felt that Benezet's abilities had reached their full expression back in 1762 with *A Short Account of That Part of Africa*. But a decade later, he was still adding to his skills.

He was also adding to his group of allies. The latest to join the list was John Wesley, Methodism's founder and one of the most influential religious figures of his day. We don't know how the two initially came in contact.[29] But when Benezet sent Wesley a copy of *Some Historical Account*, the text struck him with such force that he would confront slavery head-on for the rest of his days. Wesley noted in his journal entry for January 12, 1772, "I read a very different book, published by an honest Quaker, on that execrable sum of all villainies commonly called the slave trade. I read of nothing like it in the heathen world, whether ancient or modern and it infinitely exceeds, in every instance of barbarity, whatever Christian slaves suffer in Mahometan countries."[30]

Wesley had seen slavery up close in Georgia and South Carolina in 1736 and 1737. At the time, slavery was outlawed in Georgia, though the prohibition was often flouted. But he was exposed to the reality of plantation slavery during his visits to South Carolina and had been opposed to slavery since. In 1787 he wrote to Sharp, "Ever since I heard of it first I felt a perfect detestation of the horrid slave trade."[31] Still, slavery did not play much, if any, role in his writing or sermons until he read Benezet's book, which shifted his attention and stoked his anger at the enormity of the institution.

In May 1772, Benezet told Sharp, "My friend John Wesley promises he will consult with thee about the expediency of some weekly publication, in the newspapers, on the origin, nature, and dreadful effects of the slave trade. This appears absolutely necessary, as many well-minded people, who may have some influence, are ignorant of the case; and also because way may be thereby made for a further attempt towards the removal of this potent evil; to which we think nothing will more effectually conduce as a representation to the King and both houses of Parliament."[32] No newspaper articles materialized out of this connection, but Benezet had motivated Wesley otherwise. In 1774 Wesley wrote his own tract arguing for abolition, *Thoughts upon Slavery*, not only using Benezet's ideas and information but copying *Some Historical Account* wholesale. Not that Benezet minded. On the contrary, after Sharp sent him a copy, he immediately wrote to Wesley, "The Tract thou has lately published, entitled, Thoughts Upon Slavery, afforded me much satisfaction. I was the more especially glad to see it, as the circumstances of the times made it necessary that something on that most weighty subject, not large, but striking and pathetic, should now be published. Wherefore I immediately agreed with the Printer to have it republished here."[33]

Benezet did more than simply republish *Thoughts upon Slavery*. He took the opportunity to expand on it, adding five lengthy footnotes, four of them refuting proslavery arguments that had long been in circulation, the fifth reiterating the certainty of divine vengeance. He also added an afterword, which quoted various eyewitness sources describing the astonishingly horrible cruelties and torture murders English, Dutch, French, and, of course, American slave masters utilized in order to keep their slaves cowed and in order, without hope for relief, justice, or revenge. "I sicken at the recital of these horrors," wrote one observer. "My eyes ache with seeing them—my ears with hearing them."[34]

Benezet's attitude toward what we would call plagiarism wasn't exceptional. There were no laws against plagiarism then, and writers, including Benezet himself, often made free use of others' works. In this instance

Benezet was especially pleased to have the support; Wesley was a person of vast influence. Besides that, *Thoughts upon Slavery* didn't merely regurgitate Benezet's words; it brought a new level of firepower, which Benezet appreciated at once. Wesley's book was indeed "striking and pathetic" ("moving") even beyond Benezet's own impassioned rhetoric. Benezet was permanently sick with anger over slavery. His *Some Historical Account* triggered the same emotions in John Wesley.

But whereas Benezet's goals were to get antislavery initiatives in front of king and Parliament, Wesley addressed *Thoughts upon Slavery* to a different audience. He didn't think it made much sense to speak to the public at large. "It may inflame the world against the guilty," he wrote, "but it is not likely to remove the guilt." Nor would it help to appeal to the English nation, "never likely to procure any redress for the sore evil we complain of," nor to Parliament, too busy with issues "which seem of greater importance" to attend to slavery matters.[35] All that being the case, he has a few things to say directly to those most immediately engaged in the sore evil: the captains, merchants, and planters. Wesley's turn of mind, his tone, the acid of his excoriation separates him from even the angriest and most bitter of his antislavery allies.

First to the slave ship captains. You know the land and the people, he tells them, formerly

> so populous and fruitful, now become a dreary, uncultivated wilderness, the inhabitants being all murdered or carried away part by stealth, part by force, part made captive in those wars, which you raise or foment on purpose. You have seen them torn away, children from their parents, parents from their children: husbands from their wives, wives from their beloved husbands, brethren and sisters from each other. You have dragged them who had never done you any wrong, perhaps in chains, from their native shore. You have forced them into your ships like an [*sic*] herd of swine, them who had souls immortal as your own: (only some of them, leaped into the sea, and resolutely stayed under water, till they could suffer no more from you.) You have stowed them together as close as ever they could lie, without any regard either to decency or convenience. And when many of them had been poisoned by foul air, or had sunk under various hardships, you have seen their remains delivered to the deep, till the sea should give up its dead. You have carried the survivors into the vilest slavery, never to end but with life: such slavery as is not found among the Turks at Algiers, no nor among the Heathens in America. May I speak plainly to you? I must. Love constrains me: love to *you*, as well as to those you are concerned with.

> Is there a God? You know there is. Is he a just God? Then there must be a state of retribution: a state wherein the just God will reward every man according to his works. Then what reward will he render to *you*? O think betimes! Before you drop into eternity! Think now, *He shall have judgment without mercy that hath shewed no mercy*. Are you a *man*? Then you should have a *human* heart. But have you indeed? What is your heart made of? Is there no such principle as compassion there? Do you never *feel* another's pain? Have you no sympathy? No sense of human woe? No pity for the miserable? When you saw the flowing eyes, the heaving breasts, or the bleeding sides and tortured limbs of your fellow-creatures, was you a stone, or a brute? Did you look upon them with the eyes of a tiger? When you squeezed the agonizing creatures down in the ship, or when you threw their poor mangled remains into the sea, had you no relenting? Did not one tear drop from your eye, one sigh escape from your breast? Do you feel no relenting *now*? If you do not, you must go on, till the measure of your iniquities is full. Then will the great God deal with *you*, as you have dealt with *them*, and require all their blood at your hands. And at that day it shall be more tolerable for Sodom and Gomorrah than for *you*![36]

Wesley had the same message for merchants and planters as he did for ship captains. He claimed to be speaking to them out of love, ostensibly to convince them to stop what they were doing and repent. "Whatever you lose, lose not your soul: nothing can countervail that loss. Immediately quit the horrid trade: at all events, be an honest man."[37] But far more than love comes through in *Thoughts upon Slavery*; what comes through is revulsion and fury.

Here was a powerful ally indeed, and effective in a different way from Benezet. Benezet was a Christian moralist, Wesley a preacher with a magisterial command of the preacher's art. Benezet's writing was passionate and often moving; Wesley's was poetry disguised as prose. A close reading reveals the essentially oral nature of *Thoughts upon Slavery*, as if Wesley had composed it as a sermon to be delivered. The cadences, the direct questions, the italicized emphases, the repetitions all created a compulsiveness that would have riveted a listening congregation.

> *Do you never feel another's pain? Have you no sympathy? No sense of human woe? No pity for the miserable? When you saw the flowing eyes, the heaving breasts, or the bleeding sides and tortured limbs of your fellow-creatures, was you a stone, or a brute?*

Wesley's mastery of the sermon form was hardly surprising—Methodism was a preaching religion. Wesley didn't call his ministers "priests," the Anglican term, or "pastors," the general Lutheran and Reformed usage; he called them "preachers." He stated in his *Journal* that he "had found no congregation that his voice could not command."[38] In over fifty years he had preached thousands of sermons, often three, four, or even five a day, beginning typically at five o'clock in the morning.

More to the point, Wesley was constantly traveling, preaching in churches and open fields (like his Oxford classmate George Whitefield), enlisting even unordained itinerant preachers as well as confirmed clergy in his rapidly expanding Methodist movement. His reach in 1772 was already extensive and was increasing steadily, and after his reading of Benezet's *Some Historical Account*, abolitionism became an embedded part of his message.[39] "I would to God it may never be found more," he wrote, "that we may never more steal and sell our brethren like beasts; never murder them by the thousands. Oh, may this worse than Mohammedan, worse than pagan abomination be removed from us forever. Never was anything such a reproach to England, since it was a nation, as the having a hand in this infernal traffic."[40] The historian William Lecky considered the abolition of the slave trade "among the three or four perfectly virtuous acts recorded in the history of nations."[41] A hundred years earlier, Wesley had declared that the slave trade was the greatest reproach to England in its history as a nation.

CHAPTER FOURTEEN

Speaking Though in the Tomb

The impact of *Some Historical Account* reverberated long after Benezet's death in 1784. Much of the book was included in early editions of the *Encyclopedia Britannica.* It was, says David Crosby, "the standard early-nineteenth-century source for African history."[1]

Among those it affected was James Forten, the wealthy, Black Philadelphia sailmaker who was a major influence on William Lloyd Garrison and a supporter of Garrison's influential abolitionist newspaper, the *Liberator.* Copies of *Some Historical Account* and *A Caution and a Warning* were, Nancy Hornick writes, among Forten's valued possessions, which "formed an important link with the antebellum abolitionist movement."[2] Forten had attended the Quakers' Africans' School, which Benezet initiated as the successor to the school for Black students he conducted in his home. Together with Absalom Jones (an alumnus of Benezet's home school), Forten was a key figure in the Black abolitionist movement. Both Forten and Jones were dedicated to Black education and were instrumental in the establishment of Black schools. They not only read Benezet (we know Forten did; we can assume Jones did); in certain ways they took him (perhaps unconsciously, or perhaps not) as their model. Benezet's compassion for those undergoing extreme hardship—enslaved people, refugee Acadians, desperate Indians—was in a way mirrored by Jones and his colleague Richard Allen (who may have also been an alumnus of Benezet's school) during Philadelphia's catastrophic 1793 yellow fever epidemic, when their efforts at providing nursing and medical care for the sick and dying were heroic.

In England, two Black abolitionist leaders, Quobna Ottobah Cugoano and Olaudah Equiano, were also greatly influenced by Benezet, by *Some Historic Account* specifically. Ottobah Cugoano was kidnapped from the Gold Coast area (present-day Ghana) when he was thirteen. Enslaved for several years on a plantation in Grenada, he was bought by a Scottish plantation owner who took him to England as his servant. In England he was eventually manumitted, then employed in the household of painters Richard and

Maria Cosway, who taught him to read and write. Cugoano took advantage of their attention to educate himself in some depth. In 1787 he wrote *Thoughts and Sentiments on the Evil and Wicked Traffic of the Slavery and Commerce of the Human Species*, probably with the help of his friend Olaudah Equiano, who had also been kidnapped as a child (see chapter 8).

Thoughts and Sentiments on the Evil and Wicked Traffic was unusual in that Cugoano didn't limit himself to attacking the slave trade or slavery more generally. His may have been the first publication to link the slave trade to the injustices of colonialism globally; he took special aim at Portugal and Spain as well as England. Cugoano's book was popular. It went through three printings, and he toured England with it, visiting "upwards of fifty places."[3] He sent copies to Edmund Burke and George III, though he got no known response from either.

Cugoano had read Benezet's *Some Historical Account* and *A Caution and a Warning*. Instances of Benezet's wording and phrasing occur throughout *Thoughts and Sentiments*. He used Benezet's calculations in figuring the number of slaves carried by British shipping to the Americas, specifically acknowledging Benezet—"The worthy and judicious author of the Historical Account of Guinea, and others, have given some very striking estimates of the exceeding evil occasioned by that wicked diabolical traffic of the African slave-trade; wherein it seems, of late years, the English have taken the lead, or the greatest part of it, in carrying it on."[4]

Cugoano spent only a few of the book's 148 pages relating his own story. The bulk of *Thoughts and Sentiments* was instead taken up with religious arguments and appeals, refutations of proslavery assertions, philosophical observations, and—what was really radical—calls to end not just trading in slaves but slavery itself.

By contrast, *The Interesting Narrative of the Life of Olaudah Equiano, or Gustavus Vassa, the African*, was a true memoir, which may explain its even greater popularity. First published in 1789, *The Interesting Narrative* went through nine printings and was translated into several languages. It was one of the best-selling books of the early 1790s in England, and Equiano toured it successfully for several years. The book was a cultural phenomenon, making Equiano a celebrity author.[5]

In writing *The Interesting Narrative*, Equiano reached into Benezet's *Some Historical Account* for geographical descriptions and discussions of African civil and family life as well as of the treatment of slaves on Caribbean plantations. He acknowledged Benezet in footnotes; at the bottom of one page he noted,

"See Benezet's Account of Africa Throughout."[6] Equiano worked with Wesley on slavery issues, and with Granville Sharp. It was Equiano who brought the *Zong* massacre to Sharp's attention. The slave ship *Zong*'s crew had thrown 130 captives overboard when the ship ran low on water; then, when they reached port, the shipowners had filed a claim for insurance payment on the deceased slaves. Sharp attempted to prosecute the captain and crew for murder. His effort failed, but the incident was widely covered, which provoked a wave of public disgust and greatly stimulated antislavery sentiment.

The books by Cugoano and Equiano were far more popular than Benezet's *Some Historical Account*. For all his forcefulness, Benezet was a man talking about slavery. Cugoano had experienced it in his person. The trauma had never left him. "[The] grevious thoughts which I then felt," he wrote, "still pant in my heart though my fears and tears have long since subsided."[7]

Like Cugoano, Equiano suffered the tortures of the Middle Passage, which he described with harrowing intimacy. Lord Kames had written about "the power of language to raise emotions." Equiano and Cugoano had raised the emotions of many thousands of Englishmen, furthered and in part inspired as they were by Benezet and his works.

For all Benezet meant to Sharp, Rush, Franklin, Wesley, and Black abolitionists on either side of the ocean, his influence on Thomas Clarkson proved most consequential of all. Clarkson, as we saw previously, had won the Cambridge Senior Latin Essay Prize after reading Benezet's *Some Historical Account*. Benezet's book was, Clarkson said later, "instrumental, beyond any other book ever before published, in disseminating a proper knowledge and detestation of this trade."[8]

Some Historical Account had kept Clarkson up night after night with grief. He had expected, he said, that writing the essay would be a pleasure—thinking about his subject, inventing the arguments, composing them, arranging them. It was supposed to be, he said, "an innocent contest for literary honor." Instead, writing the essay turned out to be a severe trial. "After the perusal of Benezet," he wrote later, "I always slept with a candle in my room, that I might rise out of bed and put down such thoughts as might occur to me in the night. . . . Having at length finished this painful task I sent my Essay to the vice-chancellor, and found myself honored as before [the previous year he had won the junior essay prize] with the first prize."[9]

After the prize was announced, Clarkson was called from London to Cambridge to read his essay publicly in the university senate house. On his way back he was so agitated, thinking about what he had written, that he had to get down from his horse occasionally and walk. "I frequently tried to persuade myself in these intervals," he wrote, "that the contents of my Essay could not be true. The more however I reflected on them, or rather on the authorities on which they were founded, the more I gave them credit. Coming in sight of Wades Mill in Hertforshire, I sat down disconsolate on the turf by the roadside and held my horse. Here a thought came into my mind, that if the contents of the Essay were true it was time some person should see these calamities to their end."[10]

Clarkson was twenty-four, destined for the clergy. But he seems to have forgotten that aspiration, at least for a moment, as he found himself preoccupied with thinking about what he had learned from Benezet. "Someone should interfere," he told himself, but he couldn't think of who that might be. If he was a rich MP, he thought, maybe he could do it himself. But he wasn't, and an undertaking of that magnitude seemed to be as daunting as any of the labors of Hercules. He certainly couldn't do it without some credible "coadjutor," but where was he to find such a person? The one thing that *was* in his power, he thought, was to translate his prize essay from the Latin, publish it, and see how the public might receive it.

With that decision, he translated the first half of the essay and went to London hoping to find a publisher. On the street there he happened to run into an old family friend, Joseph Hancock, a Quaker, who told Clarkson he was just the person he wanted to see. Hancock asked Clarkson why he hadn't published his essay yet, that the London Quakers had "long taken up" the issue of slavery and that they wanted to meet with him. In particular, the Quaker publisher James Phillips wanted to meet him, also William Dillwyn, another member of the Society.

The essay contest took place in 1785, a year after Benezet's death. Clarkson met with Phillips and then Dillwyn early in 1786. Phillips was the London Society's official printer and publisher. Among the various antislavery tracts he published was Benezet's *A Caution and a Warning*. His best-known publication, though, was a graphic of the slave ship *Brooks* tightly packed with 482 bodies (supposedly its limit, though the ship had carried 638 captives on the passage before the graphic was produced and 744 on the following passage). Phillips's 1789 graphic was reproduced many hundreds of times in pamphlets, books, and posters. Clarkson said at the time, "It seemed to make an instantaneous impression of horror upon all who saw it."[11] The *Brooks* drawing became the iconic representation of the slave trade and the Middle Passage. Still being reproduced today, it continues to elicit disbelief and horror.

Not long after meeting Phillips, Clarkson spent a day with William Dillwyn at Dillwyn's home. Clarkson wrote, "I soon discovered the treasure I had met with in his local knowledge, both of the Slave-trade and of slavery, as they existed in the United States."[12] Dillwyn did know the American slave trade intimately. He had grown up and gone to school in Philadelphia, where he was a pupil and later close friend and protégé of Benezet. Dillwyn, in fact, was one of the two young miscreants who captured and imprisoned a mouse in the frequently told story about Benezet's gentle demeanor in the classroom (see chapter 6).[13]

Clarkson's meetings with Phillips and Dillwyn stimulated his enthusiasm, and he began writing to friends, sending his translated essay to them, then meeting with them. Clarkson's circle of acquaintances, and the individuals they introduced him to, included several members of Parliament, peers, and others with broad connections, all of whom hated the slave trade, shared their opinions, and offered to help. One was Sir Charles Middleton (later Lord Barham), comptroller of the navy. He told Clarkson he could procure extracts from naval journals and other sources that might be helpful. Middleton's offer opened a new avenue of information for Clarkson. Moreover, he was delighted to find that he and Middleton were neighbors. Middleton and his family lived in the great house called Barham Court in Kent (Clarkson knew it as Teston Hall), "in a park, which was but a few yards from the house in which I then was."[14]

Although Clarkson didn't know it, Lady Middleton was a good friend of Clarkson's future antislavery partner William Wilberforce, who was a frequent guest in the Middletons' home.[15] Friends also introduced Clarkson to Granville Sharp. "I could depend on [Sharp]," Clarkson wrote, "as well as the whole society of the Quakers."[16] Although the campaign he envisioned would require large amounts of money, Clarkson realized he could raise funds from "generous friends" and that "as the Quakers had taken up the cause . . . they would not be behind-hand in supporting it."[17]

Eventually Clarkson understood that if he were to take up the fight of ending the slave trade, he'd have to devote himself to it completely, that "constant exertion would be necessary" and he would have to "make it an object or business of his life." "The question was," he asked himself, "whether I was prepared to make the sacrifice."[18]

Clarkson, outraged morally and driven to do something about it, was Benezet's legitimate heir. But as motivated as he was, he didn't step into that role lightly. It was not an easy decision:

> In favor of the undertaking I urged to myself, that never was any cause, which had been taken up by man in any country or in any age, so great and important; that never was there one in which so much misery was heard to cry for redress; in which the duty of Christian charity could be so extensively exercised; never one, more worthy of the devotion of a whole life towards it. . . . Against these sentiments on the other hand I had to urge, that I had been designed for the church; that I had already been advanced so far as deacon's orders in it; that my prospects there on account of my connections were brilliant: that, by appearing to desert my profession, my family would be dissatisfied, if not unhappy. These thoughts pressed upon me, and rendered the conflict difficult. But the sacrifice of my prospects staggered me, I own, the most. When the other objections . . . occurred to me, my enthusiasm instantly, like a flash of lightning, consumed them: but this stuck to me, and troubled me. I had ambition. I had a thirst after worldly interest and honours, and I could not extinguish it at once. I was more than two hours in solitude under this painful conflict. At length I yielded, not because I saw any reasonable prospect of success in my new undertaking (for all cool-headed and cold-hearted men would have pronounced against it) but in obedience, I believe, to a higher power. And this I can say, that both, on the moment of this resolution, and for sometime afterwards I had more sublime and happy feelings than at any former period of my life.[19]

Clarkson was as methodical as he was determined. Once he had made the decision that would in fact become a lifetime calling, he began to prepare himself "by obtaining further knowledge, for the management of this great cause."[20] Everything he knew about slavery he had learned from reading, notably from Benezet. Now he began looking for people who had been personally involved, to get their stories and observations if he could. He also decided to get a firsthand look at a slave ship. London was one of the major ports for the trade. Liverpool and Bristol handled more of the Africa traffic, but the Thames was home to its own fleet. Clarkson thought, "Why couldn't I get on board them and examine for myself?"[21]

That turned out not to be a problem. A slave ship called the *Fly* was tied up to a wharf and he was allowed to come on board. From his description, it appears to have been easy; the captain and others aboard didn't seem in the least defensive or secretive about what they were doing. They didn't mind showing off and explaining the slave holds, the barricado (possibly with its swivel canons), and some of the ironware slave ships were stocked with to lock down their living cargo. Clarkson's hosts thought he was just curious about the tools of their trade. He, meanwhile, could hardly suppress his horror and indignation at what he was seeing. Later he visited Bristol, Liverpool, and other slave trading ports, interviewing hundreds of sailors and others who had worked in the trade, gathering accounts, and searching out witnesses who might be brave enough to testify in parliamentary or court hearings. In Liverpool and elsewhere he found shops selling the slave-related restraining and torture devices used on the ships: handcuffs, leg irons, chains, whips, thumbscrews, the speculum oris used to pry open the mouths of those trying to kill themselves by refusing to eat. Clarkson bought samples, which he carried with him and used to illustrate his talks.

Sailors and others who had been on slaving voyages came to him, usually surreptitiously, to tell their stories and unburden themselves of guilt by describing what they'd seen or done. But as news about his intentions spread, the places he visited became dangerous. In the major slave trading cities, large numbers of people depended on the trade for their living: sailors, outfitters, merchants, carpenters, shipbuilders, sailmakers, dock laborers, not to mention ship owners and investors. Hostility inevitably mounted. People looked at him with death in their eyes—"savage looks," he said.[22] Threats against his life multiplied. He rarely went outside without a tough, armed companion, usually Alexander Falconbridge, a former slave ship surgeon who had given it up in disgust and become an abolition crusader. Clarkson heard accounts not just of the atrocities practiced onboard to keep the hundreds of captives in order but of the brutality used by many captains against their own sailors and mates. Eighteenth-century officers often treated their seamen harshly, but the slaving enterprise encouraged the sadistic tendencies of more than a few captains, whose crews were at least partly made up of sailors shanghaied from taverns and alehouses.

In Liverpool, Clarkson heard about the murder of a mate named Peter Green by a notorious captain and began investigating. He had learned about the extremely high death rate of sailors on the slave ships, from both disease and ill-treatment, and he was gathering material he thought would be useful in the anti–slave trade campaign. Word of his interest got around, and one day when he was out walking, without Falconbridge for once, he strolled out on Liverpool's high pier, a popular lookout point:

> I was . . . with many others, looking at some little boats below at the time of a heavy gale. . . . I had seen all I intended to see, and was departing, when I noticed eight or nine persons making towards me. I was then only about eight or nine yards from the precipice of the pier, but going from it. I expected that they would have divided to let me through

> them; instead of which they closed upon me and bore me back. I was borne within a yard of the precipice, when I discovered my danger; and perceiving among them the murderer of Peter Green . . . it instantly struck me that they had the design to throw me over the pier-head, which they might have done at this time, and yet pleaded that I had been killed by accident. There was not a moment to lose. Vigorous on account of the danger, I darted forward. One of them against whom I pushed myself, fell down. Their ranks were broken. And I escaped, not without blows, amidst their imprecations and abuse.[23]

Benezet had devoted his life to recognizing Black humanity and ending the slave trade, all without leaving the Philadelphia area. By contrast, Clarkson traveled over thirty-five thousand miles, mostly on horseback, organizing, lecturing, and gathering witnesses—not only dedicating his time and energy but putting himself at grave risk. One wonders what Benezet might have thought about that, or about the antislavery organizing that London Quakers had finally initiated.

In 1782 Benezet wrote to John Fothergill and other London Quakers he knew—no doubt including William Dillwyn—enclosing copies of *Some Historical Account* and asking them to organize against the slave trade. The following year, the Society formed such a group out of its Meeting for Sufferings. In September 1783, that committee asked two of its members—one of whom was Dillwyn—to draw up a "short address to the public on the subject of the slave trade."[24] In response, Dillwyn and his partner wrote *The Case of Our Fellow Creatures, the Oppressed Africans*. The tract has often been ascribed to Benezet, although the minutes of the Meeting for Sufferings make it clear that Dillwyn and his partner drafted the first version, which was subsequently edited by the slave trade committee.[25] Since Dillwyn had been and still was close to Benezet, he likely drew ideas and inspiration, as well as specific language, from his old teacher's writings. With the new parliamentary elections of 1785, the London Meeting printed eleven thousand copies of the tract and distributed them to the king and royal family, cabinet ministers, members of Parliament, and peers and widely through the rest of British society.

Dillwyn often served as the hub of letters and tracts between Benezet and his English correspondents. Having previously lived with his brother George in Burlington, New Jersey, Dillwyn had relocated to London in 1774. Benezet wrote to George Dillwyn in 1783, "I mean to send to thy brother William every publication that may give light & strength to the Testimony, against slavery, in any publication which they may judge necessary to put into the hands of the ruling people."[26] William Dillwyn had grown up under Benezet's tutelage and worked for a while as Benezet's amanuensis; he may have transcribed some of Benezet's earlier writing from dictation. Under Benezet's direction, he spent time in South Carolina studying plantation slavery. Anstey wrote that "in his person Dillwyn epitomized Anglo-American abolitionism."[27] Clarkson believed him "capable of being made the great medium of connection" between the leading abolitionists on both sides of the Atlantic as well as among the various committees forming to further the cause.[28] In that way, and in his person, Dillwyn carried Benezet's words, feeling, and spirit into the antislavery environment that developed after Benezet's death. With all his many frustrations, Benezet planted seeds that took root in English soil, starting with the London Friends' slave trade committee of 1783.

The committee hoped their massive distribution of *The Case of Our Fellow Creatures*, along with a petition to Parliament signed by three hundred Quakers requesting abolishment of the slave trade, would create legislative movement. But they were disappointed—much as Benezet had been—to find the response was more or less inaudible. Not that they were totally surprised. There were no Quakers in Parliament (their religion disqualified them from serving, since they wouldn't swear loyalty to the king), and despite the business success many enjoyed, they were still considered a fringe element, separate from the mainstream and thus without political leverage.

When Clarkson had first met with James Phillips and William Dillwyn, they told him that their Quaker group had noticed him when they first heard about his prize essay. Since then they had been hoping they might somehow engage him with their antislavery efforts. At the same time Clarkson, sitting on the roadside in Hertfordshire holding his horse, had told himself that someone had to do something to put an end to the slave trade. He didn't think he was up to that himself, except maybe if he had the right collaborator. But where would he find such a person? The fact that the Quakers and Clarkson had met and developed a relationship was a kind of miraculous convergence of hopes and needs. Clarkson thought Providence was at work in this; the Quakers no doubt thought so too.

Now, in the spring of 1787, the collaboration between Clarkson and his Quaker friends had ripened to the point where it was semiformalized. They met more or less regularly, Clarkson reported what he had been doing, they discussed and shared ideas about how to move forward. Among his other activities, Clarkson had continued to "wait upon" parliamentarians and others who had been recommended to him, often personally delivering a copy of his published essay by way of introduction.

While James Phillips, the Quaker printer and bookseller, was printing Clarkson's translated essay, he introduced Clarkson to Granville Sharp, and the two began having interesting conversations, the start of an ongoing relationship. Another figure Clarkson became friendly with was William Wilberforce, a parliamentarian known for his reformist efforts and oratorical prowess ("the greatest natural eloquence of all the men I ever knew," said William Pitt), as well as for his beautiful singing voice and conversational wit.[29]

Clarkson's meeting with Wilberforce was another one of those fortunate happenstances. Clarkson was casting a wide net, seeking out individuals with knowledge of the trade but also meeting with any parliamentarian he thought might be responsive. Wilberforce was on his list, a likely prospect. What Clarkson didn't know was that Wilberforce was already somewhat knowledgeable about the slave trade and had already thought at length about it. "He stated frankly," Clarkson wrote about their first meeting, "that the subject had often employed his thoughts, and that it was near to his heart."[30]

Wilberforce didn't just express approval for what Clarkson was doing and offer his support, as many of Clarkson's other contacts had; he began to look into Clarkson's assertions, asking several of Clarkson's witnesses to come see him, including the former slave captain, now Anglican priest, John Newton. After he had talked with Newton and others he told Clarkson he was willing to assist him, though he didn't offer any specifics. But he did ask Clarkson to come back and let him know about his progress.

Clarkson did just that. Even while he was courting other parliamentarians, he began paying special attention to Wilberforce, who seemed increasingly interested in Africa and the fate of Africans. Before long, Clarkson was reporting to Wilberforce regularly on his ongoing research, his discoveries, the work his colleagues were doing. Meanwhile, Wilberforce continued making his own inquiries and sharing those with Clarkson. These meetings were so encouraging that Clarkson's colleagues decided the time was ripe to ask Wilberforce directly if he would lead a parliamentary antislavery campaign. At a dinner that included the painter Joshua Reynolds, James Boswell (Samuel Johnson's friend and future biographer), Sir Charles Middleton (Clarkson's former neighbor at Teston Hall), and several influential pro-abolition members of Parliament (MPs), there was a discussion. When one guest brought up the anticipated fierce opposition of the sugar and shipping interests, another guest MP declared, "Let Liverpool and the islands be swallowed up in the sea, [rather] than this monstrous system of iniquity be carried on."[31] When the question of leadership was "delicately" posed to Wilberforce, he replied "that he had no objection to bring forth the measure in parliament."[32]

That was all Clarkson and his Quaker colleagues needed to hear. On May 22, 1787, they formally constituted themselves as a committee to support a parliamentary campaign, stating that the "slave-trade was both unjust and impolitic" and that their purpose would be to gather and publish information in the interest of abolishing it. They knew their committee membership had to grow beyond the Meeting for Sufferings. Quakers simply didn't have an effective political voice. They needed Anglicans, and of course they needed Clarkson. He was the center, the galvanizing force that was connecting all the dots, doing the research, the speaking, the motivating of those who hated the trade but had seen no opportunity to get involved. They also tapped the more than willing Granville Sharp, who agreed to serve as chairman.

The one significant internal debate the newly minted committee had about its ultimate mission. Should they work to abolish the slave trade, or was their goal the abolition of slavery itself? Sharp argued the latter. He was for full emancipation, which he urged "in a loud voice, a powerful emphasis, and both hands lifted up towards Heaven."[33] The other members thought differently. Moving to abolish slavery itself, they thought, would face too many barriers. Parliament would need to abrogate the power of colonial governments. There would be huge fights over England's long-established protection of property rights. They were facing tremendous odds as it was. Knowing the prodigious power of the economic interests arrayed against them, they saw no reason to provide their adversaries with additional ammunition. The decision made, they named themselves the Society for Effecting the Abolition of the Slave-Trade, rather than the Society for Effecting the Abolition of Slavery.

The new committee (popularly known as the London Abolition Committee, or just the Abolition Committee) launched into their work immediately. They decided first to print and distribute an array of antislavery pamphlets and more substantial works to raise, as we might say, the consciousness of the British public. The time was approaching, Clarkson wrote in his *History*, "when the public voice should be raised against this enormous evil. I was sure that it was only necessary for the inhabitants of this favoured island to know it to feel a just indignation against it. Accordingly I set off."[34]

Previous attempts to directly influence Parliament through providing antislavery literature hadn't worked, so this was a shift in strategy, a kind of mass mailing campaign. To this end the committee printed and sent out tracts and pamphlets, including fifteen thousand copies of Clarkson's prizewinning essay, which he edited and condensed to make it more accessible, and 1,500 copies of Benezet's *Some Historical Account*. The cost was considerable: over one thousand pounds, which today would equal more than $200,000.[35]

Meanwhile, in his travels around England to gather evidence and raise awareness, Clarkson spoke with religious leaders and other influential individuals about creating petition drives—a strategy Benezet had used as early as 1773. The town of Bridgewater had already initiated its own drive in 1785, and Clarkson urged the town leaders to take up a new one. As knowledge of the trade and its circumstances spread, so did popular disgust for it. Organizers in Manchester were especially active, not only launching their own petition drive but urging chief magistrates in every other major town to do the same.[36] By the time its next session opened, Parliament had received over a hundred petitions signed by up to 100,000 people across the range of English social classes. During the 1794 session, petitions with 400,000 names flooded in. Clearly the movement had expanded well beyond a fringe group of religious eccentrics.

On May 12, 1789, Wilberforce put a bill before Parliament to abolish the slave trade. He was not well that day. But somehow he gathered his strength and spoke for three and a half hours in what is now considered one of history's great speeches. "The circumstances of this trade are now laid open to us," he declared;

> we can no longer plead ignorance, we cannot evade it, it is now an object placed before us, we cannot pass it. We may spurn it, we may kick it out of our way, but we cannot turn aside so as to avoid seeing it; for it is brought now so directly before our eyes that this House must decide, and must justify to all the world, and to their own consciences, the rectitude of the grounds and principles of their decision. . . . Let not Parliament be the only body that is insensitive to the principles of national justice.[37]

Wilberforce was a small man, not much more than five feet. He was frail and rarely in the best of health. But when he spoke, in his powerful yet pleasing voice, his eloquence on full display, he transformed. "I saw what seemed a mere shrimp mount upon the table," James Boswell said, "but as I listened, he grew and grew until the shrimp became a whale."[38] But whale or not, Parliament did not vote abolishment, but postponed debate until the following session, at which Wilberforce gave another forceful speech, again to no avail. The motion was turned down 163 to 88. The economic strength of the shippers and planters was simply too entrenched in England's industrial and commercial life to be overcome by argument and an ardent delivery. Wilberforce and the Abolition Committee were determined and driven, but it wasn't until 1808, nineteen years later, that the economic interests at long last crumbled and gave way. As Maurice Jackson has shown, Wilberforce used material in his speeches from Benezet's *Some Historical Account* and *A Caution and a Warning*, even including some of Benezet's language.[39] All those years after his passing, Benezet's spirit was still alive and still influencing the great debate.

Benezet died on May 4, 1784, seven months after the end of the Revolutionary War. He had written his last tract, *Short Observations on Slavery*, less than a year before, prefacing it with Jefferson's declaration "We hold these truths to be self-evident, that all men are created equal." Yet "Negroes," he wrote, "[are] still kept in slavery." To what extent was that consonant with the Revolution's declared values? "Will it not appear wonderfully inconsistent and a matter of astonishment to the whole world, that an alteration of conduct towards them has not yet taken place?"[40]

As he neared his end, though, Benezet's mind was not on the antislavery struggle that had consumed so much of his life. He thought about his wife, his close companions, his school, and the Black children who were his students. He didn't want people making speeches about him; he wanted no memorials, no statues, no remembrances of that sort. He was, he said, gifted by God to know how unimportant he was. If his friends wanted an epitaph, that was it.

Of course that was not it. Many years later Clarkson wrote, "No good effort is ever lost. For if he, who makes the virtuous attempt, should be prevented by death from succeeding in it, can he not speak, though in the tomb? Will not his works still breathe his sentiments upon it? May not his opinions, and the facts he has recorded meet the approbation of ten thousand readers, of whom it is probable, in the common course of things, that some will branch out of him as authors, and others as actors or labourers, in the same cause?"[41]

It was probable. For Sharp, Clarkson, and Wesley, Benezet had been inspirational, as he was for Black abolitionists Olaudah Equiano, Ottobah Cugoano, James Forten, and Absalom Jones. For William Dillwyn, he transmitted values and laid out a path. He played a transformative role with the Quakers, both in America and in the mother country of Great Britain. These, and the tens and hundreds of thousands who had signed the petitions that moved Parliament were his memorial in England. In that country Wilberforce's two-and-a-half-decades-long campaign had finally triumphed, ending the slave trade in 1807. Slavery itself was abolished there in 1833. In Benezet's adopted American home, abolition took a longer, rougher road. But Benezet had been there at the beginning, and he had lit a fire under that struggle as well.

In 1786 French revolutionary Jacques-Pierre Brissot wrote about him, "Where is the man in all of Europe, of whatever rank of birth, who is equal to Benezet? . . . Who was more virtuous than Benezet? Who was more useful to society, to mankind?" More than two hundred years later, Garry Wills called him "the one unquestionably authentic American saint."[42] Benezet would have been bemused; one can only imagine what he might have thought of it. As he lay on his deathbed "in the outer room about Sun-sett," he faced his end with a different assessment.[43] "I am dying," he said, "and feel ashamed to meet the face of my maker, I have done so little in his cause."[44]

The piety of Benezet's era is largely a remote memory now. But the lessons his life taught still resonate, much as they did for the Philadelphians he lived among. His humanity struck everyone who met him, his graciousness and humility, perhaps most of all his fierce insistence on the equality of those he thought of, not according to the color of their skin, but simply as his fellow human beings.

NOTES

Prologue

1. James Pemberton to John Pemberton, May 4, 1784, in George S. Brookes, *Friend Anthony Benezet* (Philadelphia: University of Pennsylvania Press, 1937), 157.

2. James Pemberton to John Pemberton, May 14, 1784, in Brookes, *Friend Anthony Benezet*, 459.

3. Anthony Benezet to Lady Huntingdon, March 1775, in Irv Brendlinger, *To Be Silent Would Be Criminal* (Lanham, Md.: Scarecrow Press, 2006), 34.

4. Quoted in Roberts Vaux, *Memoirs of The Life of Anthony Benezet* (Philadelphia: James P. Parke, 1817), 22.

5. Ibid., 134.

6. Probably Colonel Francis Johnston. Brookes, *Friend Anthony Benezet*, 162.

7. Ibid., 167–170.

8. Jacques-Pierre Brissot, "Letter Addressed to the Marquis," Paris, July 1, 1786, in *Extracts from a Critical Examination of Marquis de Chastellux's Travels in North America in a Letter Addressed to the Marquis*, quoted in Maurice Jackson, *Let This Voice Be Heard: Anthony Benezet, Father of Atlantic Abolitionism* (Philadelphia: University of Pennsylvania Press, 2009), 186.

9. W. E. H. Lecky, *A History of European Morals: From Augustus to Charlemagne* (New York, 1876), 1:161.

10. Thomas Clarkson, *The History of the Rise, Progress and Accomplishment of the Abolition of the African Slave Trade by the British Parliament* (1808; Qontro Classics, Internet Archive), 1:71.

11. John Wesley, *The Journal of John Wesley, 1840*, vol. 5, quoted in Brookes, *Friend Anthony Benezet*, 84.

12. Garry Wills, *Head and Heart* (New York: Penguin Press, 2007), 152.

13. William Armistead, *Life of Anthony Benezet* (Philadelphia: Sherman & Co., 1867), 23.

14. Bernard Bailyn, *To Begin the World Anew* (New York: Vintage Books, 2003), 3.

Chapter 1. The Man We Do Not Know

1. "Revocation of the Edict of Nantes," October 22, 1685, Modern History Sourcebook, https://sourcebooks.fordham.edu/mod/1685revocation.asp, from Isambert, Recueil general des anciennes lois francaises XIX, 530 sqq, translated, in J. H. Robinson, *Readings in European History* (Boston: Ginn, 1906), 2:180–183.

2. Bernard Douzil, "The Vaunageole and Cevenole Roots of Anthony Benezet," in *The Atlantic World of Anthony Benezet*, ed. Marie-Jean Rossignol and Bertrand Van Ruymbeke (Leiden: Brill, 2016), 7–22.

3. Michael Smithies, "The Abbé de Chaila 1648–1702: From Tourist in Siam to Persecutor," *Journal of the Siam Society* 94 (2006): 210–220.

4. Catherine Randall, *From a Far County: Camisards and Huguenots in the Atlantic World* (Athens: University of Georgia Press, 2011), 20.

5. Lionel Laborie, "W. Gregory Monahan, *Let God Arise: The War and Rebellion of the Camisards*," *Historical Review/La Revue Historique* 11 (December 2014): 190.

6. W. Gregory Monahan, "Prophets, Prophetism, and Violence during the War of the Camisards," in *The Theology of the Huguenot Refuge*, ed. Martin Klauber (Grand Rapids: Reformation Heritage Books, 2020), 53. See also "The Progress of the War," Musée virtuel du protestantisme, http://museeprotestant.org/en/notice/the-progress-of-the-war-1702-1704/?parc=21739.

7. Samuel Wayland Kershaw, *Protestants from France in Their English Home* (London: Sampson Low, Marston, Searle & Livingston, 1885), 54.

8. Margaret Jacob, "The Nature of Early Eighteenth-Century Religious Radicalism," *Arcade* 1, no. 1 (2008): 2.

9. Bertrand Van Ruymbeke, "Anthony Benezet the Huguenot," in Rossignol and Van Ruymbeke, *Atlantic World of Anthony Benezet*, 51.

10. Kershaw, *Protestants from France*, 86.

11. George S. Brookes, *Friend Anthony Benezet* (Philadelphia: University of Pennsylvania Press, 1937), 14.

12. Ibid., 15.

13. Ronald Knox, *Enthusiasm* (Oxford: Clarendon Press, 1950), 354.

14. Jacob, "Nature."

Chapter 2. The Benezets in England

1. Unidentified Dutch pastor to Presbyterian minister John Quick, quoted in Geoffrey Nuttall, "English Dissenters in the Netherlands 1640–1689," *Dutch Review of Church History*, n.s., 59, no. 1 (1978): 38.

2. Jacques Bonbonnoux letter quoted in Catherine Randall, *From a Far County: Camisards and Huguenots in the Atlantic World* (Athens: University of Georgia Press, 2011), 24.

3. Quoted in Martin Klauber, "The Apocalypticism of Pierre Jurieu," in Martin Klauber, ed., *The Theology of the Huguenot Refuge* (Grand Rapids: Michigan Reformation Heritage Books, 2020), 119.

4. David van der Linden, "Histories of Martyrdom and Suffering in the Huguenot Diaspora," in *A Companion to the Huguenots*, ed. Raymond Mentzer and Bertrand Van Ruymbeke (Leiden: Brill, 2016), 348–359.

5. Lionel Laborie, "From English *Trembleurs* to French *Inspirés*," in *Radicalism and Dissent in the World of Protestant Reform*, ed. Bridget Heal and Anorthe Kremers (Gottingen: Vandenhoeck & Ruprecht, 2017), 229.

6. William O' Reilly, "Strangers Come to Devour the Land: Changing Views of Foreign Migrants in Early Eighteenth-Century England," *Journal of Early Modern History* 21, no. 3 (June 2017): 153–187.

7. Picture in Greig Parker, "Huguenot Identity in Post-medieval London," *Assemblage* 10 (2009): 7–15, academia.edu/269334/Huguenot_Identity_in_Post_Medieval London.

8. O'Reilly, "Strangers Come to Devour," 17.

9. Lionel Laborie, "The Huguenot Offensive against the Camisard Prophets," in *The Huguenots: France, Exile and Diaspora*, ed. Jane McKee and Randolph Vigne (Eastbourne, U.K.: Sussex Academic Press, 2013), 127.

10. In Hillel Schwartz, *The French Prophets* (Berkeley: University of California Press, 1980), 75.

11. Robin Gwynn, "England's 'First Refugees,'" *History Today* 35, no. 5 (May 1985).

12. Randall, *From a Far Country*, 42.

13. Schwartz, *French Prophets*, 54.

14. Samuel Keimer, *A Brand Snatch'd from the Burning* (London: W. Boreham, 1718), 1, 2.

15. The Anglo-Catholic scholar Gregory Dix wrote in his magisterial *The Shape of the Liturgy*, "The force of a single idea [carried] the whole protestant [*sic*] movement forward. . . . That idea was the conception of a personal relation of each individual soul to God." *The Shape of the Liturgy* (London: Dacre Press, 1945), 637–638.

16. The prophet Jean Cavalier described in detail his experience of being possessed by the spirit. "Rivers of waters ran down my eyes. . . . I wept in secret continually. . . . There seemed a beating as of a hammer in my breast, which kindled a flame which took me and dispersed all over my veins and put me into a sort of leaping, which flung me down; I rose again . . . and as my heart was lifted up to God with unutterable fervor I was struck again . . . speaking and breathing with mighty groans . . . and sudden violent agitations of the head and body." Cavalier, quoted in Randall, *From a Far Country*, 54.

17. Schwartz, *French Prophets*, 154.

18. Quoted in Hillel Schwartz, *Knaves, Fools, Madmen, and That Subtile Effluviam: A Study of the Opposition to the French Prophets in England, 1706–1710* (Gainesville: University Presses of Florida, 1978), 17.

19. Quoted in Bernard Cottret, *The Huguenots in England* (Cambridge, England: Cambridge University Press, 1985), 284.

20. Quoted in Laborie, "The Huguenot Offensive against the Camisard Prophets," 129.

21. Lionel Laborie, "The French Prophets: A Cultural History of Religious Enthusiasm in Post-toleration England (1689–1730)" (PhD thesis, University of East Anglia, 2010), 73; Ronald Knox, *Enthusiasm* (Oxford: Clarendon Press, 1950), 370.

22. Schwartz, *French Prophets*, 285–292.

23. On trauma and moral formation, see Augustus White, Jon Land, and David Chanoff, *Overcoming: Lessons in Triumphing over Adversity and the Power of Our*

Common Humanity (New York: Post Hill Press, 2021), 310, 311. On intergenerational trauma, see Tori DeAngelis, "The Legacy of Trauma," *American Psychological Association Monitor on Psychology* 50, no. 2 (2019), Apa.org/monitor/2019/02/legacy-trauma.

24. Francois Marquis De Barbe-Marbois, *Our Revolutionary Forefathers*, trans. and ed. Eugene Parker Chase (New York: Duffield and Co., 1949), 139.

25. Francois Jean Chastellux, *Travels in North America in the Years 1780, 1781 and 1782*, trans. Howard C. Rice Jr. (Chapel Hill: University of North Carolina Press, 1963), 1:165–166, quoted in Maurice Jackson, *Let This Voice Be Heard: Anthony Benezet, Father of Atlantic Abolitionism* (Philadelphia: University of Pennsylvania Press, 2009), 3.

26. Samuel Wayland Kershaw, *Protestants from France in Their English Home* (London: Sampson Low, Marston, Searle & Livingston, 1885), 86.

Chapter 3. Quakers

1. Bertrand Van Ruymbeke, "Anthony Benezet the Huguenot," in *The Atlantic World of Anthony Benezet*, ed. Marie-Jean Rossignol and Bertrand Van Ruymbeke (Leiden: Brill, 2016), 48.

2. Ibid., 49.

3. Ibid., 49.

4. Ibid., 51.

5. Francois Marquis De Barbe-Marbois, *Our Revolutionary Forefathers*, trans. and ed. Eugene Parker Chase (New York: Duffield and Co., 1949), 141.

6. Peter Collins, "The Embodiment of Seventeenth Century Quakerism: An Exercise in Historical Anthropology," *Quaker Studies* 4, no. 2 (1999): 121.

7. H. Larry Ingle, *First among Friends: George Fox and the Creation of Quakerism* (New York: Oxford University Press, 1994), 190.

8. *The Journal of George Fox*, ed. Norman Penney (Cambridge, England: Cambridge University Press, 1911; rpt., BiblioLife historic reproduction), 323.

9. Ronald Knox, *Enthusiasm* (Oxford: Clarendon Press, 1950), 142.

10. *George Fox: An Autobiography*, ed. Rufus M. Jones [*The Journal of George Fox*], Project Gutenberg eBook, 2013 [EBook #43031], chap. 1, line 82.

11. Ibid., chap. 2, line 97.

12. Ibid., chap. 2, line 102.

13. Knox, *Enthusiasm*, 145.

14. Lancashire petition and Richard Baxter, both quoted in Knox, *Enthusiasm*, 150.

15. Andrew R. Murphy, *William Penn: A Life* (New York: Oxford University Press, 2019), 49.

16. In Knox, *Enthusiasm*, 160.

17. Ibid.

18. Penney, *Journal of George Fox*, 24.

19. Quoted in William C. Braithwaite, *The Beginnings of Quakerism* (London: Macmillan and Co., 1912), 105.

20. William James, *The Varieties of Religious Experience* (New York: Library of America Paperback Classic Edition, 2010), 378.

21. In Knox, *Enthusiasm*, 162.

22. Braithwaite, *Beginnings of Quakerism*, 252.

23. *State Trials*, no. 52, 269, quoted in Knox, *Enthusiasm*, 165.

24. *State Trials*, no. 52, 429, in Knox, *Enthusiasm*, 166.

25. Ingle, *First among Friends*, 148.

26. Ibid., 149.

27. In Braithwaite, *Beginnings of Quakerism*, 270.

28. Penney, *Journal of George Fox*, 243.

29. Ingle, *First among Friends*, 150.

30. Voltaire, *Letters on England*, Project Gutenberg, https://www.gutenberg.org/files/2445/2445-h/2445-h.htm.

31. Quoted in Bertha Leaman, "American Quakerism through French Eyes: Ampere and Voltaire," *Quaker History* 61, no. 2 (Autumn 1972), 119.

32. Voltaire, from Letter 1: "On the Quakers," *Letters on England.*

Chapter 4. William Penn's "Holy Experiment"

1. J-E Benezet to Prosper Marchand, December 10, 1748, Leiden University Library, courtesy of Bertrand Van Ruymbeke.

2. Ralph LeFevre, "The Huguenots—The First Settlers in the Province of New York," *Quarterly Journal of the New York State Historical Association* 2, no. 3 (July 1921): 177–185.

3. Maurice Jackson, *Let This Voice Be Heard: Anthony Benezet, Father of Atlantic Abolitionism* (Philadelphia: University of Pennsylvania Press, 2009), 6; J. William Frost, "Anthony Benezet: The Emergence of a Weighty Friend," in *The Atlantic World of Anthony Benezet*, ed. Marie-Jean Rossignol and Bertrand Van Ruymbeke (Leiden: Brill, 2016), 58.

4. Chastellux in George S. Brookes, *Friend Anthony Benezet* (Philadelphia: University of Pennsylvania Press, 1937), 456.

5. In Andrew R. Murphy, *William Penn: A Life* (New York: Oxford University Press, 2019), 150.

6. See Robert J. Lowenherz, "Roger Williams and the Great Quaker Debate," *American Quarterly* 11, no. 2, part 1 (Summer 1959): 157–165.

7. Brookes, *Friend Anthony Benezet*, 16.

8. Jean-Etienne and Judith also had siblings in England—Judith two sisters, Jean-Etienne at least one brother, Jacques, his business partner. See Bertrand Van Ruymbeke, "Anthony Benezet the Huguenot," in Rossignol and Van Ruymbeke, *Atlantic World of Anthony Benezet*, 46, 47.

9. Van Ruymbeke, "Anthony Benezet the Huguenot," 51.

10. Ibid., 51.

11. Brookes, *Friend Anthony Benezet*, 19.

12. J-E Benezet to Prosper Marchand, May 15, 1745, quoted in Van Ruymbeke, "Anthony Benezet the Huguenot," 52.

13. See Craig Atwood, "Understanding Zinzendorf's Blood and Wounds Theology," *Journal of Moravian History* 1 (Fall 2006): 31–47.

14. Andrew Frey, *A True and Authentic Account of Andrew Frey* (London: J. Robinson, 1753), 5.

15. Brookes, *Friend Anthony Benezet*, 19, 20.

16. Ibid., 20.

17. Ibid., 21.

18. Three years later Jean-Etienne broke with the Moravians too, calling them a "sect of perdition," and returned, as he told Marchand, to his "former and good Protestantism." J-E Benezet to Prosper Marchand, December 1948, quoted in Van Ruymbeke, "Anthony Benezet the Huguenot," 52. It's not known exactly what made Jean-Etienne so bitter, but it apparently had to do with his relationship with sect founder Zinzendorf. When Jean-Etienne died, in 1751, the eulogy was delivered by his friend Gilbert Tennent, a prominent evangelical Presbyterian preacher. Some thought this choice indicated that Jean-Etienne had become a Presbyterian, but there is no record to support the supposition.

19. Ronald Knox, *Enthusiasm* (Oxford: Clarendon Press, 1950), 409.

20. Katherine Gerbner, "We Are against the Traffik of Men-Body: The Germantown Quaker Protest of 1688 and the Origins of American Capitalism," *Pennsylvania History* 74, no. 2 (2007): 166.

21. Robert Barclay, *Barclay's Apology in Modern English*, ed. Dean Freiday (Newberg: Oregon Barclay Press, 1991), 134.

22. Carter Woodson, "Anthony Benezet," *Journal of Negro History* 2 (1917): 49, quoted in Jackson, *Let This Voice Be Heard*, 22.

23. Benjamin Rush, *Essays, Literary, Moral and Philosophical* (Philadelphia: Thomas & Samuel F. Bradford, 1798), 311, 312.

24. For a description of Franklin's experiment, see Thomas Kidd, *George Whitefield: America's Spiritual Founding Father* (New Haven: Yale University Press, 2004), 84, 85.

25. Perry Miller, *Jonathan Edwards* (Cleveland: Meridian Books, 1964), 133.

26. Anthony Benezet to Samuel Fothergill, quoted in Brookes, *Friend Anthony Benezet*, 223.

27. George M. Marsden, *Jonathan Edwards: A Life* (New Haven: Yale University Press, 2003), 202.

28. "The Eternity of Hell-Torments," in *Selected Sermons of George Whitefield*, Christian Classics Ethereal Library, https://www.ccel.org/ccel/whitefield/sermons.xxviii.html.

29. Kidd, *George Whitefield*, 116.

30. J. Hector St. John de Crevecoeur, *Letters from an American Farmer and Sketches of Eighteenth Century America* (New York: Penguin Books, 1986), 198.

31. Clarke Garrett, *Origins of the Shakers* (Baltimore: Johns Hopkins University Press, 1987), 111.

32. Ibid., 14.

33. Murphy, *William Penn*, 151.

34. Ibid., 128.

35. Ibid., 134.

36. Bernard Bailyn, *The Barbarous Years: The Peopling of British North America; The Conflict of Civilizations 1600–1675* (New York: Alfred Knopf, 2012), 303.

37. Ibid., 303.

38. Jean R. Soderlund, *Lenape Country* (Philadelphia: University of Pennsylvania Press, 2015), 5.

39. Bernard Bailyn, *The Peopling of British North America: An Introduction* (New York: Vintage Books, 1986), 123.

40. Quoted in Sidney Ahlstrom, *A Religious History of the American People* (New Haven: Yale University Press, 1972), 211.

41. *The Journal of George Fox*, ed. Norman Penney (Cambridge, England: Cambridge University Press, 1911; rpt., BiblioLife historic reproduction), 323.

42. George Fox, *Epistle* 19, in *The Epistles of George Fox*, vol. 1, Friends Library, https://www.friendslibrary.com/george-fox/epistles-v1.

43. Advise of London Yearly Meeting, 1789, quoted in Sydney James, *A People among Peoples* (Cambridge, Mass.: Harvard University Press, 1963), 30.

44. James, *People among Peoples*, 28.

45. The Voltaire Foundation, "Quakers in Eighteenth-Century England," https://www.voltaire.ox.ac.uk/quakers-england/. Swarthmore College's Global Nonviolent Action database estimates that eleven thousand Quakers were imprisoned and 243 "died in jail." https://nvdatabase.swarthmore.edu/content/english-quakers-campaign-freedom-religion-1647-1689.

46. Joseph Besse, *A Collection of the Sufferings of the People Called Quakers*, (London: Luke Hinde, 1753), 1:iii.

47. Quoted in John Miller, "'A Suffering People': English Quakers and Their Neighbors, 1650–1700," *Past and Present* 188, no. 1 (August 2005): 71, 72.

48. Besse, *Collection of the Sufferings*, 1:iv.

49. James, *People among Peoples*, 30.

Chapter 5. Links in the Antislavery Chain

1. Jean R. Soderlund, *Lenape Country* (Philadelphia: University of Pennsylvania Press, 2015), 184.

2. George S. Brookes, *Friend Anthony Benezet* (Philadelphia: University of Pennsylvania Press, 1937), 39.

3. Ibid., 16.

4. Ibid., 26.

5. Ibid., 26.

6. Joseph Redman to Benjamin Rush, November 14, 1798, in Brookes, *Friend Anthony Benezet*, 59.

7. Brookes, *Friend Anthony Benezet*, 39.

8. Full text, with original spelling, in Brycchan Carey, *From Peace to Freedom: Quaker Rhetoric and the Birth of American Antislavery, 1657–1761* (New Haven: Yale University Press, 2012), 76.

9. Ibid.

10. Ibid.

11. "Germantown Friends Protest against Slavery," 1688 [facsimile], Library of Congress, https://www.loc.gov/resource/rbpe.14000200/?st=text.

12. Carey, *From Peace to Freedom*, 84.

13. Ralph Sandiford, *A Brief Examination of the Practice of the Times* (printed by Benjamin Franklin, 1729), preface.

14. Ralph Sandiford, *Mystery of Iniquity* (self-published, 1730), introduction, 6.

15. Ibid., 20, 21.

16. See Jack D. Marietta, *The Reformation of American Quakerism, 1748–1783* (Philadelphia: University of Pennsylvania Press, 1984), 112; Darold D. Wax, "Quaker Merchants and the Slave Trade in Colonial Pennsylvania," *Pennsylvania Magazine of History and Biography* 86, no. 2 (April 1962): 151; Jean R. Soderlund, *Quakers and Slavery: A Divided Spirit* (Princeton: Princeton University Press, 1985), 162ff.

17. Sandiford, *Mystery of Iniquity*, 21.

18. Ibid., 7.

19. Ibid., 21, 22. Sandiford was quoting Genesis 49:5–6.

20. Marcus Rediker, *The Fearless Benjamin Lay* (Boston: Beacon Press, 2017), 58; Sydney James, *A People among Peoples* (Cambridge, Mass.: Harvard University Press, 1963), 125.

21. Ralph Sandiford, "To My Select Friends," in *Mystery of Iniquity*, 92.

22. Ibid., 92.

23. Benjamin Lay, *All Slave-Keepers That Keep the Innocent in Bondage* (Affordable Classics Limited Edition, 2020), 11.

24. Carey, *From Peace to Freedom*, 161. See also Marietta, *Reformation of American Quakerism*, 111.

25. Carey, *From Peace to Freedom*, 161, 62.

26. Maurice Jackson, Let This Voice Be Heard: *Anthony Benezet, Father of Atlantic Abolitionism* (Philadelphia: University of Pennsylvania Press, 2009), 32.

27. Sandiford, *Mystery of Iniquity*, 3, 4.

28. Jonathan Sassi, "With a Little Help from the Friends: The Quaker and Tactical Contexts of Anthony Benezet's Abolitionist Publishing," *Pennsylvania Magazine of History and Biography* 135, no. 1 (January 2011): 46.

29. In Irv Brendlinger, *To Be Silent Would Be Criminal* (Lanham, Md.: Scarecrow Press, 2007), 94.

30. Roberts Vaux, *Memoirs of the Lives of Benjamin Lay and Ralph Sandiford* (Philadelphia: Solomon W. Conrad, 1815), 37.

31. Ibid., 64.

32. Lay, *All Slave-Keepers*, 66.

33. Ibid., 16.

34. Vaux, *Memoirs of the Lives of Benjamin Lay and Ralph Sandiford*, 28.

35. Rediker, *Fearless Benjamin Lay*, 45.

36. Vaux, *Memoirs of the Lives of Benjamin Lay and Ralph Sandiford*, 26–27.

37. Benjamin Rush, *Essays, Literary, Moral and Philosophical* (Philadelphia: Thomas and William Bradford, 1798), 306.

38. Vaux, *Memoirs of the Lives of Benjamin Lay and Ralph Sandiford*, 28–29.

39. In Brookes, *Friend Anthony Benezet*, 39.

40. Rush, *Essays, Literary, Moral and Philosophical*, 313.

41. Deborah Logan to Roberts Vaux, ca. 1825, in Brookes, *Friend Anthony Benezet*, 469.

42. Jackson, *Let This Voice Be Heard*, 52.

Chapter 6. Educator

1. H. Larry Ingle, *First among Friends: George Fox and the Creation of Quakerism* (New York: Oxford University Press, 1994), 22.

2. Ibid., 44.

3. George Fox, *Epistle* 38, in *The Epistles of George Fox*, vol. 1, Friends Library, https://www.friendslibrary.com/george-fox/epistles-v1.

4. Ibid.

5. George Fox, *Epistle* 29, in *Epistles of George Fox*.

6. *George Fox: An Autobiography*, ed. Rufus M. Jones [*The Journal of George Fox*], Project Gutenberg eBook, 2013 [EBook #43031].

7. *The Great Mystery of the Great Whore Unfolded: The Antichrist's Kingdom Revealed unto Destruction*, Friends Library, 3, 4, https://flp-assets.nyc3.digitaloceanspaces.com/en/george-fox/great-mystery-great-whore/original/Great_Mystery--original.pdf.

8. Lawrence Willyer, quoted in William C. Braithwaite, *The Beginnings of Quakerism* (London: Macmillan and Co., 1912), 297.

9. Braithwaite, *Beginnings of Quakerism*, 297.

10. Ibid., 298.

11. Robert Barclay, *Barclay's Apology in Modern English*, ed. Dean Freiday (Newberg: Oregon Barclay Press, 1991), 206.

12. Ibid., 110.

13. Ibid., 111.

14. Robert Barclay, *Apology for Christian Divinity Vindicated*, quoted in Thomas Woody, *Early Quaker Education in Pennsylvania* (Washington, D.C.: Westphalia Press, 2019), 31.

15. Samuel Hanson Cox, *Quakerism Not Christianity* (Boston: D. Fanshaw, 1833), 53.

16. Howard H. Brinton, "The Quaker Contribution to Higher Education in Colonial America," *Pennsylvania History* 25, no. 3 (July 1958): 242.

17. "Advice of William Penn to His Children," quoted in Brinton, "Quaker Contribution to Higher Education," 242.

18. David Hall, *An Epistle of Love and Caution*, quoted in Sydney James, *A People among Peoples* (Cambridge, Mass.: Harvard University Press, 1963), 63.

19. Thomas Budd, *Good Order Established in Pennsylvania and New Jersey* (Philadelphia: William Bradford, 1685), 44.

20. *William Penn's Charters of Ye Publick School Founded by Charter in ye Town and County of Philadelphia in Pensilvania 1701, 1708, 1711* (Philadelphia: J. B. Lippincott, [1880?]), https://catalog.hathitrust.org/Record/011159460.

21. William Penn, *Some Fruits of Solitude*, quoted in William Kashatus, "What Love Can Do: William Penn's Holy Experiment in Education," *Pennsylvania Heritage*, Spring 1989.

22. Ibid.

23. Woody, *Early Quaker Education in Pennsylvania*, 57.

24. Paul D. Travers, "A Historic View of School Discipline," *Educational Horizons* 58, no. 4 (Summer 1980): 184.

25. Ibid., 184.

26. Ibid., 185. Also see Roberts Vaux, *Memoirs of the Life of Anthony Benezet* (Philadelphia: James P. Parke, 1817), 9.

27. George S. Brookes, *Friend Anthony Benezet* (Philadelphia: University of Pennsylvania Press, 1937), 31.

28. Woody, *Early Quaker Education in Pennsylvania*, 186.

29. Brookes, *Friend Anthony Benezet*, 34. See also Maurice Jackson, *Let This Voice Be Heard: Anthony Benezet, Father of Atlantic Abolitionism* (Philadelphia: University of Pennsylvania Press, 2009), 21.

30. Vaux, Memoirs of *the Life of Anthony Benezet*, 8.

31. Ibid., 18.

32. Anthony Benezet to George Dillwyn, August 4, 1779, in Brookes, *Friend Anthony Benezet*, 333.

33. Anthony Benezet to George Dillwyn, August 6, 1780, in Brookes, *Friend Anthony Benezet*, 349.

34. Ibid., 350.

35. Carter Woodson, "Anthony Benezet," *Journal of Negro History* 2 (1917): 4, 29.

36. Anthony Benezet to "a Schoolmaster," ca. 1752, in Brookes, *Friend Anthony Benezet*, 209.

37. Vaux, *Memoirs of the Life of Anthony Benezet*, 10.

38. Ibid., 11.

39. See Heather Zimmerman and Thomas Horejes, "Origins of Deaf Education: From Alphabets to America," chap. 6 in *Preparing to Teach, Committing to Learn: An*

Introduction to Educating Children Who are Deaf/Hard of Hearing, ed. Susan Lenihan (Logan: National Center for Hearing Assessment and Management, Utah State University, 2020), 7, https://www.infanthearing.org/ebook-educating-children-dhh/chapters/6%20Chapter%206%202017.pdf.

40. Brookes, *Friend Anthony Benezet*, 38.

41. Deborah Logan to Roberts Vaux, ca. 1825, in Brookes, *Friend Anthony Benezet*, 466–470.

42. Brookes, *Friend Anthony Benezet*, 37.

Chapter 7. A School for Black Children

1. Birgit Brander Rasmussen, "'Attended with Great Inconveniences': Slave literacy and the 1740 South Carolina Negro Act," PMLA 125, no. 1 (2010): 201–203.

2. Catechismal classes for Blacks and Indigenous people were initiated in New York in 1703 by the Huguenot refugee Élie Neau and sponsored by the Anglican Society for the Propagation of the Faith. Three evenings a week for two hours, Neau taught the rudiments of faith by drill and memorization. There was apparently no instruction in reading or writing. See David R. King, "Missionary Vestryman," *Historical Magazine of the Protestant Episcopal Church* 34, no. 4 (December 1965): 361–368.

3. Benezet wrote a letter of encouragement to a schoolteacher in Nantucket, noting that he was "not unacquainted" with the "difficulties and discouragements" of their mutually chosen profession. Anthony Benezet to Benjamin Coffin, School Master, March 9, 1755, in George S. Brookes, *Friend Anthony Benezet* (Philadelphia: University of Pennsylvania Press, 1937), 212.

4. Arthur O. Lovejoy, *The Great Chain of Being* (New York: Harper Brothers, 1936), 183.

5. Roger Bruns, "Anthony Benezet's Assertion of Negro Equality," *Journal of Negro History* 56. no. 3 (1971): 230.

6. Soame Jenyns, "Disquisitions on Several Subjects, I, On the Chain of Universal Being," in *Works* (1790 ed.), 179–185, quoted in Lovejoy, *Great Chain of Being*, 197.

7. Josiah C. Nott, *Two Lectures on the Natural History of the Caucasian and Negro Races* (Mobile: Dade & Thompson, 1844), 7, quoted in Terence D. Keel, "Religion, Polygenism, and the Early Science of Human Rights," *History of Human Sciences* 26, no. 2 (2013), 4.

8. Nott, *Two Lectures on the Connection between the Biblical and Physical History of Man* (New York: Bartlett & Welford, 1849), 7, in Keel, "Religion, Polygenism," 5.

9. Louis Menand, "Morton, Agassiz, and the Origin of Scientific Racism in the United States," *Journal of Blacks in Higher Education* 34 (Winter 2001–2002), 112.

10. For a fuller description of the general eighteenth-century prejudice against Black people see Bruns, "Anthony Benezet's Assertion," 230–238.

11. Bruns, "Anthony Benezet's Assertion," 230.

12. Benjamin Franklin to John Waring, January 3, 1758, in Leonard Labaree and Wil-

liam Willcox, *Papers of Benjamin Franklin*, quoted in Gary B. Nash, *Forging Freedom: The Formation of Philadelphia's Black Community* (Boston: Harvard University Press, 2003), 22.

13. *American Weekly Mercury* (Philadelphia), February 5–12, 1722.

14. See Stephen Bloore, "A Footnote to the Life of Franklin," *Pennsylvania Magazine of History and Biography* 54, no. 3 (July 1930): 265, 266.

15. Brookes, *Friend Anthony Benezet*, 96.

16. *Pennsylvania Gazette*, November 7, 1740.

17. Nancy Slocum Hornick, "Anthony Benezet and the Africans' School: Toward a Theory of Full Equality," *Pennsylvania Magazine of History and Biography* 99, no. 4 (1975): 402.

18. Thomas Kidd, *George Whitefield: America's Spiritual Founding Father* (New Haven: Yale University Press, 2004), 11, 112. Also see Stephen J. Stein, "George Whitefield on Slavery: Some New Evidence," *Church History* 42, no. 2 (June 1973): 254.

19. Stein, "George Whitefield on Slavery," 254.

20. George Whitefield to John Wesley, 1751, quoted in Irv Brendlinger, "Wesley, Whitefield, a Philadelphia Quaker, and Slavery," *Faculty Publications—College of Christian Studies*, George Fox University, 167.

21. See "Two Early Philadelphia Dance Masters," *Philadelphia Dance History Journal*, July 4, 2012. See also Nash, *Forging Freedom*, 19; John C. Van Horne, "The Education of African Americans in Benjamin Franklin's Philadelphia," in John Pollack, ed. *The Good Education of Youth: Worlds of Learning in the Age of Franklin* (Philadelphia: Oak Noll Press, 2009), 78, 79.

22. Nash, *Forging Freedom*, 29.

23. George Keith, *An Exhortation & Caution to Friends Concerning Buying or Keeping of Negroes, 1693*, reprinted in the *Pennsylvania Magazine of History and Biography* (1889), text viewable on the Quaker Writings Home Page, http://www.qhpress.org/quakerpages/qwhp/gk-as1693.htm.

24. Quoted in Brycchan Carey, *From Peace to Freedom: Quaker Rhetoric and the Birth of American Antislavery, 1657–1761* (New Haven: Yale University Press, 2012), 102.

25. George Fox, *Gospel Family Order*, 1676, in Stella Alexander, *Quaker Testimony against Slavery and Racial Discrimination*, (London: Friends House, 1958), Quaker Historical Books, vol. 74, Digitalcommons.georgefox.edu/quakerbooks/74.

26. George Fox, *Gospel Family Order, Being a Short Discourse Concerning the Ordering of Families, Both Whites, Blacks, and Indians*, quoted in Thomas E. Drake, *Quakers and Slavery in America* (Gloucester, Mass.: Peter Smith, 1965), 7.

27. Henry Cadbury, "Negro Membership in the Society of Friends," *Journal of Negro History* 21 (1936): 151–213.

28. George Fox, *Journal* II, 105, quoted in Thomas Woody, *Early Quaker Education in Pennsylvania* (Washington, D.C.: Westphalia Press 2019), 12.

29. Benjamin Lay, *All Slave-Keepers That Keep the Innocent in Bondage* (Affordable Classics Limited Edition, 2020), 28.

30. *Pennsylvania Gazette*, March 5, 1751.

31. Ibid.

32. Roberts Vaux, Memoirs of the *Life of Anthony Benezet* (Philadelphia: James P. Parke, 1817), 19.

33. Maurice Jackson, "The Social and Intellectual Origins of Anthony Benezet's Antislavery Radicalism," in "Explorations in Early American Culture," supplement, *Pennsylvania History: A Journal of Mid-Atlantic Studies* 66 (1999), 88.

34. Vaux, Memoirs of the *Life of Anthony Benezet*, 19.

35. Brookes, Friend Anthony Benezet, 45.

36. Anthony Benezet, *A Short Account of the People Called Quakers, Their Rise, Religious Principles and Settlement in America, Mostly Collected from Different Authors, for the Information of All Serious Inquiries, Particularly Foreigners* (Philadelphia, 1780), 2, 3, quoted in Maurice Jackson, *Let This Voice Be Heard: Anthony Benezet, Father of Atlantic Abolitionism* (Philadelphia: University of Pennsylvania Press, 2009), 22.

37. Anthony Benezet to John Smith, August 1, 1760, in Brookes, *Friend Anthony Benezet*, 241.

38. See Nash, *Forging Freedom*, 9; Jackson, *Let This Voice Be Heard*, 12.

39. Vaux, Memoirs of the *Life of Anthony Benezet*, 29.

40. Brookes, *Friend Anthony Benezet*, 45.

Chapter 8. Equality

1. Roberts Vaux, Memoirs of the *Life of Anthony Benezet* (Philadelphia: James P. Parke, 1817), 22.

2. Nancy Slocum Hornick, "Anthony Benezet and the Africans' School: Toward a Theory of Full Equality," *Pennsylvania Magazine of History and Biography* 99, no. 4 (1975): 399–421.

3. Anthony Benezet to Benjamin Franklin, March 5, 1783, in George S. Brookes, *Friend Anthony Benezet* (Philadelphia: University of Pennsylvania Press, 1937), 387.

4. See also Roger Bruns, "Anthony Benezet's Assertion of Negro Equality," *Journal of Negro History* 56, no. 3 (July 1971): 230–238.

5. Anthony Benezet, *Short Observations on Slavery*, in David Crosby, *The Complete Antislavery Writings of Anthony Benezet, 1754–1783: An Annotated Critical Edition* (Baton Rouge: Louisiana State University Press, 2013), 233.

6. Hornick, "Anthony Benezet," 403, 404.

7. Richard I. Shelling, "Benjamin Franklin and the Dr. Bray Associates," *Pennsylvania Magazine of History and Biography* 63, no. 3 (July 1939): 283, 284.

8. Peter Moore, *Life, Liberty, and the Pursuit of Happiness* (New York: Farrar, Strauss and Giroux, 2023), 112, 113.

9. Hornick, "Anthony Benezet," 419.

10. See David Frost, "Anthony Benezet: The Emergence of a Weighty Friend," in *The Atlantic World of Anthony Benezet*, ed. Marie-Jean Rossignol and Bertrand Van Ruymbeke (Leiden: Brill, 2016).

11. PMM Minutes, March 30, 1770, in Thomas Woody, *Early Quaker Education in Pennsylvania* (Washington, D.C.: Westphalia Press, 2019), 240.

12. Gary B. Nash, *Forging Freedom: The Formation of Philadelphia's Black Community* (Boston: Harvard University Press, 2003), 68, 111.

13. Julie Winch, *A Gentleman of Color: The Life of James Forten* (New York: Oxford University Press, 2003), 24, 25.

14. Woody, *Early Quaker Education in Pennsylvania*, 242.

15. Vaux, Memoirs of the *Life of Anthony Benezet,* 21.

16. Hornick, "Anthony Benezet," 419.

17. J. P. Brissot De Warville, *New Travels in the United States of America, Performed in 1788* (Dublin, 1792), 262, 263.

18. Ibid., 262–268.

19. Thomas Clarkson, *The History of the Rise, Progress, and Accomplishment of the Abolition of the African Slave Trade by the British Parliament*, vol. 1 (London: Richard Taylor and Co., 1808), 70, 71.

20. Nina Reid Maroney, "Benezet's Ghost," in Rossignol and Van Ruymbeke, *Atlantic World of Anthony Benezet*, 214.

21. Crosby, *Complete Antislavery Writings*, 113.

22. Ibid.

23. For a review of some examples, see Maurice Jackson, *Let This Voice Be Heard: Anthony Benezet, Father of Atlantic Abolitionism* (Philadelphia: University of Pennsylvania Press, 2009), 226.

24. Irv Brendlinger, "Anthony Benezet, the True Champion of the Slave," in *Truth's Bright Embrace*, ed. Paul Anderson and Howard R. Macy (Newberg, Oreg.: George Fox University Press, 1996), 81.

25. Brookes, *Friend Anthony Benezet*, viii.

26. Woody, *Early Quaker Education in Pennsylvania*, 242.

27. Anthony Benezet to Robert Pleasants, March 17, 1781, in Brookes, *Friend Anthony Benezet*, 352.

28. Jackson, *Let This Voice Be Heard*, 24.

29. Quoted in Jackson, *Let This Voice Be Heard*, 227.

30. Anthony Benezet to George Dillwyn, ca. 1783, in Brookes, *Friend Anthony Benezet*, 374; Anthony Benezet to Granville Sharp, May 14, 1772, in Brookes, *Friend Anthony Benezet*, 290.

31. Vaux, Memoirs of the *Life of Anthony Benezet,* 19.

32. Hornick, "Anthony Benezet," 410; Carter Woodson, "Anthony Benezet," *Journal of Negro History* 2 (1917): 42.

33. Vaux, Memoirs of the *Life of Anthony Benezet,* 29.

34. Hornick, "Anthony Benezet," 400.

35. See Matthew C. Ward, "An Army of Servants: The Pennsylvania Regiment during the Seven Years War," *Pennsylvania Magazine of History and Biography* 119, nos. 1–2 (1995): 75–93.

36. Darold Wax, "Quaker Merchants and the Slave Trade in Colonial Pennsylvania," *Pennsylvania Magazine of History and Biography* 86, no.2 (April 1962): 145.

37. Jackson, *Let This Voice Be Heard*, 193–200. There is controversy over the place of Equiano's birth—whether it was in Africa, as he wrote in his autobiography, or in South Carolina, as suggested by several archival sources. If it was the latter, Equiano must have fabricated the story of his birth and capture in Africa and experience of the dreaded Middle Passage. The scholarly disagreement between "Americanists," who believe the South Carolina references, and "Africanists," who defend the veracity of Equiano's account, is recounted in Brycchan Carey's "Olaudah Equiano: African or American?," *1650–1850: Ideas, Aesthetics, and Inquiries in the Early Modern Era*, vol. 17, article 12 (2010), 229–248, https://repository.lsu.edu/sixteenfifty/vol17/iss1/12. Carey judges the argument to be inconclusive. This author believes that the emotional integrity of the book as a whole indicates the accuracy of Equiano's telling.

38. Olaudah Equiano, *An Interesting Narrative* (Middletown, Del.: Decades Press, 2019), 66.

39. Thomas Drake, *Quakers and Slavery in America* (Gloucester, Mass.: Peter Smith, 1965), 21.

40. See Thomas Slaughter, *The Beautiful Soul of John Woolman, Apostle of Abolition* (New York: Hill and Wang, 2008), 9.

41. Hornick, "Anthony Benezet," 399.

42. Bruns, "Anthony Benezet's Assertion," 230.

Chapter 9. Entering the Antislavery Lists

1. Thomas P. Slaughter, *The Beautiful Soul of John Woolman, Apostle of Abolition* (New York: Hill and Wang, 2008), 132.

2. David Crosby, "Anthony Benezet's Transformation of Anti-Slavery Rhetoric," *Slavery and Abolition* 23, no. 3 (2002): 46, DOI:10.1080/714005242.

3. Brycchan Carey, *From Peace to Freedom: Quaker Rhetoric and the Birth of American Antislavery, 1657–1761* (New Haven: Yale University Press, 2012), 184.

4. John Woolman, *Some Considerations on the Keeping of Negroes* [1762], in *The Journal and Major Essays of John Woolman*, ed. Phillips P. Moulton (Richmond, Ind.: Friends United Press, 1971), 199.

5. Ibid., 200.

6. Ibid.

7. Ibid., 202.

8. Ibid.

9. George S. Brookes, *Friend Anthony Benezet* (Philadelphia: University of Pennsylvania Press, 1937), 80, 81.

10. Maurice Jackson, *Let This Voice Be Heard: Anthony Benezet, Father of Atlantic Abolitionism* (Philadelphia: University of Pennsylvania Press, 2009), 53. See also Geoffrey Plank, "Anthony Benezet, John Woolman, and Praise" in *The Atlantic World of Anthony Benezet*, ed. Marie-Jean Rossignol and Bertrand Van Ruymbeke (Leiden: Brill, 2016), 93.

11. Brookes, *Friend Anthony Benezet*, 81.

12. In David Crosby, *The Complete Antislavery Writings of Anthony Benezet, 1754–1783: An Annotated Critical Edition* (Baton Rouge: Louisiana State University Press, 2013), 8.

13. Woolman, *Some Considerations*, 207.

14. *An Epistle of Caution and Advice,* in Crosby, *Complete Antislavery Writings*, 8.

15. Ibid., 9.

16. Ibid., 10.

17. Ibid.

18. "Germantown Friends Protest against Slavery," 1688 [facsimile], Library of Congress, https://www.loc.gov/resource/rbpe.14000200/?st=text.

19. Ibid.

20. Carey, *From Peace to Freedom*, 195.

21. Gary Nash, "Slaves and Slaveowners in Colonial Philadelphia," *William and Mary Quarterly* 30, no. 2 (April 1973): 229.

22. Churchman quoted in Robert Daiutolo Jr., "The Role of Quakers in Indian Affairs during the French and Indian War," *Quaker History* 77, no. 1 (Spring 1988): 6.

23. Ibid.

24. Full text available at "A Declaration from the Harmless and Innocent People of God, Called Quakers," https://quaker.org/legacy/minnfm/peace/A%20Declaration%20to%20Charles%20II%201660.htm.

25. *The Journal of George Fox*, ed. Norman Penney (Cambridge, England: Cambridge University Press, 1911; rpt., BiblioLife historic reproduction), 323; George Fox, *Epistle 19*, in *The Epistles of George Fox*, vol. 1, Friends Library, https://www.friendslibrary.com/george-fox/epistles-vi.

26. William Penn, quoted in Sydney James, *A People among Peoples* (Cambridge, Mass.: Harvard University Press, 1963), 28.

27. Anthony Benezet to Jonah Thompson, April 24, 1756, in Brookes, *Friend Anthony Benezet*, 220.

28. Jack D. Marietta, *The Reformation of American Quakerism, 1748–1783* (Philadelphia: University of Pennsylvania Press, 1984), 115.

29. Woolman, *Journal and Major Essays*, 92.

30. Slaughter, *Beautiful Soul of John Woolman*, 118, 119.

31. Ibid., 240.

32. Woolman, *Journal and Major Essays*, 92.

33. Marietta, *Reformation of American Quakerism*, 115.

34. Jean R. Soderlund, *Quakers and Slavery: A Divided Spirit* (Princeton: Princeton University Press, 1985), 34.

35. Marietta, *Reformation of American Quakerism*, 115.

36. Woolman, *Journal and Major Essays*,92.

37. Ibid., 92–93.

38. Ibid., 93.

39. Ibid.

40. Ibid.

41. Brookes, *Friend Anthony Benezet*, 83; Jackson, *Let This Voice Be Heard*, 55, 56.

42. Anthony Benezet to Samuel Fothergill, October 1, 1757, in Brookes, *Friend Anthony Benezet*, 222.

43. Anthony Benezet to Samuel Allinson, July 16, 1774, in Brookes, *Friend Anthony Benezet*, 313.

44. Benezet to Fothergill, October 17, 1757.

45. Philadelphia Yearly Meeting, *Minutes*, September 23, 1758, in Carey, *From Peace to Freedom*, 207. The "disunion" the minutes noted was only partial. Full disownment for slave owners had to wait until 1774.

Chapter 10. A New Antislavery Language

1. Quoted in *A Brief Statement of the Rise and Progress of the Testimony of the Religious Society of Friends, against Slavery and the Slave Trade* (Philadelphia: Joseph and William Kite, 1843), Library of Congress, https://tile.loc.gov/storage-services/service/rbc/rbaapc/10000/10000.pdf.

2. Elaine Letki, *Captives of the French and Indian Wars 1676–1763: English Slavery in Canada* (master's thesis, East Stroudsburg University, 2019), 54.

3. For a list, see the Cornell University Library's Garland Library of North American Indian Captivity Narratives: 18th Century, https://guides.library.cornell.edu/Garland/18thcentury.

4. Quoted in *A Brief Statement of the Rise and Progress.*

5. Roger Bruns, "Anthony Benezet's Assertion of Negro Equality," *Journal of Negro History* 56, no. 3 (July 1971): 230.

6. George S. Brookes, *Friend Anthony Benezet* (Philadelphia: University of Pennsylvania Press, 1937), 248ff; Sydney James, *A People among Peoples* (Cambridge, Mass.: Harvard University Press, 1963), 203, 204; David Crosby, *The Complete Antislavery Writings of Anthony Benezet, 1754–1783: An Annotated Critical Edition* (Baton Rouge: Louisiana State University Press, 2013), 12; Maurice Jackson, *Let This Voice Be Heard: Anthony Benezet, Father of Atlantic Abolitionism* (Philadelphia: University of Pennsylvania Press, 2009), 27.

7. Anthony Benezet, *Observations on the Enslaving, Importing, and Purchasing of Negroes*, in Crosby, *Complete Antislavery Writings*, 15, 16.

8. Ibid., 16.

9. Ibid.

10. Ibid., 13.

11. Ibid., 15.

12. I owe the Cobb story to Augustus White, the first African American chief of service at the Harvard hospitals. Augustus White and David Chanoff, *Seeing Patients: Unconscious Bias in Healthcare* (Cambridge, Mass.: Harvard University Press, 2011), 279.

13. Bruns, "Anthony Benezet's Assertion," 230.

14. Jean R. Soderlund, *Quakers and Slavery: A Divided Spirit* (Princeton: Princeton University Press, 1985), 175.

15. Julie Winch, "Friends, Family and Freedom in Colonial Philadelphia: A Black Slave-Owner Settles Her Accounts," in *Quakers and Their Allies in the Abolitionist Cause*, ed. Maurice Jackson and Susan Kozel (Abingdon-on-Thames: Routledge, 2015), 162–164.

16. Donald W. Pfaff, *The Altruistic Brain* (New York: Oxford University Press, 2015), 6, 10, 102ff.

17. Aristotle, *Nicomachean Ethics*, Book 8, in *The Ethics of Aristotle*, trans. D. P. Chase (New York: E. P. Dutton and Co., 1950).

18. Crosby, *Complete Antislavery Writings*, 9.

19. Benezet, *Observations*, 16.

20. Ibid.

21. Stuart Masters, "A Glimpse of Heaven on Earth," *Friends Journal*, June 1, 2021, https://www.friendsjournal.org/a-glimpse-of-heaven-on-earth/.

22. *An Epistle of Caution and Advice*, in Crosby, *Complete Antislavery Writings*, 9.

23. Benezet, *Observations*, 16.

24. Ibid.

25. Maurice Jackson, *Let This Voice Be Heard: Anthony Benezet, Father of Atlantic Abolitionism* (Philadelphia: University of Pennsylvania Press, 2009), 81.

26. David Crosby, "Anthony Benezet's Transformation of Anti-Slavery Rhetoric," *Slavery and Abolition* 23, no. 3 (2002): 42, DOI:10.1080/714005242.

27. Louisiane Ferlier, "The Circulation of Early Quaker Antislavery Books: A Transatlantic Passage?" in *The Atlantic World of Anthony Benezet*, ed. Marie-Jean Rossignol and Bertrand Van Ruymbeke (Leiden: Brill, 2016), 163.

28. Benezet, *Observations*, 16.

29. Jackson, *Let This Voice Be Heard*, 81–88.

30. Benezet, *Observations*, 18.

31. Albert van Dantzig, "William Bosman's *New and Accurate Description of the Coast of Guinea*: How Accurate Is It?," *History of Africa* 1 (1974): 105; Benezet, *Observations*, 17.

32. Benezet, *Observations*, 17.

33. See David Crosby, "The Surgeon and the Abolitionist: William Chancellor and Anthony Benezet," *Pennsylvania Magazine of History and Biography* 137, no. 2 (April 2013): 125–131.

34. Benezet, *Observations*, 18.

35. Ibid., 20.

36. Crosby, "Anthony Benezet's Transformation," 50.

37. Lord Kames, *Elements of Criticism*, quoted "Anthony Benezet's Transformation," 52.

38. Crosby, "Anthony Benezet's Transformation," 48.

Chapter 11. Two Streams of Morality

1. Anthony Benezet, *Observations on the Enslaving, Importing, and Purchasing of Negroes*, in David Crosby, *The Complete Antislavery Writings of Anthony Benezet, 1754–1783: An Annotated Critical Edition* (Baton Rouge: Louisiana State University Press, 2013), 19.

2. Ibid., 20.

3. Anthony Benezet, *A Short Account of That Part of Africa Inhabited by the Negroes*, 28, in Crosby, Complete Antislavery Writings, 28.

4. Ibid., 28, 29.

5. Ibid., 40.

6. Ibid., 30.

7. Maurice Jackson, *Let This Voice Be Heard: Anthony Benezet, Father of Atlantic Abolitionism* (Philadelphia: University of Pennsylvania Press, 2009), 78.

8. David Crosby, "Anthony Benezet's Transformation of Anti-Slavery Rhetoric," *Slavery and Abolition* 23, no. 3 (2002): 55, DOI:10.1080/714005242.

9. Benezet, *Short Account of That Part of Africa*, 30.

10. Ibid., 34. Also see Crosby's notes, *Complete Antislavery Writings*, 77.

11. Benezet, *Short Account of That Part of Africa*, 34.

12. Ibid.

13. Ibid., 43.

14. Ibid., 44.

15. See chapter 10.

16. Benezet, *Short Account of That Part of Africa*, 56, 57.

17. Lay's 1737 *All Slave-Keepers* contained a number of brief graphic descriptions scattered throughout the disorganized text, which Benjamin Franklin, who printed the tract, attempted to organize. Benjamin Lay, *All Slave-Keepers That Keep the Innocent in Bondage* (Affordable Classics Limited Edition, 2020).

18. Benezet was quoting from Emanuel Bowen's *Complete System of Geography (1747)*.

19. Benezet, *Short Account of That Part of Africa*, 55.

20. Estimates, The Trans-Atlantic Slave Trade Database, https://www.slavevoyages.org/voyage/database.

21. Benezet, *Short Account of That Part of Africa*, 54.

22. "The Middle Passage," Digital History, https://www.digitalhistory.uh.edu/disp_textbook.cfm?smtid=2&psid=446#:~:text=At%20least%202%20million%20Africans,or%20during%20the%20Middle%20Passages.

23. Benezet, *Short Account of That Part of Africa*, 56.

24. Crosby, *Complete Antislavery Writings*, 26.

25. Benezet, *Short Account of That Part of Africa*, 49.

26. Ibid., 50.

27. John Coffey, "I Was an Eye-witness: John Newton, Anthony Benezet, and the Confession of a Liverpool Slave Trader," *Slavery & Abolition* 44, no. 1 (2022): 181–201, https://doi.org/10.1080/0144039X.2022.2113716.

28. Ibid. (no page numbers given in online version).

29. Ibid.

30. Crosby, *Complete Antislavery Writings*, 80n79.

31. Jackson, *Let This Voice Be Heard*, 57. Foster was not Scottish but British, though he received an honorary doctorate in divinity from the University of Aberdeen.

32. Jackson, *Let This Voice Be Heard*, 276n27.

33. See Henry J. Cadbury, "Anthony Benezet's Library," *Bulletin of Friends Historical Association* 23, no.2 (Autumn 1934), 63–75.

34. David Brion Davis, "New Sidelights on Early Antislavery Radicalism," *William and Mary Quarterly* 28, no. 4 (October 1971): 587.

35. T. H. F. Fletcher, "Montesquieu's Influence on Anti-slavery Opinion in England," *Journal of Negro History* 8, no. 4 (October 1933): 416.

36. See Sydney Ahlstrom, *A Religious History of the American People* (New Haven: Yale University Press, 1972), 395ff.

37. Roger Anstey, *The Atlantic Slave Trade and British Abolition* (Atlantic Highlands, N.J.: Humanities Press, 1975), 217.

38. Benezet, *Short Account of That Part of Africa*, 45.

39. Ibid., 47.

40. Ibid., 47, 48.

41. "The Deleted Passage of the Declaration of Independence," BlackPast, August 10, 2009, https://www.blackpast.org/african-american-history/declaration-independence-and-debate-over-slavery/#:~:text=Jefferson's%20passage%20on%20slavery%20was,removed%20from%20the%20final%20document.

42. Benezet, *Short Account of That Part of Africa*, 45.

43. Anstey, *Atlantic Slave Trade*, 214.

44. Anstey, *Atlantic Slave Trade*, 215.

45. Jonathan Sassi, "With a Little Help from the Friends: The Quaker and Tactical Contexts of Anthony Benezet's Abolitionist Publishing," *Pennsylvania Magazine of History and Biography* 135, no. 1 (January 2011): 45.

46. Roger Bruns, "Anthony Benezet and the Natural Rights of the Negro," Pennsylvania Magazine of History and Biography 96, no. 1 (January 1972), 105. Bruns is quoting from Frederick Tolles's 1948 book *Meeting House and Counting House: The Quaker Merchants of Colonial Philadelphia*.

Chapter 12. A Shift to England

1. David Crosby, *The Complete Antislavery Writings of Anthony Benezet* (Baton Rouge: Louisiana State University Press, 2013), 87.

2. Crosby, *Complete Antislavery Writings of Anthony Benezet*, 28.

3. Ralph Sandiford, *Mystery of Iniquity* (self-published, 1730), 3, 4.

4. Crosby, *Complete Antislavery Writings*, 104.

5. According to the United Kingdom National Archives, Britain was the world's

dominant slave trading nation between 1640 and 1807. "It is estimated that Britain transported 3.1 million Africans (of whom 2.7 million arrived) to the British colonies in the Caribbean, North and South America and to other countries." "A Brief Introduction to the Slave Trade and Its Abolition," National Archives (U.K.), https://www.nationalarchives.gov.uk/help-with-your-research/research-guides/british-transatlantic-slave-trade-records/.

6. Anthony Benezet to Joseph Phipps, May 28, 1763, in Roger Bruns, ed., *Am I Not a Man and a Brother* (New York: Chelsea House, 1983), 97.

7. Ibid., 99.

8. Anthony Benezet, *A Short Account of That Part of Africa Inhabited by the Negroes*, in Crosby, *Complete Antislavery Writings*, 40.

9. Jonathan Sassi, "With a Little Help from the Friends: The Quaker and Tactical Contexts of Anthony Benezet's Abolitionist Publishing," *Pennsylvania Magazine of History and Biography* 135, no. 1 (January 2011): 48 and n43.

10. Simon Schama, *Rough Crossings* (New York: Harper Collins, 2006), 23.

11. This account follows Simon Schama's description in *Rough Crossings*. Also see Maurice Jackson, *Let This Voice Be Heard: Anthony Benezet, Father of Atlantic Abolitionism* (Philadelphia: University of Pennsylvania Press, 2009), 139–153; Irv Brendlinger, *To Be Silent Would Be Criminal* (Lanham, Md.: Scarecrow Press, 2007, 19–22.

12. Thomas Clarkson, *The History of the Rise, Progress and Accomplishment of the Abolition of the African Slave Trade by the British Parliament* (1808; Qontro Classics, Internet Archive), 1:24–25.

13. Roger Anstey, *The Atlantic Slave Trade and British Abolition* (Atlantic Highlands, N.J.: Humanities Press, 1975), 221.

14. Jackson, *Let This Voice Be Heard*, 141.

15. Ibid.

16. Extract from *A Representation of the Injustice and Dangerous Tendency of Tolerating Slavery, or Admitting the Least Claim of Private Property in the Persons of Men in England*, Evans Early American Imprint Collection, https://quod.lib.umich.edu/cgi/t/text/text-idx?c=evans;cc=evans;rgn=div1;view=text;idno=N09401.0001.001;node=N09401.0001.001:8.

17. Schama, *Rough Crossings*, 38, 39.

18. Ibid., 38.

19. Ibid., 33, 34.

20. Granville Sharp to Anthony Benezet August 12, 1772, in George S. Brookes, *Friend Anthony Benezet* (Philadelphia: University of Pennsylvania Press, 1937), 429.

21. Quoted in "Somerset v Stewart," Wikipedia, https://en.wikipedia.org/wiki/Somerset_v_Stewart.

22. Crosby, *Complete Antislavery Writings*, 112.

23. Adam Hochschild, *Bury the Chains: Prophets and Rebels in the Fight to Free an Empire's Slaves* (London: Pan Books, 2012), 68.

24. Anthony Benezet to SPG, April 26, 1767, in Bruns, *Am I Not A Man*, 137, 138.

25. Ibid., 138.

26. Hochschild, *Bury the Chains*, 67.

27. Benezet to SPG, 138.

28. Ibid.

29. Daniel Burton (SPG) to Anthony Benezet, February 3, 1768, in Bruns, *Am I Not A Man*, 138.

30. Ibid., 139.

31. Anthony Benezet to Thomas Secker, in Brookes, *Friend Anthony Benezet*, 273. Brookes indicates the letter was undated. Jackson gives the date as 1758. Jackson, *Let This Voice Be Heard*, 138.

32. Sassi, "With a Little Help," 50.

33. Ibid.

34. Ibid.

35. Benezet, *Short Account of That Part of Africa*, 40.

36. Anthony Benezet to George Dillwyn, August 17, 1783, in Brookes, *Friend Anthony Benezet*, 400; Nancy Slocum Hornick, "Anthony Benezet and the Africans' School: Toward a Theory of Full Equality," *Pennsylvania Magazine of History and Biography* 99, no. 4 (1975): 412.

Chapter 13. Going Public

1. Anthony Benezet to George Dillwyn, September 11, 1779, in George S. Brookes, *Friend Anthony Benezet* (Philadelphia: University of Pennsylvania Press, 1937), 337.

2. David Crosby, *The Complete Antislavery Writings of Anthony Benezet, 1754–1783: An Annotated Critical Edition* (Baton Rouge: Louisiana State University Press, 2013), 107, 108.

3. Crosby, *Complete Antislavery Writings*, 107.

4. Anthony Benezet, *A Caution and a Warning*, in Crosby, *Complete Antislavery Writings*, 99.

5. Benjamin Rush to Granville Sharp, May 1, 1773, in Brookes, *Friend Anthony Benezet*, 446.

6. Anthony Benezet to Samuel Allinson, November 5, 1770, in Brookes, *Friend Anthony Benezet*, 280.

7. Anthony Benezet to Sam Fothergill, October 24, 1771, in Brookes, *Friend Anthony Benezet*, 280, 281.

8. Granville Sharp to Benjamin Rush, February 21, 1774, in Brookes, *Friend Anthony Benezet*, 447.

9. Benezet to Allinson, November 5, 1770, in Brookes, *Friend Anthony Benezet*, 280.

10. Benezet to Fothergill, October 24, 1771, in Brookes, *Friend Anthony Benezet*, 281.

11. Crosby, *Complete Antislavery Writings*, 113.

12. Ibid., 118.

13. Nancy Slocum Hornick, "Anthony Benezet: Eighteenth Century Social Critic, Educator and Abolitionist" (PhD diss., University of Maryland, 1974), http://hdl.handle.net/1903/24740.

14. Anthony Benezet to the Gurney brothers, January 10, 1772, in Brookes, *Friend Anthony Benezet*, 284.

15. Ibid., 285.

16. Anthony Benezet to Benjamin Franklin, April 27, 1772, in Brookes, *Friend Anthony Benezet*, 288.

17. Anthony Benezet to J. Fothergill, April 28, 1772, in Brookes, *Friend Anthony Benezet*, 303.

18. Benezet to Franklin, April 27, 1772, in Brookes, *Friend Anthony Benezet*, 288–289.

19. Ibid., 289.

20. Anthony Benezet to Granville Sharp, April 4, 1773, in Maurice Jackson, *Let This Voice Be Heard: Anthony Benezet, Father of Atlantic Abolitionism* (Philadelphia: University of Pennsylvania Press, 2009), 151.

21. "The Sommersett Case and the Slave Trade, 18–20 June 1772," Founders Online, National Archives, https://founders.archives.gov/documents/Franklin/01-19-02-0128.

22. Benjamin Rush to Benjamin Franklin, May 1, 1773, in Lyman Henry Butterfield, ed., *Letters of Benjamin Rush* (Princeton, Princeton University Press, 1951), vol. 1, 80–81, quoted in Jackson, *Let This Voice Be Heard*, 121.

23. Benjamin Rush to Granville Sharp, May 1, 1773, in John A. Woods, "The Correspondence of Benjamin Rush and Granville Sharp," *Journal of American Studies* 1, no. 1 (April 1967): 2.

24. Donald J. D'Elia, "Dr. Benjamin Rush and the Negro," *Journal of the History of Ideas* 30, no. 3 (July–September 1969): 417.

25. Jackson, *Let This Voice Be Heard*, 118.

26. Benjamin Rush to John Adams, July 20, 1811, Founders Online, https://founders.archives.gov/documents/Adams/99-02-02-5659.

27. The course of this legislation through the Pennsylvania assembly and English authorities is discussed by Darold Wax, "Negro Import Duties in Colonial Pennsylvania," *Pennsylvania Magazine of History and Biography* 97, no. 1 (January 1973), 41ff.

28. Granville Sharp to Anthony Benezet, August 21, 1772, in Brookes, *Friend Anthony Benezet*, 420; Prince Hoare, *Memoirs of Granville Sharp* (London: Henry Colburn, 1838), 102, in Jackson, *Let This Voice Be Heard*, 150.

29. Brycchan Cleary, "John Wesley's *Thoughts upon Slavery* and the Language of the Heart,'" *Bulletin of the John Rylands University* Library of *Manchester* 85, nos. 2–3 (Summer/Autumn 2003): 275.

30. Nehemia Curnock, ed., *The Journal of John Wesley* (London, 1840), vol. 5, in Jackson, *Let This Voice Be Heard*, 154; Brookes, *Friend Anthony Benezet*, 84.

31. John Wesley to Granville Sharp, October 11, 1787, quoted in Frank Baker, "The Origins, Character, and Influence of John Wesley's Thoughts upon Slavery," *Methodist*

History 22 (1984): 76, Centers for Studies in the Wesleyan Tradition, https://divinityarchive.com/handle/11258/38969.

32. Anthony Benezet to Granville Sharp, May 15, 1772, in Brookes, *Friend Anthony Benezet*, 291.

33. Anthony Benezet to John Wesley, May 23, 1774, in Brookes, *Friend Anthony Benezet*, 318.

34. Anthony Benezet, "Notes to John Wesley's *Thoughts upon Slavery*," in Crosby, *Complete Antislavery Writings*, 212.

35. John Wesley, *Thoughts upon Slavery* (London: G. Paramour, 1792), Project Gutenberg eBook, vols. 1–3, https://www.gutenberg.org/cache/epub/68144/pg68144-images.html.

36. Ibid.

37. Ibid.

38. Richard Heitzenrater, "John Wesley's Principles and Practice of Preaching," *Methodist History* 37, no. 2 (January 1999): 92.

39. Baker, "Origins, Character and Influence," 83ff.

40. V. Green, *John Wesley* (Lanham, Md.: University Press, 1987), 156.

41. W. E. H. Lecky, *A History of European Morals: From Augustus to Charlemagne* (New York, 1876), 1:161.

Chapter 14. Speaking Though in the Tomb

1. David Crosby, *The Complete Antislavery Writings of Anthony Benezet, 1754–1783: An Annotated Critical Edition* (Baton Rouge: Louisiana State University Press, 2013), 113.

2. Nancy Slocum Hornick, "Anthony Benezet and the Africans' School: Toward a Theory of Full Equality," *Pennsylvania Magazine of History and Biography* 99, no. 4 (1975): 416, 417.

3. Ottobah Cugoano to Granville Sharp, n.d., quoted in Adam Hochschild, *Bury the Chains: Prophets and Rebels in the Fight to Free an Empire's Slaves* (London: Pan Books, 2012), 136.

4. Quobna Ottobah Cugoano, *Thoughts and Sentiments on the Evil and Wicked Traffic of the Slavery and Commerce of the Human Species* (London, 1787), 97.

5. John Bugg, "The Other Interesting Narrative: Olaudah Equiano's Public Book Tour," PMLA 121, no. 5 (2006): 1424, 1426.

6. Maurice Jackson, *Let This Voice Be Heard: Anthony Benezet, Father of Atlantic Abolitionism* (Philadelphia: University of Pennsylvania Press, 2009), 195.

7. Cugoano, *Thoughts and Sentiments*, 10, 11.

8. Thomas Clarkson, *The History of the Rise, Progress, and Accomplishment of the Abolition of the Slave Trade by the British Parliament*, (London, 1808; repr., Lexington, Ky.: Filiquarian Publishing/Qonto, 2016), 1:57.

9. Ibid., 1:70, 1:71.

10. Ibid., 1:71.

11. Clarkson, *History of the Rise,* 2:35.

12. Ibid., 1:72.

13. George S. Brookes, *Friend Anthony Benezet* (Philadelphia: University of Pennsylvania Press, 1937), 34.

14. Clarkson, *History of the Rise*, 1:75.

15. "Village of Teston," Internet Archive, web.archive.org/web/20070930204716/http://web.ukonline.co.uk/johnno/test.htm.

16. Clarkson, *History of the Rise*, 1:76.

17. Ibid.

18. Ibid., 1:77.

19. Ibid.

20. Ibid., 1:79.

21. Ibid.

22. Ibid., 1:121.

23. Ibid., 1:135.

24. Patrick C. Lipscomb III and Edward C. Milligan, "A Note on the Authors of 'The Case of Our fellow Creatures, the Oppressed Africans,'" *Quaker History* 55, no. 1 (Spring 1966): 48.

25. Ibid., 50.

26. Anthony Benezet to George Dillwyn, August 17, 1783, in Brookes, *Friend Anthony Benezet*, 400.

27. Roger Anstey, *The Atlantic Slave Trade and British Abolition* (Atlantic Highlands, N.J.: Humanities Press, 1975), 248.

28. Clarkson, History of the Rise, 1:65.

29. Tim Thornborough, "William Wilberforce's Lesser Known Campaign," The Good Book Company, June 21, 2018, https://www.thegoodbook.com/blog/interestingthoughts/2018/06/21/william-wilberforces-lesser-known-campaign/?srsltid=AfmBOooj_MelEHcxCSarLvI-j-VPaAvpu_DY3VxUD1WsWxHd-uOn1opl.

30. Clarkson, 1:81.

31. Ibid., 1:85.

32. Ibid.

33. Hochschild, *Bury the Chains*, 110.

34. Clarkson, *History of the Rise*, 1:108.

35. Anstey, *Atlantic Slave Trade*, 257.

36. Ibid., 266.

37. "Abolition," Emerson Kent: World History of the Relaxed Historian, emersonkent.com/speeches/abolition.htm.

38. Stephen Tomkins, *William Wilberforce: A Biography* (Grand Rapids, Mich.: Eerdmans Publishing, 2007), 39.

39. Jackson, *Let This Voice Be Heard*, 166, 167.

40. Crosby, *Complete Antislavery Writings*, 229.

41. Clarkson, *History of the Rise*, 1:89.

42. Jacques-Pierre Brissot, in Jackson, *Let This Voice Be Heard*, 186; Garry Wills, *Head and Heart* (New York: Penguin Press, 2007), 152.

43. James Pemberton to John Pemberton, May 14, 1784, in Brookes, *Friend Anthony Benezet*, 459.

44. Roberts Vaux, Memoirs of the *Life of Anthony Benezet* (Philadelphia: James P. Parke, 1817), 132.

INDEX